Swansea 'til I Die

a century of supporting the swans

Swansea 'til I Die

a century of supporting the swans

Edited by Martin Johnes. Layout by Huw Cooze.

The stories and memories here have been collected as part of a Heritage Lottery Fund - supported project to celebrate the history of the Swans. The project is a partnership between Swansea University and Swansea City Supporters' Trust. It is assembling an online archive of memories, documents and memorabilia at www.swans100.org.uk. Much of the text in the book is taken from the early responses to a fans' survey hosted on the website. Please be part of the club's history by adding your own memories and completing the survey.

Thanks for their help and permissions are due to Phil Bethell, Huw Bowen, Cathy Duncan, Gwilym Games, Keith Haynes, Patricia Jones, Alan Lewis, Stuart McDonald, Will Morris, Peter Stead, Phil Sumbler, and to everyone who wrote stories, filled out the Swans100 survey and helped the project.

Images have been supplied by the South Wales Evening Post, Dimitris Legakis, Athena Picture Agency, The Press Association, Swansea City FC, Swansea City Supporters' Trust, Swansea Metropolitan University, and the Western Mail and are reproduced with permission. The South Wales Evening Post have a range of Swansea City photographs for sale. For further details please visit www.dipintosales.co.uk/thisisSouthWales/

The Heritage Lottery Fund (HLF) sustains and transforms a wide range of heritage through innovative investment in projects with a lasting impact on people and places. For more information please visit: www.hlf.org.uk

Swans100 project patrons:
Mrs Esme Allchurch, Joe Allen, Wyndham Evans, John Hartson, Kevin Johns MBE, Mal Pope, Professor Peter Stead, Lee Trundle

Introduction - a game of stories

Football is a game of stories. There are the stories of individual matches, each with their own anticipation, characters and expectations; each with their beginnings, middles and ends. There are the stories of the seasons: the ones that started badly but exploded into life, the ones that did completely the opposite, and the ones that never promised or managed to go anywhere. Then there are the stories of clubs: the tales and the memories of past glories and failures, of what was and what might have been, the stories of local rivals beaten or lost to and of strikers full of pace, power and panache and of those best forgotten.

There are also the stories of fans: the memories of going to games, of the sights, the smells, the sounds and the colours. There are the trips there and the trips home again. There's the singing, the drinking and the fighting. There's the happiness and the sadness. And there's the watching, the listening and the talking it all over with friends and family. Football is not something we do on our own. Even when we know no one else in the crowd, watching a game is something done with other people. Even if we're watching on tv, somewhere else someone is doing the same.

This means that football is interwoven with the course of our lives. Where we live, how much time and money we have, what other interests and commitments we have all determine the place football plays in our day-to-day existence. It's part of our relationships too, something to share or argue about. A match might last 90 minutes but football takes up so much more time, energy and emotion than that.

This is a book of stories from fans and about fans. It's a scrapbook of memories and snapshots. It's a book not just about the Swans but about family, friendship, culture, belonging and identity. It has moments of love and moments of hate. It has moments of glory and moments of despair. In these Premier League times, it's easy to forget that the Swans have had more bad days than good ones. But the victories are sweeter when they're less frequent and less expected.

The stories, memories, writings and pictures in this book tell of both the extraordinary and the ordinary. They might not always be quite what happened but they are what people remember. There are very few now who can recall the club's first few decades and probably none at all who can remember its first. But while players, managers, tactics, formations, kits, songs, fashions and even the stadium have changed, the supporters have remained. Over the course of a hundred years people have cared about the Swans. We might not all have quite the same reasons but we all have the same club.

At its best Swansea City has given us a tension-laden mix of excitement, passion and unpredictability. At its worst it's given us dull, boring and predictable football. But football is a game that never stops. There's always another season, full of hope and promise. We may have very nearly gone out of business twice but we survived. The club is still here because people have cared about it. This book tells you why.

Martin Johnes

My first match

My first visits in 1924-5 were as a babe-in-arms. My first conscious memory of the Vetch Field I have been able to establish as on Thursday 11 March 1926. Of course, at that age I knew nothing about the game (has this changed since?) but I knew that 'our side' wore white – all except one who wore a red jersey. I must have thought he was something special as he was my hero. In my memory on that fateful day, he took off his red jersey and handed it to one of the others. I was heartbroken to see that he was just like the others underneath. The match was against Sheffield Wednesday and what I had seen was the goalkeeper Jack Denoon sent off – the first Swans' player to be sent off in a Football League match.

John Conibear (89), Swans 100 survey

Oh, 1929 I think. I wasn't working due to the depression so I couldn't afford the sixpence to get in. Used to wait outside until the doorman let us in one at a time at halftime. The team wasn't too great then, and there was plenty of space to sit down and stretch out.

'HTH' in Love, Peace and Swansea City, 5 (March/April 1993)

I remember going to watch the Swans in the season 1929-30 when they played Grimsby Town in league division 2... I went with my uncle ... by car ... It was 45-odd mile from Llandysul ... We sat in the front row of the double decker. ... There wasn't a very big crowd but there was the usual shouting. ... I didn't see them more than one or two games in that period between 1929 and 1935 because I wasn't very well and the distance between Llandysul and Swansea were a bit excessive.

Ieuan Jones, Swans100 interview

My mother took me to stand behind the goals Town End to see West Bromwich Albion where my Dad still worked, having been sent there during WWII. I was hooked. [I remember the] Large crowd standing on the railway sleepers. Much pleasure because the people had been starved of football due to WWII.

Peter Miles (76), Swans100 survey.

A packed Vetch. Standing at the very top of the open North Bank – not seeing a thing. A sailor saw my predicament and went down the back and brought up an empty 50 gallon drum. He stood me on it, giving me the best view in the house. The match was in the last years

of 'war time' football 1945/46 and was against Newport County. Swans won.

Tommy Vaughan (80), Swans100 survey.

My first match was at the end of 45-46 season against Wolves. I was 11 years old and stood under the double decker. I didn't see a player or a blade of grass, only the ball when it went in the air. But I was hooked and have been a supporter ever since.

My Dad was home on leave from the Army and kept saying 'I would never brought you if I knew there would be this many here! We went with my dad, his mate, my brother and his 2 mates. We walked.

Eileen Morgan (77), Swans100 Survey

Because of poor transport facilities from the Rhondda to Swansea it only became possible to attend the Vetch when a family member bought a car and one of our first trips was to Swansea to experience a game. [I remember] standing on wooden sleepers on the East Terrace and watching a 4-2 victory over Ipswich Town – with Mel Charles scoring from the centre circle.

Brian John (73), Swans100 survey.

About 1949, the opponents were Blackburn. There were terrific crowds in those days. You had to queue for ages to get in. I think it was sixpence for schoolboys to enter back then. We all went down the front of the North Bank.

'IGR' in Love, Peace and Swansea City, 5 (March/April 1993)

Went with an uncle I think it was in 1951 and the opponents were Grimsby Town. Very exciting and scary for a young boy but I was hooked.

Allan McPherson (74), Swan100 survey

Forest or Bristol City. Long time ago. [I went] By train alone.

Norman Mathias (72), Swans100 survey

Too long ago to recall. With my father. By bus from Llanelli.

Peter White, Swans100 survey

About 1955, because it was my home town club and we had some real stars, my favourite being Cliff Jones. My love for the Swans is still as strong as it was when I first went in 1955.

Geoff Whittaker (65), Swans100 survey

Notts County? 1951. Being in the small bank and struggling to identify the teams. My father took me.

Geoff Evans (65), Swans100 survey

Standing on an orange box at the front of the enclosure under the double decker. Ivor Allchurch scoring the winning goal.

Anon (65), Swans100 survey

1959, Man Utd 25000 attendance. Played like a cup tie. United won 6-4, Mel Charles scored all for Swans. Been a Jack ever since

Alun Davies (67), Swans100 survey

Ivor Allchurch played. George Heyes made a good save and I sat in the upper West Stand with my Dad and Huw and Wyn Jones from Three Crosses. I was surprised by the chanting on the N Bank and also surprised that they chanted Swansea and not The Swans! I think the Swans won 1.0. I was hooked.

Anon (55), Swans100 survey

Started supporting in 1961 / 62 season. I used to live close to the ground and the noise of the crowds first attracted my interest as a child. I managed to persuade my father to start taking me to the Vetch.

Andy Reilly (58), Swans100 survey

I was 9 or 10 went with my dad who took me under duress from my nagging, he was more of a rugby man. It was an evening game, we sat in the south stand, and I clearly remember the brightness and vibrancy of the experience. I would at that age never have been in a crowd of that size, to see football in colour "Incredible".

Paul Williams (57), Swans100 survey

1962, as a 9 year old, I lived in Brynmill, and finally my mother allowed me to walk down to the Vetch with a group of friends. She told me to keep a look out for any "Teddy Boys"!

Geoffrey Thyer (59), Swans100 survey

1963. I believe it was a 3-0 win against Brighton? I went with my father and his friends who were regulars in the double decker. I was 9 years old and I thought the whole thing was brilliant.

Anon (58), Swans100 survey

It was 1965 and Bristol Rovers. My grandmother had died and my Uncle Charlie who lived in London took me to the game to give my parents some peace. I remember being in the Double Decker and not liking it very much!

Alan Hughes (56), Swans100 survey

QPR 1965. The grass, the white nets and the atmosphere. I had previously gone to watch rugby at St Helens with my father but once I went to the Vetch I didn't want to go anywhere else.

Anon (58), Swans100 survey

1966, my father took me in when they used to open the gates in the 2nd half down the Vetch and was hooked from then

Stephen Francis (57), Swans100 survey

My Grandfather took me to see Swansea Town Reserves v Cardiff City Reserves at the Vetch in the spring of 1967 or 1968 and this was followed by watching Swansea Schoolboys v Neath Schoolboys. I remember the Swansea boys wore orange shorts and Neath were in all blue. A very diminutive Brian Flynn was playing for Neath. I can't remember the scores of either game now, but both games were well attended and the atmosphere of a real football match captivated me. I was 'hooked' and my early years of watching the Swans were shared with my grandfather, literally making them a priceless memory.

Keith Roberts (48), Swans100 survey

1966/67, Reading. We were doing badly in the 3rd Division and there had been talk of a fan boycott but the crowd seemed big to me as a ten year old. Stood at the front of the old West Bank and we won 5-2. I remember how close the action at our end seemed and how exciting the goals were. I'd been on the big bank at St Helen's with my Dad but that seemed a long way away from the players. Also the floodlights and the sparks as people lit cigarettes on the North Bank. Reading wore a bright sky blue that season which stood out under the lights. I immediately adopted Willie Humphries as my favourite player and got my Mum to sew a 7 in ribbon on the back of a white top I had - well before replica kits. We lost 1-0 to Mansfield the next time and my parents thought I'd get bored then but I was hooked!

Peter Dawson (55), Swans100 survey

I was 11. Went with my sister's boyfriend. I had no idea that the Swans were so exciting to watch. It was in colour too, LOL. We had a black and white TV at the time and I'd never seen a footy match in colour. Swans won 4-2, jaw dropping experience. Knew nothing about the Swans before that game. Noisy atmosphere.

Jack Flack (52), Swans100 survey

1969/70 Heart of Oak. Pre-season friendly. I remember the goalkeeper making lots of saves and I was behind the goal in the double decker end with my Dad. I think the Swans were in orange and maybe Ivor Allchurch was playing.

Steve Garland (51), Swans100 survey

1970 My dad wasn't a football fan and I pestered him for weeks to go to a game. Eventually he gave in and my first match was Oldham which the Swans won 4-0, a dream start.

Richard Thomas (52), Swans100 survey

1972 was when I first saw the Swans. The following year I had my first season ticket. I did two paper rounds to save enough money. Sat upstairs in the old double decker.

Andy Carolan (53), Swans100 survey

1971/2. Can't remember who Swansea were playing, but attended with my father, grand father and great uncle. At that time we used to stand in the bottom tier of the west 'double decker ' stand, and I remember the people in the upper tier stamping their feet on the wooden floor whilst chanting.

Paul Davies (50), Swans100 survey

Walsall, 1971. I was 9 and my uncle took me to see Swans v Walsall. He put me on the wall at the side of the lower level of the old wooden double decker stand.

Anthony Hill (49), Swans100 survey

I went to the Xmas fixture at home to Aston Villa in 1971. Sat in the Double Decker and remember it being a big game. [I recall] Nothing about the game but I remember the atmosphere and a fight breaking out on the North Bank which could be clearly seen from the Double Decker.

Simon Short (47), Swans100 survey

Rochdale, 1974. Poured with rain. My scarf was soaking. Dad and I both caught a cold. Just remember the floodlights and the smells.

Tudor, Swans100 survey

I first became a supporter at the age of around 6/7. I remember being on my uncle's shoulders and watching the Swans lose 2-1 to QPR. The North Bank went all the way back then and I remember thinking of how many people were there.

Andy Robinson (43), Swans100 survey

My dad took me when I was 13 in 1974 as it was my brother's 7th birthday present, and I have supported them ever since.

Liz Jones (50), Swans100 survey

I went with my dad at a young age. I can remember seeing matches from 1975-76 season onwards, though my dad says he took me a lot earlier than that.

Adrian Byrne (45), Swans100 survey

Newport County 1976. Newport played in bright orange adidas shirts which had the 3 stripes in black and I thought it looked brilliant! Charlo scored a couple of goals. My Dad and I sat in the old double decker. Think we won 4-2?

Huw Mellor (46), Swans100 survey

Scunthorpe, 1976. I liked playing football so wanted to see my local team.

Dylan Williams (46), Swansea

Barnsley 27/8/1977, sitting upstairs in the Double Decker. Everything seemed so big. I went with my Dad, we'd been to Everton a couple of weeks before while on holiday, but we were visitors there; this was different, this was "ours" and I immediately felt a connection. It was

all magical, buying a programme for 15p(!!!), a "Cashcade" lottery ticket (Jackpot £1000!), the build up, the noise - I was smitten and have been ever since!

Rob Jenkins (46), Swans100 survey

Chesterfield 1979? Toshack scoring with a header. The place going mental. I'm convinced it's that atmosphere that got me hooked as a 7year old.

Gareth Morgan (39), Swans100 survey

My father took me to Tosh's first game against Watford in 1978, the 3-3 draw. I was 9. I attended a number of games around that time, but was a bit young to fully get into it. I stopped going around 1980 just in time to miss the 'glory years!' My first game back was Birmingham home in December 1982. I was 13. It was a dire midweek 0-0 draw but I was hooked. I watched around a dozen games that 2nd season in division 1 and have been a fan ever since.

Stephen James (42), Swans100 survey

Hartlepool, 1978. We won 8 nil. I played football with a coke can up against the front wall of the North Bank. The game passed me by though, I was only 6!

Wayne Davies (40), Swans100 survey

Halifax Town 1978. We won promotion to division 3. Tosh scored and we all ended on the pitch after the final whistle

Alan Whiffin (43), Swans100 survey

Watford 1978. Queue and being squashed outside the double decker with my Dad to go into the game. Winning.

Diane Morris (52), Swans100 survey

Tranmere Rovers 1978. Stood on the West Terrace at the front nearest the South Enclosure. Smell of stale beer, fags, pipe smoke and people eating cockles. Big crowd, a couple of police on the gate at the front of the West and the whole crowd going bananas at Swans scoring their 4th goal which helped us win 4 -3. Oh and most boys/teenagers wore a scarf, silken or woollen.

David Richards (42), Swans100 survey

My uncle took me when the Swans were in division 2 in 1978 and I sat in the posh stand to see us lose 2-0 I think to Leicester. I was only 9 so everything seemed big and noisy as I'd never seen football fans in the flesh before.

Ian Derrick (43), Swans100 survey

My older brother and his mates took me down to the Vetch for my first game, I was around 12 at time and it was against Newport County. We ended up going in the away end and we lasted about 15 minutes before the fighting started and we were all kicked out! I was hooked from that day on.

Michael James (46), Swans100 survey

In my mind it was against Newport County in the Welsh Cup. We were winning comfortably and my dad insisted that we leave 5 minutes before the end to avoid the rush. As we were leaving I heard two roars, one minute apart, as the Swans scored twice. I've never left a game early since. My dad doesn't recall the game and I can't find any record of it. It would have been around 1978 and I'd love to know which game it was.

Paul Ashley-Jones (45), Swans100 survey

My Dad liked John Toshack and took us down as a family [from Merthyr] when he took over in the late 70's.

Martin Wilson (39), Swans100 survey

Blackburn 1981. Standing on east terrace with my (football hating) dad and my mate Mark, watching what seemed to be men playing in incredibly bright kits. The sound and movement on the North bank - it was exciting and scary. Like a living thing.

Richard Davies (40), Swans100 survey

Man City 1981. I cannot remember a lot at all, just the atmosphere and the smell of the place, the people who went there. It felt like a adventure going to Swansea from Pembrokeshire. I was hooked from that day on.

Matt Parry (40), Swans100 survey

I had just moved to Swansea and started work at the beginning of January 1982. The first game I went to was Man United in the old first division. I went with my new friends/housemates so it was a great opportunity to meet people and get to know them. I had been to first division football before at QPR and elsewhere. The whole thing was great fun - the atmosphere on the North Bank was just tremendous, it was impossible not to get caught up in the excitement. And the Swans won 2-0! What an introduction to the club and the city as a whole.

Phil Bethell (53), Swans100 survey

Like most kids I had a favourite First Divison side. My dad took me to the occasional Swans match but it was only around 1982 when I was old enough to travel by train [from Carmarthen] that I really became a fan.

Paul Ashley-Jones (45), Swans100 survey

I remember very little as was too young - just that we played a team in red and I've always presumed it was Nottingham Forest. Sat in West Stand and always remember how rickety it was.

Anon (39), Swans100 survey

Stockport County 1984? Being a young boy I was very excited to actually be at the home of my heroes. I travelled by train from Morecambe to Swansea and I arrived very early. Swans won 3 0.

Jeremy Lunn (43), Swans100 survey

My first match was against Man City 1983. We were in the old first division, going down as it turned out but I didn't know that then. Even though I was starting my life as a Swans supporter, I was most excited about the fact that Joe Corrigan was in goal for Man City. I had an annual (probably Shoot) with a big picture of him in. There weren't pictures of Swans players in annuals in those days.

I grew up 40 odd miles west of Swansea and neither of my parents liked football so I was never going to be a regular as a kid but my Dad was taking me for my 10th birthday treat. We sat in the upper section of the old wooden double decker. I think we sat on a bench rather than a seat. There was a kid in front of me who had a very long black and white scarf, Tom Baker as Dr Who style. I really wanted that scarf.

I was amazed at men shouting and swearing without taking any notice of anyone around them. I remember sitting there wondering what was going to happen when we scored. (I don't think it it occurred to me that we might not score.) When we did score everyone jumped up and the noise was immense. I was a bit late joining in but it was great. And we scored three more times that day. I can't remember who scored though.

I think I assumed every game would be like that. Unfortunately they aren't. Like that day, the crowd have sometimes been more interesting than the football.   **Martin Johnes, Swans100 archive**

Crewe 1989. As I was only 15 it was quite intimidating. I remember Robbie Savage was playing for Crewe.

Jason Morgan (39), Swans100 survey

I was taken by my father to a home friendly in The Vetch against Chelsea which I believe was in the late 80's or early 90's (can't find any records online and was very young at the time). My only memories of the game are that it was midweek, we sat in the East Upper and were eating Rhubarb and Custard boiled sweets. After that I was next taken to a home game against Middlesbrough sometime in the early 90's (I think it was FA Cup) and carried on from there.

Lewis (27), Swans100 survey

Aged 8 (1992) I was introduced to the North Bank by my mother believe it or not!

Gareth Mugford (27), Swans100 survey

1993. Went to watch a game with a friend. Never had any interest in football before then.

Clare Ridley (37), Swans100 survey

6 years old and I was a bit dazed because I had never been to the Vetch or to a live football match before. I had a pastie and we sat in the front of the East Stand. I remember my friend 'Gemma' fancied Andrew Legg. I really enjoyed myself and took an interest in the club but my friend moved away and I had no-one else to go down with, until 6/7 years later my mum got a job there and the rest is history. I've still got my first programme. The Vetch was big, the pasties were nice and Andy Legg was ugly!!!

'Amber' (29), Swans100 archive

My first match

I went along to a night game in the early 90s when they started the 2 kids go free scheme. I went because they were my local team and I was excited by the prospect of seeing live football at a big stadium with my mates from school... and without my parents being around!

J. Borley (34), Swans100 survey

My dad took me down the old North Bank in 1996 when I was 5 years old. I remember loving the smells, noises, cheering, roaring, sights and just the general buzz around The Vetch Field on game day. Floodlight games were extra special.

Ben Ace (21), Swans100 survey

I started supporting the Swans at the age 14 in the summer of 1997 when a few of my mates decided to go to the first game of the season against Brighton. I wasn't a big football fan at the time, but decided to tag along anyway. We caught the X75 Stagecoach bus to Swansea on a warm sunny day. The game was very poor but Tony Bird headed a late winner in front of the East Stand to send the North Bank crazy, and from that day I was hooked on the Swans.

It's become a passion these days. But it's also become a major social part of my life, as I meet up with my friends every home game.

Geraint Davies (28), Swans100 survey

Horribly I can't remember my first home game. But it would have been in the East Stand at the Vetch. One of my earliest memories is Tony Bird scoring a diving header against the opponent. He became my favourite player after this.

Jack Taylor (22), Swans100 survey

I remember it being a dull game. The weather was horrible and the bleak weather reflected our league position.

Daniel Brown (20), Swans100 survey

First Match I saw Swansea vs Stoke, I was 5 or 6, so 1997 or 8! All my family are Swansea City fans and my uncle took me. Giovanni Savarese scored twice. Absolute classic and have never looked back!

Benjamin Wood (19), Swans100 survey

My first home game was Shewsbury Town. All I remember is a very cold day and a lot of grown up men and women shouting (I was only 1 and a bit!).

Becca Williams (19), Swans100 survey

Port Vale 2008. 5 of us caught the bus from Brecon. It was a grey, rainy day but the Swans won 2-0.

William Price (19), Swans100 survey

A season ticket book from the 1966 - 1967 season

SWANSEA CITY AFC

32 Red

"Why I love Swansea City"

by

Daniel Russell
Age 9

Y. G. G. Gellionnen

Competition winner

Ever since I could talk I've asked my Dad to take me to watch the Swans play. We go to all their home matches and if I'm lucky enough, my Dad takes me to away matches too. I love sitting in the stadium with the excited roar of the crowd filling my ears as the Swans team run onto the pitch. Everytime the Swans score a goal I shout and cheer until my throat hurts. It's the best feeling in the world when the Swans win. I love it when the crowd goes wild with excitement and the air is filled with thousands of happy voices chanting and cheering until they're hoarse.

I wear my Swans kit to ever match. Actually I wear it whenever I can - once I even wore it to bed. Every Christmas I get the new kit it's always my favourite present. I poke and prod all the parcels to work out which is my kit so I can open it first and put it on.

My favourite toy is a big teddy dressed in my very first Swans kit. I wore it when I was a baby. My teddy even has his own togs. He sits at the end of my bed and he keeps me company when I watch the Swans on tele. My bedroom is decorated with posters of the team. My favourite player is Ashley Williams. I would love to meet him. I've got a Swans duvet cover and pillow case and a football bedside lamp.

I keep all my football programmes in a special box that I've decorated with Swans stickers. My favourite photo is a framed picture of me with Cyril the Swan. I met him in the eisteddfod last summer. At Christmas my best friend gave me a Swans mug and pen and I bought all my family presents from the shop in the Liberty Stadium. My dad really liked his magnet of Scott Sinclair.

I'm in the school football team. We train on Wednesday's. Every night after school I go to the park to play football with my friends. If it's pouring with rain we play FIFA on my PS3 instead. I've got every FIFA game. My sister thinks I'm mad but I have loads of fun playing them.

My great grandad was a Swans supporter, so is my grampa and so is my Dad. My great grandad was six when the Swans team started to play so my family have been supporting the Swans for a hundred years and we'll support them for the next hundred too.

When I went to Margam Park to see the Queen with my Cubs group last month, I saw Brendan Rodgers as well and I took a photo of him smiling at me. It was really exciting.

My ambition is to play for the Swans. That would be amazing. I'm really proud to be a Swans fan they're the best football team in the world.

SWANSEA CITY F.C. announce the setting up of a

Season Ticket
Purchase Savings Scheme

From now on, all supporters wishing to purchase
SEASON TICKET SAVINGS STAMPS –
Value 25p each
may apply to the
VETCH FIELD TICKET OFFICE

They will be provided with a SAVINGS BOOK to which all stamps purchased must be affixed. Stamps may be purchase at any time during normal opening hours, only at the Vetch Field Ticket Office.

Stamps may be redeemed only when purchasing a Season Ticket; they *cannot* be redeemed for cash.

Postal applications must include a stamped addressed envelope.

The Club will not accept responsibility for lost books or damaged or defaced stamps.

All enquiries to Mrs. Abramson, at the Vetch Field Ticket Office.

Match programme,
4 March 1980

Look back with real pride

I suppose I was hooked on the Swans when my father took me down the Vetch one evening, entering this unique football ground to stand on the William Street embankment and, whilst in my position, looking straight ahead and admiring for the first time the glow of the floodlights beaming down on the ever so emerald green pitch.

When the teams emerged through a narrow tunnel which seemed to me as if it was within touching distance from where I was standing, I couldn't help being impressed by the contrast in colours of the kits of both teams against the background of lights and pitch.

The experience for me of this spectacular event as an eight year old became even more enhanced when we made our way to the United Welsh bus garage, but, of course, stopped for chips before taking our seats upstairs on the orange double decker bus. The smell of its green leather upholstery and the smell of chips remains with me as a 53 year old today. The misted up windows indicated that we were not the only supporters indulging in this treat.

I started watching the Swans when Roy Bentley was manager and have seen the ups and downs throughout the years. It's difficult now to remember individual seasons/players without the help of reference books to pin point the years, but here are a few of my random memories which include the hilarious events of trying to start a broken down smoking generator which was brought in for our evening fixture against Shrewsbury Town and having to come back the following morning to see the game. The game where our manager at the time - Harry Gregg – was not, to say the least, impressed with our goalkeeper Tony Millington having a full blown conversation with the Evening Post photographer who had positioned himself directly behind Millington's goalpost sat on his stool whilst the game was in full flow.

Herbie Williams, our goalscoring contact-lensed centre forward / come centre half, speaking to me at the players entrance and addressing me as "alright nipper".

Using my brand new Swans crested shiny red autograph book and approaching my first ex-player to sign- it was Ivor Allchurch, who readily added his autograph as he sat in isolation at the back of the Centre Stand and at that time for me not truly understanding the magnificent player he was as it was before my time but my Dad put me right!

My first Sunday game at the Vetch, a team sheet for a ticket,

methinks it was against Workington Town. The chant of "animals" against Bradford in the next Sunday game. The removal of row M from the Centre Stand which meant a move to new season ticket seats.

Sitting in the Centre Stand, arriving early for games there was always a silence that was always broken by the unique sound of someone who would lower their plastic seat in this stand that would cause a chain reaction of the clattering of other seats along the same row.

Away matches that stand out for me:- Reading away at Elm Park where we played in Green and Red striped kit with Stevenson and Morris at the heart of defence. Wimbledon Plough Lane where as we exited the tube station to make our way to the ground. It seemed that all the people there were heading off to watch Chelsea as they had the Chelsea shirts on. My experiences of Ugo's away trips in D coach number 1 bus luxury, with videos and quiz, to the smaller airport express no heating buses for the hardened supporters. Being filmed by police getting off our coach in Plymouth when the coach was mainly filled with OAPs. Monaco, great holiday. Stayed in Nice and swapped my terrace ticket for a stand ticket and seeing us lose 8 - 0 in front of the onlooking Pele but not again realising the quality that we were up against and the total mismatch.

Geoff Thomas a midfielder, what a terrific shot he had in his locker. Seeing the rise of Curtis, James and Charles. The attacking flair that Harry Griffiths encouraged to the Toshack years and the historic rise through the divisions and seeing the rise of journalist Peter Jackson with comments in his articles such as "Class will out". Our Yugoslavs Ante and Jimmy.

Autoglass trophy Wembley highs in a penalty shoot out against Huddersfield and Jan Molby play off Wembley blues against Northampton.

Seeing John Bond coaching Saunders and Mardenborough in training out in Fabian Way to seeing Lee Chapman being cold shouldered by Molby in his session. Gwyther training at Paradise Park ash pitch and returning to play against us for Rotherham in a 4-4 thriller and years later on sitting along from me in the Centre Stand with Brian Evans, a talented Wales international. I recalled that game as Brian and Dai were leaving and Brian simply said 'thanks for remembering' which for me sums up this entire project. Seeing his son become physio with the Swans and seeing him leave this

Adrain Forbes score the last league goal at the Vetch Field against Shrewsbury Town with England's Joe Hart comfortably beaten

club to move to Wigan with Roberto Martinez.

Funniest moment seeing a player from Magdeberg roll around in agony in front of the North Bank and suddenly a medical crutch being thrown onto the pitch to aid his recovery!

Fastest hat trick of quality finishing has to be Ian Walsh against Sliema Wanderers.

I think also of all the opposition players who played against us who were unknowns at the time who went on to become stars at other clubs and colleagues of mine saying to me that you are not going down to watch that rubbish whilst we lingered in the lower leagues. A recent example that someone reminded me of was that Joe Hart featured in goal for Shrewsbury in one of our last games at the Vetch and now he is Manchester City's and England's number one goalkeeper.

Seeing Tommy Smith tackle on Argentine world cup winner and Spurs great in front of this Centre Stand was special. Friendlies and testimonial games deserve their own mention, the Len Allchurch game against Sheffield Utd with some great long range shooting. Wyndham Evans' game against Everton, Herbie Williams and groundsman Harold Woolacott deserve mention.

I also want to mention the game against Jamaica's reggae boys and their very vociferous supporters which impressed me to send a letter into the Evening Post which was published with a photo of their flag waving support. The flare that set fire to the seats in the top corner of the East Stand let off by the supporters of Panthanaikos.

The East Stand that was opened by the Pearly Kings and Queens before the game against West Ham and the building bonds scheme that we had to subscribe to in order to retain our season ticket seats position in the Centre Stand.

Cup matches stand out with John Hollins' side beating West Ham in the FA Cup after a replay. The three matches against Crystal Palace which ended in our favour at Ninian Park with the news that one of our supporters had died, which reminded me of the trip to Rotherham and not knowing until after the game that one of our supporters had been trampled to death by a police horse in the narrow lane which I had walked up earlier to enter the ground.

Not to forget all the reserve and youth matches I attended over the years and the voice of Ron Walton booming out "second ball". Unsung heroes of mine , Pat Lally, Dave Bruton, Eddie May, Danny Bartley, George Smith, Mel Nurse, Geoff Thomas, Herbie Williams,

Dai Gwyther, Brian Evans, Micky Conway, Kevin Moore, Alan Waddle, Tony Millington, Jimmy Rimmer, John Cornforth, Jan Molby etc. etc.

Sad to see the fans after the Wrexham game ripping the Vetch field into pieces which I personally couldn't understand why it was allowed to happen, I thought the place deserved much more respect than this.

Great games, obviously the day at Preston when we achieved Division One football, the opener against Leeds. The eight nil demolition of Hartlepool. More recently the play off against Forest and play off final against Reading and wins against Arsenal and Manchester City in the Premiership and the style of football which has got us to where we are.

All the minute silences I have stood for at the Vetch and Liberty should also have their unique place in the 100 years history.

In summary all the above has provided me and my family with fantastic entertainment, a range of emotions from anger with Petty almost ending our club to elation of promotions and trophies and a pride in being a Swan. But for all true supporters it's about keeping our club alive and kicking for all future generations in whatever league we happen to be in and a wish that everyone in Swansea and surrounding areas can look back with real pride over the last 100 years and look forward to more exciting times.

Lawrence Molloy

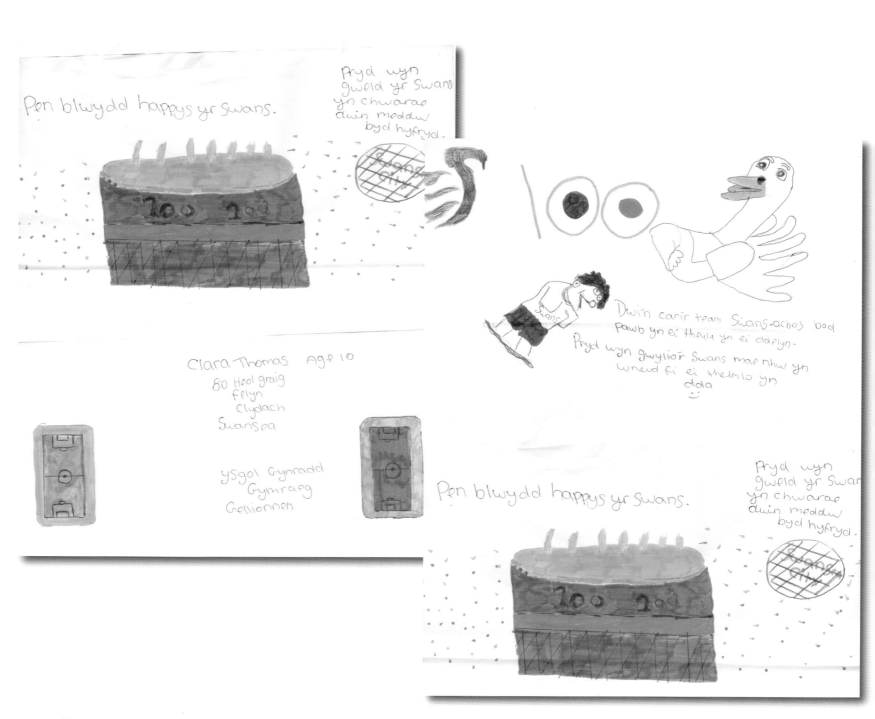

Pen blwydd happys yr swans.

Pryd wyn gweld yr Swans yn chwarae dwin meddw byd hyfryd.

Dwin carir team Siaans achos bod pawb yn ei theulu yn ei dofelyn.

Pryd wyn gwyliof Swans mae nhw yn wneud fi ei theimlo yn dda :)

Clara Thomas   Age 10
80 Heol graig
Felyn
Clydach
Swansea

Ysgol Gynradd
Gymraeg
Gellionnen

Pen blwydd happys yr swans.

Pryd wyn gweld yr Swan yn chwarae dwin meddw byd hyfryd.

That's Why I Love Swansea City

Swansea the town by the Sea, home to the mighty Swansea city.

Winning at Wembley Where we took the trophy, That's Why I love Swansea City.

Against all odds we are in the top flight

Newcastle, Arsenal and Man city felt our fight.

Sigurdsson, Sinclair and Britton are so strong

Everyone on the North Bank are singing the songs.

All the fans love our Brendan, he's one of a kind

Can't believe we have had him, "oh what a find".

Independant we stand to applaud all the team

Thank the Lord I'm from Swansea

Yes, I am SWANSEA CITY.

by Leoni John age 9
Brynhyfryd Junior School

Matchday routine

Matchday routine has changed simply as it is no longer possible to leave pub at the 2.55 and still make it to your spot before kick off.

Laura Williams (24), Swans100 survey

Always went early to get the best view in the enclosure.

Tommy Vaughan (80), Swans100 survey

Always entered same turnstile, supposed to be my lucky one, not always was unfortunately.

Peter Miles (76), Swans100 survey

I had my own car, travelling [from Llanelli] very fast ... Just on my own. I used to stand under the double decker or in the enclosure. There was no need for a season ticket at that time.

Ieuan Jones, Swans100 interview

As a child in Brynmill I walked to the Vetch. When I grew up and moved to Morriston I either went by bus or car. Now, I drive down to Brynhyfryd, park in a car park, go to the Plough and Harrow and walk from there to the Liberty.

Geoffrey Thyer (59), Swans100 survey

Many years ago when we were pre and early teens we would catch the supporters bus from outside the "Railway Hotel" in Ammanford at 1pm for home games. Myself and a friend would always have a sort of guardian on the bus (arranged by my dad) who would be charged with "Keeping an eye on us". Brian and myself would ALWAYS have a "Vetch Pasty" at half time. In later years a pint or two in the "Queens" or the "Builders Arms" was taken prior to all matches. Now a cup of Hot Chocolate in the ground or if we are very early a coffee in "Starbucks" (Comes with old age I fear).

Paul Williams (57), Swans100 survey

Rush home after my son's football, gulp down some dinner quickly. Dropped off by my wife near the ground, watch the game, walk back to the Wern in Siloh Road for a couple of pints whilst the traffic dies down until my wife picks us up again.

Barry Roberts (49), Swans100 survey

Sat in the Double Decker or stood under it with my Dad. Then back to my great Aunt's house on Argyle Street for the end of Grandstand at tea.

Simon Short (47), Swans100 survey

In the 1970s it was two pints of Manns stout and a cheese and onion roll in the students bar on Union Street. From the mid 1990s it was two pints of bitter in the Brunswick Inn with my father and on to the Vetch. Since the Liberty Stadium opened it's still 2 pints of bitter in the Brunswick.

Phil Roberts (50), Swans100 survey

Fabian Way at ten past seven and I'm bogged down in City traffic, the glow rising from the Vetch Field floodlights being the only sign of the impending spectacle. After dumping the car at Dai's parent's place, I got a lift with his Dad (thanks Gwyn) down to M&S, and ran from there through a stream of Vetch bound Jacks, to rendezvous with Dai and Chris at The Jack and pick up the precious prize of the evening – a ticket for the match tonight. Having just made it, we hot foot it to the turnstiles, The Vetch tannoy already echoing off the North Bank.

Report on SCFC v West Ham in the FA Cup in Jackanory, 11 (Feb/Mar 1999)

I used to catch a bus into Swansea from Dunvant to the bus garage then walk to the old Vetch, and then a bus back home afterwards. Now we take the car, walk to Rossi's and have fish and chips before each match. We then buy a programme, and wander around the ground, then into the club shop. We always take a radio so we can listen to Anthony O'Connell's live commentary.

Cath Dyer (46), Swans100 survey

At The Liberty, it's, walk to the stadium, few drinks inside, then walk home, possibly via a pub. At The Vetch, it was, bus into town, few drinks in a pub or two on the way to the ground, and on the way home, which was on a bus.

Gary Fisher (49), Swans100 survey

Last years at the Vetch, my son and I would have lunch and a drink in 'Brunswick'.

Colin Short (75), Swans100 survey

I have fond memories of the Vetch but my life was different then, and changing circumstances bring different routines and habits. It used to be lots of beer in the Singleton and then chips at Macaris. Now it's parking at the Landore Social, (and a quick pint) a leisurely walk down the hill, match programme and a pint in the ground, before a quick getaway at the end to ditch the car and commence the postmortem at the Dunvant Workingmen's Club! Routines change but the talk and emotion is the same!

Keith Roberts (48), Swans100 survey

Lawr yn y Vetch, mynd i'r Clarence, wedyn cael burger tu ol i'r North Bank, gosod fflag ar y North Bank ac yna lawr i Wind St ar ol y gem! Erbyn nawr mwy o brofiad o jyst mynd i'r gem.

Dewi (31), Swans100 survey

Vetch: Dump the car in Oxford St. The car fire place car park. Into the Builders pub and into the North bank. Liberty: Park in Battery centre car park. Food at Rossi's then into the West Stand

Jack Flack (52), Swans100 survey

Leave home at approx 11.30 am (Saturdays) by car with my son also a lifelong fan (now 40 years). Arrive at Liberty at 12.45 pm to meet friends and discuss Swans matters.

Brian John (73), Swans100 survey

I won't wear any away team colour clothing, Stop off in Frankie and Bennys for a pint. Car to Eaton Road and walk down from there.

Anon (46), Swans100 survey

I don't drink as much as I used to pre match as the pubs are not so convenient to the Liberty!

Dai Little (44), Swans100 survey

I travel by car for home games, car or train for away games.

Phil Williams (44), Swans100 survey

This year due to the overwhelming amount of fans wanting to go to the games because of our Premiership status, I've been forced to get a season ticket alone as my friends couldn't get one, however before that it was always with friends. It's not the same celebrating the

goals with strangers. I don't know if I will carry on going on my own.

Rhys Buckney (22), Swans100 survey

I used to travel by car but now I catch the bus as it drops me off right outside the stadium

Daniel Brown (20), Swans100 survey

Living just under an hour away, we drive 2-2 1/2 hours early to the ground. On big games we wait to see the buses arrive and see the players. We walk down to Morrisons to get our weekly pasty and sweets and take a walk round the ground until kick off. We have started going to Rossi's the fish and chip bar across the road lately.

Georgia Watts (15), Swans100 survey

Matchday routines depend on one's age, one's fellow supporters and other circumstances. My routine as a student differed from my routine now as a parent. When I was much younger and attended matches with friends, we usually had a few beers both before and after matches. We would walk to matches at the Vetch. Now I go with my son to the Liberty. We drive up, park in the streets in the Hafod and walk to the ground. Afterwards, we usually call in at the Brunswick pub in town for a couple of pints.

Tim Pegler (55), Swans100 survey

Over time I have attended with mother, father and other siblings and friends. Life events such as death, divorces, marriage etc. have had their effect.

Anon (58), Swans100 survey

Who I go with has changed over the years. Started with family, then schoolfriends. I now sit with friends that I have made through attending matches at the Vetch.

Peter Watkins (58), Swans100 survey

I go with my son, at times my daughter, my godson and his father and 4 close mates and their sons. I started off with my father, then local Sandfields and Uplands boys, then my cousin and finally with mates from Dunvant and West Wales, 10 in total.

David Richards (42), Swans100 survey

Matchday routine

Collect my grandson early, drive to near the ground, go for lunch then the club shop. My grandson likes to go in early and watch the players warm up, I usually chat with friends in the concourse. I used to have plenty of superstitions but not anymore though I do tend to walk the same way prior to each game and always buy my programme from the same seller.

Anon (58), Swans100 survey

Always wear an odd number of items with Swans 'ID' on it e.g. scarf, shirt, jacket, jumper, badge, coat. i.e. one or three of the list! If we lose I will change the turnstile I go in to ground at next visit.

Anon (58), Swans100 survey

We always have hotdogs for lunch before a 3pm k/o - it would be unlucky not to. We drive to games, and it's always good to get back to the car to listen to 5live/Radio Wales to find out how the pundits felt we did.

Gareth Howe (23), Swans100 survey

This season I park, get rissole and chips from Rossi's get a programme then go into ground about 40 minutes before kick off. This has only not been followed once against Man Utd and we lost

Mike Duffy (52), Swans100 survey

I have to sit with my feet crossed under my seat!!!! Will only go in through turnstile 1 and the stairs on the left of the concourse. We drive and walk along the river.

Diane Morris (52), Swans100 survey

I have a lucky scarf and socks. Travel down from Cardiff in the morning, have lunch with parents and then walk over to the ground. Usually try and have a drink in the ground.

Anon (48), Swans100 survey

On Matchdays I only drink my tea from 'lucky' Swans mug.

Gareth Francis (25), Swans100 survey

Lucky Scarf, lucky Shirt, lucky parking space; you name it, I've got a lucky routine for it! These days my matchday routine is up at 6am, leave my home in Colchester at 7 for the 5 hr drive to Swansea. 1st

stop, Sainsbury's, Jn 22 M25 for tea & toilet around 8.15; next on to Leigh Delamere on the M4 for stop 2 around 10.30'ish; then it's non-stop to my mother's house in Killay for lunchtime. A quick bite to eat, change into my lucky shirt & off to the match. Park in Bowen St in the Hafod & 10 minute walk to the ground. Quick look round the club shop (a hangover from the old Vetch routine) & into the ground. Visit to the toilet, then a cup of tea & up to my seat. The routine's pretty much the same as it's always been, just the distance travelled has changed!

Rob Jenkins (46), Swans100 survey

My routine hasn't really changed throughout the 15 years of supporting the Swans really ... I still wear my swans shirt with leggings, boots and my scarf!

Becca Williams (19), Swans100 survey

My latest superstition is to not have a superstition. Had lucky everything down the years.

Simon Stranaghan (48), Swans100 survey

We always listen to music before the game, builds up our singing voices prior to the game.

Owain Ashley-Jones (16), Swans100 survey

I had a soft drink at the Vetch, bought a programme and watched the game. The only thing that has changed is that now I drink an alcoholic drink!

Daniel Brown (20), Swans100 survey

Why the Swans matter to me

The lights of Dynevor School Hall shone brightly as "Toad of Toad Hall", the school's dramatization of Kenneth Grahame's novel "The Wind in the Willows" drew to a close. My parents, like many others, dutifully attended that night as I had purchased 3 tickets some weeks before. My father was in a subdued mood as he sat through the school production, watching the pupils' efforts on stage, many of which had, I'm sure, been cajoled into appearing under the spotlights.

This night, you see, was Tuesday 18th February 1964, when the Swans were entertaining Stoke City in a F.A. Cup 5th Round replay, having drawn 2-2 at Stoke a few days earlier.

As the audience spilled out of the school yard and down onto the Kingsway, my father anxiously sought out the result of the game. On reaching St Mary's Church for the No.42 bus back home to Llansamlet, my father and I received the news that the Swans had won 2-0. Little did we know at that time that the Swans were to progress to the F.A.Cup semi-final, beating Liverpool en route.

It was also the night when I realised what the Swans meant to me. That moment when the passion for your team is ignited. Little did I know at that time what a roller coaster of a ride following the Swans was to be.

My trips to the Vetch prior to that season were sporadic affairs and, as a youngster, I was one of many placed on the supporting wall of the west stand (Double Decker), so that I could see over the crowd of adults before me. Health & Safety wasn't so prominent in those days! From my vantage point I could see the likes of Noel Dwyer, Herbie Williams, Keith Todd and my favourite player at that time, Barrie Jones.

It wasn't long, however, before the roller coaster ride took its first "dip" as the Swans were relegated at the end of the 1964-65 season. Despite this setback, my enthusiasm for following the Swans remained undiminished and the return of Golden Boy, Ivor Allchurch, brought hope of success for me and many others. Unfortunately, even Ivor's return could not prevent the Swans having a mediocre season, although they did win the Welsh Cup and entered European competition for the first time, losing 1-5 on aggregate to Slavia Sofia in the European Cup Winners' Cup.

In the following years, following the Swans become an integral part of my life with the calendar year being intertwined with the football season from August to May. I progressed from the Double Decker to the North Bank, leaving my father and his friends for a more raucous existence at the back of the stand. Whatever the game, or size of the crowd, there was always a sense of anticipation when approaching the Vetch Field, always the hope that the Swans would win, no matter how poor they had been the previous week or how dire their league position was. The tone for the weekend was decided on 90 minutes of football at the Vetch.

Night time games had an atmosphere all of their own, whether it be on a Tuesday or Friday night. Excitement rose as the Vetch floodlights appeared in view, where heavy rain was often magnified in the glare of the lights. As the crowd made their way to the ground the Garibaldi, Builders, Clarence and other pubs in the vicinity quenched the thirst of many, whilst Macari's chip shop satisfied the pre match hunger of many more. Inside the ground, under the North Bank, the aroma of pasties, hotdogs and burgers arose from the temporary makeshift counters. Directly opposite was the less savoury odour that escaped from the Gents toilet. On rainy days most North Bank regulars will remember the pool of water that accumulated at the entrance. You either jumped over it or waded through it. The surrounding wall behind it was topped with barbed wire from which the occasional plastic bag would flutter in the breeze. To the occasional visitor it must have looked a formidable sight.

The Vetch could be an intimidating place to visit when the North Bank was in full voice, no more so than in its latter years, when the Swans' very league survival was at stake. In years gone by, many games stick out in the mind. One such game was the 4th round F.A. Cup match against Arsenal in front of what I believe was a record 32,796 crowd on 17th February 1968. A game which the Swans lost 1-0 to a Bobby Gould header. In those days the likes of Herbie Williams, Keith Todd, Brian Evans and Willie Humphries appeared in Swans colours. It was to be another 10 years before the John Toshack revolution was to take the Swans to the top of the First Division.

I remember Toshack's Swans debut at the Vetch in front of 10,000 fans. In an exciting game, the Swans drew 3-3 with Watford. Swans fans of that era will not need reminding of the rise and fall of the club in the years to follow. The first season in the First Division was very memorable, after many of us travelled to Deepdale, Preston to witness promotion being secured. It was only after getting on the Supporters bus after the game that the reality dawned on me that the likes of Liverpool, Manchester United, Arsenal were to be the visitors the following season. The entire summer was spent in a state of anticipation of the fixture list being published. It is amusing to think that Chelsea were a mid-table Second Division side at that time.

Great games were to follow, as the Swans beat Leeds United 5-1 in the first game of the season and I visited Old Trafford to see the Swans lose narrowly 1-0 to a Garry Birtles goal. We continued throughout the season in a kind of football fantasy land, as Lokomotive Leipzig visited the Vetch in the European Cup Winners' Cup and Cardiff City were beaten in a 2 leg Welsh Cup Final.

I, like others, felt considerable disappointment as the Swans were relegated at the end of their second season in the First Division. That disappointment was to last quite a while, as the Swans slid back down to the lower reaches of the league where they lingered until the now well documented game versus Hull City, when Football League survival was secured. The build up to that game was unbearable, when it dawned what the Swans meant to me and many others.

Since then following the Swans has been much more palatable, as local business men and the Swansea City Supporters Trust saved the club, "steadied the ship" and now run the club on a sound financial basis. There followed successes when the Football League Trophy was won on 2 occasions and the climb back up the Football League began. As a member of the Swans Trust Board, I have been in a position to see how much hard work has been put in by those connected to the club on a daily basis. In addition, successive Managers have played their part in improving the club, from Kenny Jackett, Roberto Martinez, Paulo Sousa to Brendan Rodgers.

It was with a sense of pride that I witnessed the building of the Liberty Stadium. Little did I realize the amazing games that I would witness in the next few years, culminating in the joy I experienced when Darren Pratley finally secured our Wembley Play-Off Final place with a shot from the half way line into an empty net. The final itself is up there with one of my greatest moments following the Swans , as the team, in true Swans tradition, made its supporters sweat by almost giving up an apparently unassailable 3-0 lead before Scott Sinclair secured his hatrick and our Premier League place with a successful penalty.

Leaving Wembley, it was amazing to think that once again, 30 years later, I was waiting in anticipation for the fixtures to be issued.

The big clubs were still there, joined by Chelsea this time! In the current era of unparalleled Premier league sponsorship and big money transfers, the Swans have managed to hold their own and drawn admirers from far and wide with their superb, passing game.

I will, however, never forget those days at the Vetch as they have been an huge part of my life and, despite the trials and tribulations of following the Swans, I wouldn't want it any other way.

Will Morris

Liverpool away 1964

Why? Because it becomes an addiction that's cost me a fortune over the years but "I just can't get enough!"

Nigel Jarman (59), Swans100 survey

1946. I was involved in starting up a junior soccer team in a rugby stronghold village and it went from there.

Tommy Vaughan (80), Swans100 survey

30,000 crowd will see Preston in action
There will be a rousing reception for last season's Third Division champions when they take the field this afternoon against Preston North End, relegated First Division team, past Cup winners and team of great tradition.

If there is a regret at the Vetch Field to-day it is that the club lacks the accommodation to cater for all who want to see this afternoon's match, and with all main and west stand seats sold to season ticket holders, early queuing was expected for the unreserved parts of the ground.

From quite an early hour football enthusiasts were arriving in Swansea from outlying areas, and a capacity crowd was expected to see the big game.

Preston would have been attractive visitors in any event but the inclusion of men like Tom Finney, Beattie and Langton - all internationals - aroused unusual interest.

South Wales Evening Post, 20 August 1949

I've supported them through every league and now it's such a pleasure to see how they play against the best teams.

Eileen Morgan (77), Swans100 Survey

Football has been a tribulation as well as a triumph to us in the years since 1966. Financial crises, historical promotion campaigns, Welsh Cup wins, FA cup disasters, crowd problems, location debates all have been perennial visitors. Yet, the game remains; eleven visions in white on a green field chasing a white ball, chasing our most sincere hopes and aspirations.

The Jack, issue 6 (April 1994)

Summer is here, and hope springs eternal!! Soon another season will be with us and the disappointments of last will be blown away by the North Bank winds.

The London Swan, July 1989

I have been interested since childhood when I would go to the Vetch to watch training. I was thrown out once by John Charles. My father influenced me. He had watched in the 1920s and talked about Jack Fowler goals.

Colin Short (75), Swans100 survey

[I first got interested in] the early 1950s because of the style of football played by the legends i.e. Ivor Allchurch, Cliff Jones, Mel Charles, Terry Medwin, Barrie Jones etc. [Today I follow the club] Because of my love of football and passion for Swansea City and also the attachment I feel for the city of Swansea over such a long period of time.

Brian John (73), Swans100 survey

I feel such strong connections with the club and the players from the early days of following the Swans. I played local football so did not watch them regularly after the 60's until the season they almost dropped out of the league. Although I don't go to watch now I think that season they almost dropped out of the league made me closer to the club and I follow games on the radio and TV.

Rob Samuel (63), Swans100 survey

Once a Jack always a Jack! Despite living abroad for many years am still passionate about the Swans

Gilbard Honey-Jones (59), Swans100 survey

Continuing love of soccer, and will do until I'm in my wooden box.

Peter Miles, Swans100 survey

Because I love Swansea City.

Stephen Bresnan (62), Swans100 survey

Because it's in my blood.

Peter White, Swans100 survey

When it's in your blood, it becomes a compulsion. It's also a bond formed with friends from school - it's our common interest.

Andy Reilly (58), Swans100 survey

Parents (from England) both followed football and supported Manchester United as they were students there in late 1940's. I got more interested after tv coverage of 1966 World Cup (I supported England) and asked to be taken to a game. I was an instant convert and have followed Swans first and United second ever since.

Peter Dawson (55), Swans100 survey

c1966 in St Gabriel's church choir, head choirboy Mark Hamilton was a Swans fan and went to home and away games with his dad. World Cup had lit my interest in football but my dad was a rugby man so I was never able to go to live games.

Tim Douglas (54), Swans100 survey

I think it is very important to support your local team, unlike some other big teams.

Andy Carolan (53), Swans100 survey

The style of football is excellent and it is a total social occasion not just a game.

Tonny Pettican (51), Swans100 survey

I moved to Swansea in 1973 and saw a couple of games in the 1974/5 season. I really became hooked in the 1976/7 season. [First game?] Apparently it was Doncaster United in 1974. I went with my Dad. Made a day of it. There were a lot of goals but I can't remember the score. Afterwards we went to the Wimpy Bar on Oxford Street. [Why do you follow the club today?] Cannot give a rational answer. It is as close as I get to having a religious belief.

Phil Roberts (50), Swans100 survey

I've still got the same feeling on match days as when I was a boy.

Paul Davies (50) Swans100 survey

Blind loyalty.

Tudor Evans (49), Swans 100 survey

You can change jobs, move house, change wives, even change sex nowadays - but you can't change the football club you support - just not possible.

David Hurst, Swans100 survey

Swansea is my city therefore the Swans are my club.

Paul Evans (45), Swans100 survey

Mates I have made through football are amongst the best I have and following the Swans is part of me - luckily my wife understands.

Ian Derrick (43), Swans100 survey

Once it's in your blood it don't leave. If you are a true Jack you are married for life. It's like having children. You love your children irrespective of what they do, you love the Swans through good and bad. I just can't get enough.

Martin Bowen (49), Swans100 survey

It's in my blood. I've spent countless days of my life watching, travelling to and thinking about SCFC.

Steve Close (47), Swans100 survey

I have supported the club since I was a boy. It's a huge part of my life. I watch all home games, 5-10 away games, sometimes attend reserve fixtures and visit websites several times a day for updates and news.

Simon Short (47), Swans100 survey

I love the club it's become part of who I am today.

Micheal James (46), Swans100 survey

Quite simply, they're MY club! Swansea born & bred, it's in my blood. Even though I now live in Colchester, Essex (270 miles away), The Swans are the only club for me. Now that my children have grown up, I have the time & money to follow them home & away as much as possible.

Rob Jenkins (46), Swans100 survey

The Swans always have been and always will be part of who I am.

Dai Little (44), Swans100 survey

When I was a young boy [in Morecambe] I supported Liverpool (as my father was a Liverpool fan). John Toshack was my idol and when he left Liverpool to take over as Swansea City manager I was so devastated that he had gone that I decided to 'follow' him and started supporting the Swans and have done now (through thick and very thin!) for over 30 years.

Jeremy Lunn (43), Swans100 survey

I enjoy the style of the team, and also strongly identify myself as a Swansea person. It therefore makes sense to me to follow them closely, and now that they are so successful, it made sense to get a Season Ticket to ensure that I could attend every game - last year I attended about 15 home games anyway, so I could have got a Season Ticket last year too. A number of friends attend, and there is also a real buzz about the sport amongst colleagues, so it is great to have a shared interest and a point of debate!

I would describe myself as a committed fan now, though cricket remains my favourite sport. However, it takes up a lot more time to watch cricket! I'm more committed now, as I have a son who also likes football, I have a Season Ticket, and because I know more people who are big fans. I wouldn't say I was a fanatic, though, and I think I am still a bit detached from it all, but I would say I am a bit detached in life generally. I prefer to keep my following in some sort of perspective, and not to depend on it too much for making me feel happy or sad. It is only a game after all, but in some ways, I wish I was a more wholehearted supporter.

Anon (44), Swans100 survey

The Swans are a big part of my life. If they win or lose it can dictate my mood for the day or longer.

Phil Cox (42), Swans100 survey

For the passion of the game and a sense of pride in following a club that's my local professional club that I have followed through thick & thin!

Matt Parry (40), Swans100 survey

Having met a group of Swansea lads on holiday in Spain, we kept in touch and decided to visit each other every year. My first year down in Swansea, the Swans were in the old League Division 2, and it was a

terrible 0-0 draw against Rotherham on a Friday night at the Vetch - yet I was still hooked on them! I'd actually seen them twice before as a kid, playing friendlies against my team Hibernian at Easter Road in the 1980s, and had always been drawn to the white strip. I later found out that Hibs had been invited to the Vetch to open the floodlights back in the Sixties, so there was a ready-made link! Since then I've watched them whenever I've been down, been to Wembley and a couple of other far-flung places to see them away, and am now with a Swansea girl for good measure!

Colin Leslie (40), Swans100 survey

It's my club, it represents my city. It's the only club I have ever supported or will ever support. The first love is always the deepest.

Richard Davies (40), Swans100 survey

Remember starting going with friends around 78/79 quite regularly, and then getting a season ticket for the famous 81/82 season. How could you go every week for 30 yrs+ (from Hartlepool to Plymouth, etc) and not care? Now I go to every home game with my wife and daughter (who travels home from university to attend).

Anon (44), Swans100 survey

I follow the club because I love Swansea City. It is and will always be my way of life. I just love supporting MY football team, not some team that people follow and don't know how to get there.

Andy Robinson (43), Swans100 survey

I've no choice. It's just part of me now after all this time. Loving the football more than ever the past few years mind.

Gareth Morgan (39), Swans100 survey

It's quite simply a part of me. It's in my blood and part of my daily life and routine. If there is a game it's the excitement and if there's not then it's the news, discussion and comment about what is happening in and around the club!

Jim White (36), Swans100 survey

My father would take me to a few games when I was very young and I have attended majority of home games since around 14 years old. The reason I suppose was social although I never really made a

conscious decision, it's just something I did.

Thomas Jackson (35), Swans100 survey

1982 - My dad took me to see the Swans play Wolves in Wolverhampton. My granddad was a Wolves fan so as my dad had studied at University in Swansea I followed the Swans. We won 1-0 and went top of the first division. My team were the best in the land. Once a Jack always a Jack.

Anthony Dews (35), Swans100 survey

They are my team, my local team. Regardless of the division they are in, they are in my blood, my skin and my heart.

J. Borley (34), Swans100 survey

Loyalty, enjoyment. A sense of belonging and togetherness you feel with fellow fans you don't even know. To me, once I started supporting the Swans that was it, even in the dark days there was always hope it'll get better.

Anon (33), Swans100 survey

Because I'm from there. It's part of my identity. And I love the club as much as I love my nearest and dearest.

Luke Thomas (33), Swans100 survey

I first became a supporter in the mid- to late-1980's. My grandfather had been a supporter going back to the 1920's and other kids in my street began supporting the team at the same time. I've followed the team, attending matches both home and away, religiously since the early 1990's. Following the Swans is part of the fabric of my life, I cannot conceive what life would be like if the Swans were not a focal point for my activities and a structure for my time. The last few years have been a halcyon period in my life because of the success we've had in that time. Very simple really.

Buying a season ticket is a major financial commitment for me, and involves saving and budgeting over the entire year. Doing this has made me savour and appreciate the Swans more I feel. Obviously, following the Swans from the bottom in 2003 to the Premier League has filled that "gap" I felt hearing stories from those that were there between 1978 to 1981, and I (and others) feel a part of that movement and change over time.

My career as a Swans supporter has structured my life. I cannot put it any more strongly. Relationships have come and gone (and the Swans have played a part at times), my career has changed and my life circumstances have altered, but the Swans have been a constant throughout it all. Even though the fortunes of the team have fluctuated wildly over the years I have supported them, the club have always played a huge role in the background of my existence, and have been the thing I have planned my everyday life around. Without the Swans, how would I idle away time on rumours or arguments on forums? How would I plot the months between August and May? What would I do? No idea. Supporting the Swans is a kind of totalising world revealing, in that I cannot envisage there not being a Swans to support, even in the darkest days of Petty and May 2003 (ironically, that became the greatest day - even against May 30th 2011). My friends, my social life, my moods - all intricately dependent upon the Swans. I celebrate this, rather than bemoan it! STID :)

Leighton Evans (32), Swans100 survey

I moved to Canterbury 5 years ago, and now struggle to afford the time and cost. The internet has been a blessing for remote support. Swansea's my home, and there's no other team I could consider supporting.

John Richards (31), Swans100 survey

Pan o ni'n crwt - teimlo ei fod yn rhan bwysig/hanfodol o fy hunaniaeth lleol/rhanbarthol/cenedlaethol.

Dewi (31), Swans100 survey

They play excellent football and I have given up playing myself.

Paul Dicks (31), Swans100 survey

I always have followed the club through good times and bad. It is part of me, my heritage and where I come from.

Tom Lloyd (30), Swans100 survey

I was born a Swansea fan due to my father being an avid fan. Didn't have a say in the matter when I was young and impressionable. Swansea City is now a part of me and I'm proud to say that I follow my local team and have done for my whole life.

Laura Williams (24), Swans100 survey

As a boy supported West Ham. Moved to Swansea as student in 2006 and began to follow results of Swansea. Was taken to game in 2008 and began to take ever keener interest in the Swans since and have over past few seasons become the club I follow most keenly.

Anon (24), Swans100 survey

I first went to the Vetch with my dad when I was about 4 years old, in the early 90s. My dad has been a lifelong supporter, and in essence I was indoctrinated into the Jackarmy life. From when I first went aged

4, I haven't looked back. SCFC is like a family member to me. I was at the Vetch with crowds of 3000, I'm there now in the Premiership, and if we went back to League 2 with crowds of 3000 I'd still be there.

Gareth Howe (23), Swans100 survey

I became a supporter having moved to Swansea [from Merthyr] to start University - after attending a few games I was hooked and eventually became a season ticket holder.

Matthew Harrison (23), Swans100 survey

I'm a committed Swans supporter who attempts to attend every home game and would attend more away if the process for disabled supporters was made easier. I've grown up with club. It still holds the same values as all those years ago. The Swans play fantastic football with great support.

Mark Phillips (22), Swans100 survey

I follow the Swans today because it's like an addiction. You can not beat the feeling of a win, and there isn't a worse feeling in the world than when you lose. I also love the banter between the fans.

Daniel Williams (22), Swans100 survey

There's something special about Swansea - the feeling it generates is electric. When I go and see them play there is nothing I'd rather be doing. Whether it's James Thomas beating relegation from League 2, Trundle's showboating or Scott Sinclair getting us into the Premiership, supporting Swansea's like watching a classic film. You never know what'll happen next but they never fail to disappoint!

Benjamin Wood (19), Swans100 survey

I first followed Swansea City when I began my first year as a student at Swansea University. I began as a casual supporter, simply checking on their form every so often, although since their promotion to the premier league (which has given me easier access to viewing their games) I have become a more active fan. I feel that it is important to support the club which is a representative of the area in which I live.

Grant Jenkins (20), Swans100 survey

My father was an avid Swans fan who first started supporting the

club in the 60's. He began to take me down The Vetch at around the age of 6. I caught the bug at a young age and became very passionate about supporting the club. I have since then started to follow Swansea City home and away, making many friends in the process. The match day has become an important social occasion and a chance to catch up with these friends.

Jack Carter (19), Swans100 survey

I first became a supporter of Swansea City when I was sat in the back seat of my father's old Citroen down Ffordd y Gorllewin by the old Quadrant Bus Station. It was towards the end of the 1999/2000 promotion season because it was a sunny Spring day as I remember. He rolled the window down and told me to listen, we listened to the North Bank in full flow. At the time I was more into rugby, following Llanelli - but hearing the North Bank made following football, and the Swans specifically, seem like there was something extra to the experience.

Anon (18), Swans100 survey

Why I Love Swansea City Part Two!!

SCfC
1912-2012

I will always love Swansea City, through thick and thin. My brother, Thomas, plays for Swansea City Centre Of Exellence Under 9's, I am Very proud of him, I feel like I know one of the players, YaY! I am also very happy to be welsh when the Swans are on the pitch. And I am Very proud of the players for BEATING Manchester City in March. WOW I still Can't belive We beat one of the Best and Richest teams in the World!

17:00

Swansea City 1
Manchester City 0

90:00
Full Time

SCfC

I Hope You Enjoyed My Mini Project On Why I Love The Swans. I Wish Them Good Luck For Next Season !!!

This is a picture of me with the N-Power Cup from Wembley When it came to my School. I kissed it twice. :) Just like the players! :)

Why I Love Swansea City

SWANSEA CITY AFC
1912-2012

By Mia Griffiths
Aged 10
Dunvant Primary School

Why I Love Them   Part 1

I love Swansea City because, Well, there is just so many reasons! I will tell you my top two reasons now!

1) They are an inspiration to Welsh football: My reasons for this is Swansea City football Club is the only Welsh Squad in the Premier Leauge, And they are just really nice people, giving up their free time for Charity events and Signings.

2) Their Courage:
After their four Consecutive losses they bounced back with a 3-0 win at home against the Strugglers, Blackburn Rovers, and the Celebration talk in the centre circle was a Photo finish, Well done Swans!
!There Will Be More On Why I Love The Swans Soon!

SWANSEA CITY AFC

WHY I LOVE THE SWANS

THE SWANS ARE GREAT!! From winning league one it only took them three years to get into the Premier-league! Plus, they are the first ever Welsh club in the league!

I am very proud of the team. I went to the Play-Off-Final at Wembley - this was a great moment; it was one of the proudest experience for me. I have been lucky to be able to go to a few other Swans games, though I would love a season ticket with my dad and my brother!

The big reason why I love the Swans is that they just don't give up and they always work hard to complete the goals their manager sets them. I do hope Brendan Rodgers will stay with us. He's an awesome manager, who has done a lot for the club and has made the guys and the squad more confident in themselves. I think Michel Vorm is an exceptional goalkeeper. There is another special reason why I like him....... And that's because I'm half Dutch, my mum is from the Netherlands! Maybe one day my little brother could be the goalie for the Swans - its his dream!

My favourite midfield player is Gylfi Sigurdsson. I met him once he is a very nice guy. I also admire the way he plays football - I would like to learn how he scores his long-range shot goals. I would also like to meet all the players and have a training session with them and my friends.

I've just started playing football myself at a local side, Bishipston. I really like it there. I usually play anywhere in midfield, we are a good side!

I'd be very grateful if I win this competition and I will keep the prize safe forever!

Happy 100th Birthday, Swansea City!!!

By Duncan Lloyd Evans (age 10)
Grange Primary School, West Cross (year 5)

What do the Swans mean to me?

What do the Swans mean to me? Everything really (after my family, of course, but even they understand as they have been season ticket holders with me since the stadium move). I could and should have moved out of the city for a better job, but how could I?

Rather than go off on one and write a thousand words expressing my undying love for the club I just thought I'd relive some memories from the past. I'm sure most of you will remember much of this, but everyone will remember it differently.

My first memory was in the late seventies when I persuaded my Dad to take me to the Vetch on a cold day Friday night to see Wimbledon . We'd all been watching their cup runs on TV and I think I wanted to see Wimbledon more than the Swans. We sat in the front of the Double Decker Stand and watched the Swans win 3-0 (I think?) and I remember that the charismatic Wimbledon goalkeeper Dickie Guy really was rubbish.

I never really attended the Vetch prior to my teenage years. My Dad was heavily involved in the local Swansea Senior Leagues and I was usually playing twice on a Saturday – once for the school and once in the junior league. We usually had an early kick off and I remember starting to rush to the Vetch after the game with some of my teammates. We used to stand right at the front of the East Terrace behind the goal, and I just wished that I was knowledgeable enough to appreciate these times (I was only about 11 or 12). This was the start of the Toshack era, and I suppose I took our success for granted in those days.

My two greatest memories of that era came from the same game where we won promotion in a night game by beating Chesterfield 2-1. I remember standing right behind the net at the front of the East Terrace when Geoff Crudgington totally missed a cross from a corner to send us one down. There was total silence in the ground (except for Crudgington who didn't seem very happy with himself and was shouting very loudly (most of the words began with F)).

Then late in the second half Toshack bulleted a header into the same corner of the net and promotion was secured – I might have even run on the pitch at the end!!

Other memories from those times:
- My first away game at Plymouth (a 2-2 draw) in front of thousands of away fans, and all the buses rushing home because we were actually on Match of the Day. Remember this is an era before video recorders!
- Regularly beating Newcastle, Chelsea , Sunderland and other top teams at home. Robbie James always seemed to score!
- Alan Waddle's hat trick against Southend to win 3-2 when we were losing very late on in the game
- Not being allowed to go to Preston for the promotion game and listening to the game on the radio.

The First Division was great but we were just delusional. We took it for granted that we would beat Liverpool, Man Utd, Arsenal, etc every week, but it was great for a 14 year old to see these players in the flesh (just as it is today for the Family Stand to see the stars of the Premier League).

My memories are odd of our time in Division One. I remember Alan Curtis scoring a fantastic winner against Southampton, Ante Rajkovic's tackling and thinking is there anyone in the world who can run as fast as Trevor Francis!

In my late teens other interests became prevalent, and I am ashamed to say that as the Swans dropped down the leagues my love affair with them was put on hold. I returned when the club was in financial trouble, and have not been away since.

The Sharpe years were memorable, and never dull. And whatever did happen to Kevin Cullis? Silver Shield?

I remember
- Tommy Hutchinson turning his full back inside out every week.
- Joe Allon's excitement at scoring a goal (nearly matched by Paul Raynor)
- Away trips to far flung outposts – Hartlepool, Hull , Wigan, Gillingham, Rochdale, Exeter . Not an all seater stadium in sight!
- Roger Freestone taking penalties
- Standing on a tiny terrace in the pouring rain to see us beat Torquay in the second leg play off final. Remember Peter Guthrie's saves!
- Jan Molby's free kick to beat Peter Shilton in goal for Leyton Orient 1-0 on a typical fierce, muddy Saturday afternoon
- Poor Alan Davies
- Molby standing in the centre circle at the Wembley play off final against Northampton and not seeming to move for 90

Streaker at the Liberty

What do the Swans mean to me?

minutes
- Frank Lampard in a Swans shirt
- Panathanaikos and Monaco in the European Cup Winners Cup
- Jimmy Gilligan and Terry Connor scoring 5 between them in a pre season friendly against high flying West Brom. We were convinced we were going to win the league and went straight to the Bookies – we finished mid-table
- Joe Moreira at left back – remember him!
- Losing 8-0 at Liverpool in the FA Cup, getting home at dawn and going straight to work
- Loving the Autoglass Final day out and Wembley
- Chopper Harris and Keith Walker at centre-half – I thought they were great

Then there was the year we nearly went out of the league. It was the time our club's fortunes changed for the better, but you can only realise that with hindsight. At the time it was awful!

I remember losing crucial games at home to Carlisle and Exeter and feeling total despair. The final game against Hull was torture and I'll never forget the third James Thomas goal – to me the greatest in our history.

We progressed magnificently then – I think we can safely call them the 'Trundle Years' and who can begrudge him. Everyone has a Trundle story, and I have not heard a negative one yet. He had (and continues to have) time for anybody and everybody, and Swansea has become a true home for him.

We had great, noisy crowds at the Vetch at this time and it led to some wild games. I remember Trundle winding up Huddersfield and getting 2 of their players sent off, and Mansfield having 3 sent off, including one for biting, and Lee Williamson for kicking Leon Britton in the head.

And who can forget Cyril the Swan wrenching the head off the Millwall mascot and dropkicking it towards the North Bank!

Leaving the Vetch was not the upheaval for me as it was for others. I love my seat, the people around me and it's great to see the young families attending in Swans shirts.

The memories of this era are already growing:
- 7-1 against Bristol City
- The streaker in front our first full house against Yeovil – and what about Trundle's lob!
- First seeing Akinfenwa as a non-playing spectator and wondering how someone of his size could actually run. He did turn out well for us though, and did complement Trundle up front
- Wondering why did we buy Rory Fallon when we never crossed the ball from the by line
- Kevin Amankwah!
- The play off final at the Millenium Stadium. I still blame referee Lee Mason for that. I'm convinced that he should have sent off Bobby Hatchell for striking Leon Knight in the penalty area when we were 2-1 up. I never thought we were going to lose that game – not until Akinfenwa's penalty anyway.
- Beating high-flying Leeds 3-2 with 10 men
- Jason Scotland up front – what a finisher!
- Winning the league at Brighton, and the magnificent way they let us celebrate in style at their ground
- Jodie Gomez's diving
- Bodde scoring from long distance (and his over the top tackling)
- Proving everyone wrong and thriving in the Championship by playing good football
- The euphoria at Pratley's goal against Forest
- Hymns and Arias at Wembley against Reading , and the smiles on the M4 all the way back. Wasn't it great!

I don't want to talk about the Premier League yet. I want to enjoy and savour these times as much as I can. This season has been great so far, and the players, club and fans are making me very proud of our city. Long may it continue!

Anonymous

Can't help falling in love with you

My love affair with the Swans began in 1964 when I enrolled as an undergraduate student at the University. Shortly before I arrived Glyn Williams, the former Cardiff and Wales international wing half who had seen me play for Aberystwyth, had recommended me to Trevor Morris for a trial at the Vetch. But I turned down the offer. My heart was set on studying history at the feet of Glanmor Williams, that Lilliputian remembrancer from Dowlais who was transforming our outlook on the history of Wales. I also knew in my heart that I wouldn't make the grade with the Swans and that it would make better sense for me to try to win my place in the University team. Swansea was the place to be in the Swinging Sixties. As everyone knows, sexual intercourse had been invented in 1963 and although that kind of malarkey seems to have passed me by, I do recall that as hairlines got longer hemlines got shorter. I vividly remember Julie Driscoll singing her wonderfully raucous version of 'Wheels on Fire' at some college gig and that the campus was brimming with posters of Marx (Karl not Groucho) and Che Guevara. I've never forgotten the sights, smells and sounds of Swansea market and the big red double-decker buses which invariably seemed to go to Cwmrhydyceirw.

But my most abiding memory is going down the Vetch and witnessing first-hand the full-throated roar emanating from the North Bank. Since I'd managed to gain a place in the University first team, my visits to the Swans' dream palace were usually confined to midweek fixtures. It was always a struggle to see much amid the bobbing heads and the incessant drizzle, but the atmosphere was magical even though the pies and the toilets were execrable. The only thing I remember of my first visit was that Keith Todd chalked up a late equalizer against Coventry. The Swans were on a downward spiral at the time and the manager Trevor Morris, who had always struck me as being more of an accountant than a genuine football man (and who had come from Cardiff City!), was living on borrowed time.

I first encountered Morris during a midweek friendly played at Fairwood between the University and Swansea during the 1964-5 season. Since Peter Davies, formerly of Arsenal, was marking me, I didn't get a sniff of the ball. Not that anyone noticed. All eyes were on a young, gangling centre forward whom the Swans players called Giorgio. He was a real box of tricks. Every time the ball was played up to him he would flick it up on to his head or chest or bamboozle our defenders with his flashy back-heels and step-overs before giving the ball away. His showy pyrotechnics infuriated Morris, who spent most of the game leaping up and down on the touchline and cursing this 17 year-old apprentice who, we later discovered, was none other than Giorgio Chinaglia. After the game the Swansea lads told us some hair-raising stories about how the young Italian spent most of his time drinking, clubbing and thieving, and of how Walter Robbins, the team's coach, used to tell him that he'd end up selling ice cream in his native land. Morris couldn't handle this young hell-raiser and Giorgio's father (who was a chef in Cardiff) was so incensed by the manager's negative attitude towards his son that he threatened him with a meat cleaver. As everyone knows, Swansea got rid of him and the tearaway got his revenge by winning the Scudetto with Lazio, winning 14 caps for Italy and joining the New York Cosmos where he played with Pelé and Beckenbauer. When he died earlier this year, memories of that arrogant performance at Fairwood came flooding back and who knows how much money Swansea might have made had he not been thrown out by the club.

Another indelible memory is of the return of the Golden Boy to the Vetch in the 1965-6 season. I had of course seen him play several times for Wales, but was thrilled by the opportunity of watching this wonderful playmaker at close quarters until his retirement in 1968. Although thinning on top and carrying a few more pounds than was the case in his heyday, Ivor alone was worth the admission price. Perfectly balanced, he could turn on a sixpence, and his feints, body swerves and long, raking passes created countless openings for the journeymen forwards who struggled to keep up with him. His speed off the mark was striking and his thunderous rising shots into the top corner of the net were legendary. I found myself watching him rather than following the course of the ball. Ivor was simply mesmerizing. True football stars are 'born in the brain' rather than in the womb and the sheer footballing genius of the elder Allchurch seared itself on my memory. By caressing his boots at the fine statue of him outside the Liberty Stadium, I pay regular homage at all home games to a remarkable player.

When Ivor retired in 1968 and the world came to an end, I took up a lecturing post in darkest Aberystwyth (where one of my star pupils later on was a certain Huw Bowen). Three years later I became besotted from afar with a beautiful, feisty librarian who worked in the town. Thanks to the good offices of a mutual friend, a blind date was arranged. Since I prided myself on knowing how to give a girl a good time, I took her in my battered Triumph Herald (whose number plate just happened to bear the initials of my lovely passenger) to the Vetch. The occasion was an international match between Wales and Czechoslovakia on 21 April 1971. En route I regaled her with tales of how Tony Millington, the only Swansea player in the team, was living proof that all goalkeepers were crazy. I promised her that he would entertain us by swinging on the crossbar and cartwheeling across the penalty area before swapping sweets with the crowd. I thought it best not to mention the fact that it was bound to rain, that the wooden seats in the stand were even more uncomfortable than pews in Calvinistic Methodist chapels, and that sampling the cheap and cheerful meat pies was not a good idea. She sat in silence for most of the game. The Wales manager Dave Bowen pinned his faith on the aerial power of Wyn and Ron Davies, and had John Toshack been fit he would probably have fielded his entire RAF front-line. A penalty by Ron Davies set us on our way, but the mercurial Millington blotted his copybook by conceding a soft goal. The Czechs couldn't believe their luck and eventually won 3-1.

To her eternal credit, my companion took pity on me (her words!) and agreed to meet me for another date on the strict condition that the Vetch was not involved. I readily agreed, we fell in love, and were married in July 1972. I deliberately arranged the wedding date so that our ruby wedding anniversary would coincide with Swansea's

centenary year! So when members of the Jack Army around us in the East Stand raucously sing 'Can't help falling in love with you', as far as I'm concerned they're serenading my beloved spouse as well as my beloved Swans.

By Geraint H Jenkins

SPECIAL NOTES

This ticket is issued on the distinct understanding that in case of any accident the holder shall have no claim against the Swansea Town Association Football Club Ltd., as the Company cannot hold itself responsible for any accident which may occur on or in the vicinity of the ground, whether such accident be due to the negligence of the Company or their servants or otherwise.

All the family are involved. Wife, 2 kids, brother, nephew, mother and father all have season tickets. Main topic of conversation!!

Anon (46), Swans100 survey

Now I travel alone and meet my friends there. The number diminishes as years go by. We lost Frank (an ex-miner) in the summer and decided that we were going to beat Stoke City 'For Frank'.

John Conibear(89), Swans 100 survey

In 1978 I started going to home games with a colleague from work, Alcwyn Richards, who was then in his 60s and had been a devoted supporter of the Swans for over 50 years. One of my best memories is of his sheer joy, happiness, pride and disbelief when the Swans got promoted to the First Division. He was then aged 66 and never

thought he'd see them play at the top level. I have to say it was a pleasure and privilege for me to attend all those first division home games in his company especially with the Swans doing so well in that first season.

Alan Hughes (56), Swans100 survey

It's in my blood. My wife, my grandson and friends have always looked forward to match days.

Tommy Vaughan (80), Swans100 survey

My uncle was Chairman (Abe Freeman). Never got a free ticket, never.

Linden Rees (60), Swans100 survey

At first I went with family - though I was allowed to go on my own;

Mum would drive down to pick me up and come in after the exit gates opened. Then school friends, and when I came back to Swansea a particular friend, Graham, during the Toshack years. Now I sit with the same two friends every game, men a bit older than me I met on the North Bank, but we don't meet before games. I tend to be independent and rarely go with a big group. A particular pleasure these days is watching with my son at odd games - he's currently a student in Liverpool, and after a spell away when music took over, is quite passionate himself. My wife enjoys football and comes occasionally but finds it too nerve-wracking! She liked it better when we weren't very good. (Her first game was the FA Cup defeat v Minehead - what a date!)

Peter Dawson (55), Swans100 survey

My wife did once breast feed our youngest son in the old vice-presidents' lounge during a game against Yeovil and no-one batted an eyelid.

Anon (55), Swans100 survey

When I proposed to my wife, I took her to a special place to do it. Outside the VETCH FIELD.

David Seward (53), Swans100 survey

After the wife left me, I found myself returning to the lads and the pub and all the things I had really missed since I married and divorced Elaine. She ruined my life for two years. It was only after I got back in to watching the Swans that I realised just how much I love the team and football.

'Paul's Story' in Keith Haynes (ed), Come On Cymru: Football in Wales (1999), p.41

Watching Swansea has given me so many memories that I could bore the pants off everyone. Taking my elder son to his first game (lost to Scarborough). Wembley in 1994 and 1997. Flying back from Germany to watch our FA Cup replay against Nuneaton, not realising that it was all ticket and Robin Sharpe getting me tickets. The emotion of Hull and the last game at the Vetch. Pratley's goal in the play off semi final last season was a bittersweet moment as while I knew that it had taken us to Wembley I also knew that my dad, who had taken me to my first ever game, wouldn't be able to come as he

was very ill. He died the next day but the rest of us took my mum to Wembley. It was a very emotional time.

Paul Ashley-Jones (45), Swans100 survey

Always with my father (he has been an ardent supporter since 1946 and is now 77!). Have made dozens of good friends over the years - all down to watching the Swans - and am eternally grateful for this.

Robert Dixon Miles (42), Swans100 survey

My dad was a big supporter like myself. He died in 2011, before he could have a smile about us being in the Premiership. I remember crying at Wembley after we had beaten Reading 4-2 because the only person I wanted to share my elation with was my dad, and he wasn't here anymore. He left me a mint copy of Swansea vs Preston at Villa Park, semi final of the FA cup 1964. It seems quite apt that Swansea's first Prem away win was at Villa Park, and I was there. I looked up to the sky and just smiled. I think my dad knew why.

Andy Robinson (43), Swans100 survey

What can I say, supporting The Swans is one hell of a rollercoaster ride!!! We've seen it all - from the depths of Division 4, to the top of Division 1; dropping back to the foot of the league, all but going out of business twice on the way; then the rise back to the promised land first under Martinez, then Brendan & that glorious day at Wembley. Following The Swans is NEVER dull, a 550 mile round trip for every home game (further for me than most away games I go to!) is a small price to pay for the privilege of watching MY team play at MY stadium in MY town. My only regret is that my Dad isn't around to see us back there. Sadly he passed away in 1998 & the last game we saw together was Brighton at The Vetch in November 1996. We won 1-0, it was absolutely freezing. We started the journey together in 1977, I wish we were still going to the games together. He was there in spirit at Wembley though, I took his lucky cap to the game & I took hold of it in my pocket just seconds before Ashley Williams deflected the shot onto the post & Gary Monk blocked Hunt's goal-bound follow-up shot. Perhaps he is still at the games with me after all...

Rob Jenkins (46), Swans100 survey

1978, my father took me to the Vetch to see the Swans against Tranmere Rovers, most likely as it was Ian Callaghan's first game for the Swans. My mother and father used to go in the 1950s and my Grandfather in the 1920s. I have taken both my kids since 2001.

David Richards (42), Swans100 survey

Have followed the club for 30 years, and currently attend with my husband and children. It is great to all be there to support them together, and they have been great during the last few years as they have been helpful to us as a family with regard to our daughter who has not been well for years.

Cath Dyer (46), Swans100 survey

All the family are involved

Two goals in two minutes at Wembley. Think I cried a bit as my best mate, who was Swans mad, had died of cancer a couple of weeks before.

Anon (42), Swans100 survey

Following the Swans is a great thing! I have made good friends, had great times and watched some great (and some very mediocre) football. I was introduced to the Swans by my dad and have since introduced my nephew (now 18) and my son (Jack aged 8).

Wayne Davies (40), Swans100 survey

Who I've gone with has changed hugely over time. Guess it reflects your life. Went with parents/grandparent. Then the day out in Swansea with your pals when a teenager, then the progression to drinking with mates (Clarence) before the game. More recently it's just a trip purely for the fix of football. Driving down to Swansea, picking up my father on the way.

Gareth Morgan (39), Swans100 survey

Went with my father as a young child, then with school mates as a teenager. I now attend with my father again, and the same mates (and some new ones!)

Thomas Jackson (35), Swans100 survey

A group of around 15 friends have been attending for over a decade. We now sit in separate small groups, which is an unfortunate consequence of the rise in season ticket prices and the move to an all seater stadium, but I sit next to a mate that I stood next to on the North Bank since 1998, and we've been constant over that time.

Leighton Evans (32), Swans100 survey

They are in my blood. My father supports the Swans, I support the Swans and my future son or daughter will support the Swans.

Stuart Middleton (30), Swans100 survey

I started watching games with my Grandad, and occasionally my Dad. My Grandad and I bought a season ticket in 2005 and up until 2010 attended games with him. Due to his bad health, I now attend games with my friends who are also season ticket holders.

Daniel Brown (20), Swans100 survey

The Swans

I Love the Swans because they make me smile with Joy every Saturday

My best player is Scott Sinclare because he scores all the goals. Plus Michele vaugn stops all goals from going into the back of the net

SWANS ARE FAB

Scott Sincare

Ruby Flynn
Age 6.
Danygraig Primary School

Ben Fulford
Year 5
Mrs Bond

Why do I love the Swans?

Were you there at Wembley when 50,000 Swans fans sang, screamed and bit their nails down to their knuckles? When me, my dad and uncle Chrissy hugged total strangers at the final whistle, that day I will remember forever.

Why do I love the Swans?

In the yard I'm usually Dyer or Gylfi when Lewis is always Danny Graham doing his celebration when he scores!, while goalie Connor might actually be better than Vorm!!!

Why do I love the Swans?

I've only managed to go and watch them 3 times this season but I haven't missed a game thanks to the Internet, but I still coax my mom to let me watch match of the day2 on Sunday night, just to watch them again.

Why do I love the Swans?
Because I'm a jack!! Who are we? Jack army!!!!

On the 7.25am Swansea to Paddington

We're on the 7.25am Swansea to Paddington, the train is rocking, the beer flowing. A Swans fan is running up and down the carriage dressed in only his boxers, while the carriage vibrates to the old classics such as "Swansea 'til I die" and "Falling in love with you". An elderly Chinese lady is sitting with her eyes shut, valiantly ignoring the chaos. My usual partner in crime Neil and I have no intention of keeping calm and join in enthusiastically with the chorus of "Swansea O' Swansea". It's the first game of the 2008-09 season, Charlton away and a return to the Championship after some 25 years. The bloke opposite offers us a bottle of wine as he says he's brought too much. We turn down his kind offer, after all it is half past eight in the morning! The Swans, backed by 2500 travelling Jacks lost 2 – 0 that day, but it was no big surprise as the English FA's trusty fixture computer always gives us a tough away game to open the season.

Like many Jacks, following the Swans is important to Neil and me, well it's not just important, it's REALLY BLOODY IMPORTANT! For, despite coming from Swansea, we have both been undercover for nearly 20 years. Yes that's right we live and work in Cardiff, doing "missionary work" as I often say. However, what doesn't kill you makes you stronger, and we get more fanatical by the season, as our long suffering wives will testify. As season ticket holders for many years, the trek down the M4 come sun, rain or snow (literally on a few occasions) and regular pilgrimages to away games is what we do, we can't help it. It's what we live for.

My own Swans journey started in 1974-75 as a 7 year old living in Gowerton, when my Dad took my brother and I to the Vetch to see Herbie Williams' testimonial. Don't ask me the score as I spent most of the game tearing up and down the West terrace underneath the old Double decker. Like others, I learned to love that place, graduating from the West to the East and eventually settling on the North Bank behind a great big pillar (I know I can't explain it either)! Tastefully located next to Swansea prison, with wind and rain whipping in off the Mumbles and no sinks in the North Bank toilets, it was never the most welcoming of places, but it always felt like home and on a good day the atmosphere was electric. On a bad day, the Builders, Queens, Garibaldi and Clarence were only round the corner!

We are at the Liberty now of course and strutting our stuff in one of the best leagues in the world. Neil's working his way through the burgers of the Premiership – apparently you can't top the ones at Aston Villa and "Jackarmy points" is now one of our major talking points. We made good friends at the Vetch and continue to make new ones at the Liberty. There's Mike, Danny and Andrew from Morriston and Keith from Bridgend to name but a few. Andrew recently caused a bit of a stir on Twitter when one well known Swans player while dining with a group of fellow players tweeted that the service in the restaurant was slow, to which Andrew sitting on the next table with his girlfriend tweeted "You should know about crap service". Funny enough the said player (who I won't name, but is actually very good in fairness to him) didn't tweet back. Football is all about opinions I suppose. I did laugh!

You'll find us these days near the back of the East stand, in front of those Swans' heavyweights Sumbler and Haynes (have you seen the size of Haynes these days?) and next to Mal Pope's brother (now that is name dropping). You can also find Neil around the astroturf pitches of Cardiff supporting his son Dan. Dan's easy to spot, he's the 7 year old dressed in full Swans kit, with Sinclair written on the back! Old habits die hard I'm pleased to say.

Haydn Llewellyn

The Vetch Field, 1929

I am a committed supporter, renewed passion - boyhood and juvenile fanatic, slumped a little in my 30's but back with a vengeance in my 40's! The course of your life and the changes that result often impact on the amount of commitment you give. It's a roller-coaster in more ways than one!

Keith Roberts (48), Swans100 survey

Got more time now. Played Pembrokeshire League for 20 years.

Norman Mathias (72), Swans100 survey

During the 2010-11 season I decided that, regardless of where Swansea City finished in the league table, it would be my last as an active supporter. My decision can be attributed in the main to old age and dislike of evening matches, particularly in the winter months.

Cliff Davies (71), Swans100 survey

I was an ardent supporter for most of my life. As one ages the support wanes.

Alun Davies (67), Swans100 survey

I haven't lived in Swansea for 40 years but once a Jack...

Anon (65), Swans100 survey

Whilst I have not always had a season ticket it has varied over the years. However the last 4 or 5 years I have missed very few home games. Why? More time on my hands and the effect of the Liberty stadium.

Paul Williams (57), Swans100 survey

Moved to London. Awful experience of dropping down through the leagues in late 80's. Now young family and difficult to commit. Also difficult to get tickets of course now.

Anon (55), Swans100 survey

Started as a few when I was younger. Became season ticket holder in early 70s. Gave that up because team were poor and I had 4 years away as a student 74-78, so occasional then. Season ticket holder again in early 80s. Fairly regular then for next 20 odd years, got season ticket for last season at Vetch and have had same seat at Liberty since the move. More away games this season partly because

of Premier League and partly retirement.

The current success of the team has made me more enthusiastic, especially about away games, but even if we'd gone to the Conference I would still attend games. The emotional attachment comes first - then the enjoyment of the actual football!

Peter Dawson (55), Swans100 survey

Frequent visitor to the Vetch in the 70s. Married in 1980 and moved to London then Cheshire. Saw occasional games (Wembley v Huddersfield, West Ham, Chester, Stockport, West Brom play-off). Then since the Paint Pot final at the Millennium I was fairly regular at away games and a few homes each season. This season I'm a home and away season ticket holder (home ST purchased in March 2011 - Plastic???)

Tim Doulgas (54), Swans100 survey

Regular attendee till 1969. (Couple of seasons was a junior season ticket holder). Then started playing Saturday afternoons. So number of games went down. Moved away from Swansea 1977. Caught a few away games. Then joined RN 1980. Caught a few games on leave. In London from 1985 - saw Swans when they were in the capital. The year we almost went out of the league started attending regularly - you don't know how important something is until you almost lose it! Attended regularly ever since. Season Ticket Holder last 4 seasons. Also - an Away season ticket holder this season.

Anon (54), Swans100 survey

When I was younger I was a regular, but family and other priorities took over

Anon (54), Swans100 survey

Due to financial reasons I did not attend any games at the Vetch as my husband and son had season tickets. Financially better off as the years have passed and thus attended as many games as possible.

Dorothy Chafey (52), Swans100 survey

I first attended games during the First Division days and kept supporting them during the following seasons. However when my family was very young my priority was to be with the family on weekends and my support of the Swans suffered somewhat! When my sons became old enough to enjoy and appreciate the games my attendance improved and has been good ever since - the last 16 years.

Huw Landeg Morris (51),Swans100 survey

Although the Jewson Stand has been constructed, it's hardly ever full. Dads and mums just can't afford to bring their kids; the reasons being unemployment and higher admission prices. Indeed those who occupy the Jewson Stand most Saturdays are the kids from the penalty competitions.

Love, Peace and Swansea City, 4 (Jan/Feb 1993)

Since I stopped playing, watching has become far more important to me.

Simon Short (47), Swans100 survey.

I am committed and that level of commitment is as strong as it ever has been. The only time it has diminished was after the Hull match. Despite survival I was so emotional and drained by it all that I consciously took a step back and didn't renew my season ticket for a couple of years. I realised that it was affecting my life. Soon got over that blip though.

Paul Ashley-Jones (45), Swans100 survey

I followed them from the newspapers and TV from the late 1970s, but became a regular visitor to the Vetch from 1986. My father was a rugby fan, and my interest in football in my early years was confined to Match of the Day and Shoot! magazine. As a result, I tended to follow those clubs who were more visible, and as they arose through the divisions, the Swans became more visible too. However, by the early 1980's, my father had died, and I did not attend any rugby or football matches in person for several years. However, when I had a new neighbour, who was a big fan, I started to go regularly with him, and have been a fan ever since.

Anon (44), Swans100 survey

In the 1990s, as the Whites were entertaining and successful, I preferred watching them even more. However, in the last few years, I have found the brand of rugby played by the Ospreys to be too dull, and I have come to follow the Swans more. Their success has also

had a difference, and as I now have a Season Ticket, I attend every game, as well as a few more away games. For a while, 10 years ago, children prevented me from attending so regularly anyway, and my interest did wane a bit, but my son now loves football, and is old enough to come regularly. He has a Season Ticket too.

Anon (44), Swans100 survey

Dear 'Jackmail', I hope you print this letter and I hope Vetch Field officials take note of my problem. I am 14 years old and therefore qualify to enter the Vetch at the juvenile rate. So why is it that game after game I'm quizzed about my age? On two occasions this season I've been refused entry through the juvenile turnstile. Are the Swans so hard up they have to resort to making under 16s pay £3.80? I can't afford to pay this and I've also seen other younger fans turned away because some turnstile attendant thinks they're over 16. Who needs this hassle when you're going to the game? Thanks,
Angry Young Fan, Burry Port.

Jackmail, 16 (June 1991)

The course of your life

The number of games has changed from going to every game I could as a young man to going to games when I can depending on family/work commitments. The amount of games I attend varies through the years, but I have put blood, sweat, and when we left the Vetch, tears into Swansea City and always will until my last breath.

Andy Robinson (43), Swans100 survey

I was probably watching around 5-10 games a season up until 2003 when the fight for survival reignited my passion. I've been there for virtually every home game since then.

Stephen James (42), Swans100 survey

I have never stopped following the club from the good days to the bad. It is only since I stopped playing football myself three years ago that I have become a season ticket holder. Before then I just bought tickets from the Ticket Office if I could make a game. I am definitely more committed now as I have got more spare time and I can involve the whole family.

Colin Jones (42), Swans100 survey

I now rely on friends who can't attend and use their season ticket.

Phil Cox (42), Swans100 survey

Used to be with the lads in the East Stand - now the wife and 2 kids all season ticket holders

Mark Griffiths (41), Swans100 survey

Once I started working, I was able to go down the Vetch for every home game.

Richard Davies (40), Swans100 survey

I'm still committed but not as fanatical as previously.

Anon (39), Swans100 survey

Haven't seen as much since move to Liberty due to ease of just turning up at Vetch. This year it is nearly impossible to get a home ticket although did go to Newcastle! I am missing out but with media coverage so good it's easy to keep up to date.

Martin Wilson (39), Swans100 survey

I used to go regular but due to money, family life and being almost impossible to get tickets these days - only been once this season.

Ian Taylor (35), Swans100 survey

When I was younger it was more affordable. Now my son comes with me and it's just an extra cost that's not always affordable. Plus there are less tickets available as the well off plastic fans are now occupying the real supporters', who aren't so well off, seats.

Martyn James (34), Swans100 survey

I'd say I'm physically more committed these days as I live nearer and have more money to go to away games than I once did. However I wouldn't say I am more committed than I used to be, more circumstance allows me to be. Me and my brother were only saying a couple of weeks ago that winning away at Villa feels no better or worse than winning away at Cheltenham. Winning away feels as it ever did, excellent.

Anon (33), Swans100 survey

I have attended less away matches over the last 3 years due to finances and time pressures through studying. Previous to that, despite being a season ticket holder, I attended less home matches due to the 300 mile round trip it involved (and Jackett's football). During my teen years and early 20's 40+ league matches a season were normal.

Leighton Evans (32), Swans100 survey

When I was younger I used to play football a lot and therefore it was not always possible to get to as many games as I would have liked. Over the last 8 years or so I have attended many more games due to the fact that I now play football less and also because I am now able to finance my hobby through my job.

Carl Smith (30), Swans100 survey

Always thought of myself as being committed but as the years go on and it gets more expensive it's harder to do.

Matt Read (31), Swans100 survey

My dad used to go to the Vetch as a youngster, and so I always followed the results long before I went to see a live match. I still follow every result and article, even though I can not afford to go to any matches these days.

Waeffe, Swans100 survey

The Liberty stadium is much closer to where I live so have had a season ticket every year since it opened. And as I've gone older I've taken more of an interest in the club. Not so much away games because of expense.

Jack Taylor (22), Swans100 survey

As a child I supported Manchester United along with the Swans, like all glory hunters, but as I grew up I completely lost interest in a club which I had no ties to.

Rhys Buckney (22), Swans100 survey

Still a massive fan, totally hooked on the club, can't get tickets as regularly as I used to be able to but always keep an eye out for the news, lineups and watch the games on TV where possible. An affinity to the club that seems like more of a religion than a corporation.

Tom Giffard (20), Swans100 survey

Thought my enthusiasm waned after leaving the Vetch but it's returned since the beginning of the 2009-10 season when my girlfriend surprised me with tickets to see Derby County. The first Swans game I went to in 2 years. I had lost interest but since Fede Bessone (of all people!) scored the winner that day I've rekindled my passion for the Swans.

Anon (18), Swans100 survey

I'm no less committed than I have been in the past despite going to less games. Obviously it isn't always feasible to go but I will never support anyone else. It doesn't mean I'm not still Swansea till I die.

Benjamin Wood (19), Swans100 survey

Some of the biggest Swans fans
I know haven't been for years

You don't have to attend to be a fan. Some of the biggest Swans fans I know haven't been for years, for a variety of reasons.

Pete Jones (39), Swan100 survey

Left:
South Wales Evening Post
12 February 1952

Inspector Merryweather bore the weight of his twenty-five years very heavily. And on this night he became increasingly morose as he considered his age, because it seemed to him that he was expending the best part of his life in the dark. Yes, and in the bloody lonely dark, too—sharing it with seven men who could not possibly comprehend the earth-shaking importance of the recent football defeat suffered by Swansea against West Ham. The tragic news had come over the London wireless just before Merryweather departed for patrol and he had not had a chance to discuss the disaster with anyone. And so he brooded, for Merryweather came from Swansea and he wished he was back in Swansea where the nights were cool instead of wretchedly humid. Yes, back in Swansea there would be a good many chaps willing to explain how West Ham knocked up a score of four whilst Swansea managed only one. A whacking good game it must have been, though.

Ernest K. Gann, Soldier of Fortune (1954)

I only missed one home game from 27 Feb 1960 until I moved away in September 1972. The game missed was in August 1969 v Aldershot. I read the newspaper report of the game whilst on a beach in Spain.

Mike Davies (67), Swans100 survey

My first memories of following the Swans were all on the radio - I wasn't allowed to go to Swansea on my own and anyway, we didn't have the money. Used to spend Saturdays at my Gran's with my sister and mum. It was always the same, get down there early

Memoirs of a long distance Swans Supporter

David Farmer

When you live more than 150 miles from the Vetch, it's tough enough keeping in touch with your team; but when your job takes you around the world it becomes even more difficult. The following piece was written during a business trip I recently took to South East Asia and the U.S.A. I hope that it conveys something of the feelings of a keen Swans supporter 'on the move'. It is written exactly as it was first produced and while some people might consider the Ian Callaghan comment to be coincidence, I have a feeling that there are things in this life which are difficult to explain. Was I receiving a message from someone? Anyone else out there had similar experiences?

When your job takes you to various parts of the world, people are inclined to envy you. The fact that waiting around airports for flights to here or there is less than fascinating is rarely of interest. Nor that you tend to live out of a suitcase and flop down in a variety of hotel rooms which are more or less the same wherever you go. But these and other problems all count for little when as a serious Swans fan you are cut off from the Vetch and its news.

What is John Toshack up to? Has Cally scored that 50th goal, (I've a feeling he'll get it soon)? Is Robbie bewildering the opposition? How is Phil Boersma getting along? These and many other questions remain unanswered. But when you are far away, the biggest need you have is to know the score.

Take the situation as I write. I am in Penang in Malyasia. The U.K. is seven hours behind local time. Thus, when the Swans kick off, it's 10 p.m. here. Would the morning paper carry the result? Maybe I'd

Page Eighteen

have to wait until Monday. But no. The 'New Sunday Malaysia Times' arrived first thing the following morning and there it was in the sports section; Swans 1 Charlton Athletic 0. Up the Swans!

It sounds like it was a tight game. Was it one of those where we might have had six? Crumbs, it's frustrating. Then there's always that lingering doubt about misprints and things. Like the occasion in Sweden when the Fourth Division results included Newport County 2 New York 0. A heck of a way to come to go home empty handed.

The sweetest result I ever read in my travels was in Paris. That was last season when we were fighting for promotion out of Division 3. Having dropped a point at home we badly needed a result at Blackpool. French papers aren't always helpful with English League soccer results, so I had to seek out an English paper. There near the Arc de Triomphe I bought one - Blackpool 0, Swans 3. My paper sailed into the air as I let out a 'Yahoo!' Those among the Sunday morning throng looked across as if to say 'Les Anglais . . .' Little did they know I was Welsh.

Back to South East Asia. Next stop was Hong Kong, where the Chelsea result did little to cheer, though the following day the news of the FA Cup draw was a brighter message. It's blooming frustrating though; I can't even shout the boys on. So when you're soaking up the Vetch atmosphere, give a thought to those roamers of the world who would rather be there than wherever they are. Give the lads a shout for us please, and let them know that we're doing our best to will them on from a distance, even it it is 3 a.m. local time. We've got to get our priorities right after all!

Swans v Crystal Palace, Programme, 5 January 1980

morning, collect and read my comics (Eagle, Beano, Roy of the Rovers), then dinner, then spend some time chatting to Gran, then retire to the kitchen to listen to Swansea Sound broadcasting the Swans games either at home or at some glamorous place like Hull, Barnet et al. I can remember vividly the Preston game when we got promoted to division 1 the first time. For a change we were at home and I didn't have a radio so was on tenterhooks waiting for the result. My dad, a miner, was asleep upstairs when the result came in. I couldn't help myself and cheered so loud I woke him up! He was not happy, but I didn't care!!

Richard Davies (40), Swans100 survey

I'd like to say 'thank you' to all the 'big game' Swansea fans (?) who crawled out of the woodwork for Liverpool, and were forced out of their cosy beds on Boxing Day to obtain their vouchers. Never has an away supporters chant rung so true as when the Cardiff supporters taunted the North Bank with 'You're only here for the vouchers'!

Voice of the Vetch, issue 2, 1990

And, what if 15,000 haven't seen Swansea play two consecutive games since 1979, we all feel for and support the same team.

The Jack, issue 6 (April 1994)

You hold dear those things that remind you of home. No matter where I am in the world I follow the Swans. You know that on cold, wet Nov afternoons the pitch will cut up quickly, the wind will howl in off the bay, the tea will be tepid and dishwater tasting and the pasties will be over cooked and give you heartburn for 3 days!!

Neil Jones, writing in 1999. Swans100 archive

I stopped this season, simple reason I couldn't afford a season ticket for my son and myself and foolishly thought that I could turn up like I have been doing for the last few seasons. How wrong was I. The demand is huge and getting a ticket is just impossible so I have to rely on media coverage! There's Sky, internet links that freeze often, radio, various websites. I do miss going to games, not just because we are playing in the Premier league, but that whole live experience, being there soaking up the atmosphere which has just got better and better since last season.

Stephen Howell (45), Swans100 survey

BBC web pages, BBC TV, SKY Sports. At my age I don't feel I'm missing out by not attending. I can follow fully via media these days.

David Lewis (67), Swans100 survey

I always try to buy tickets for home games but generally I watch games on the internet and television

Alun Davies (67), Swans100 survey

Via websites such as scfc.co.uk, planetswans. Yes I do feel I miss out, especially this, our first PL season as tickets are so hard to come by.

David Hurst, Swans100 survey

I listen on radio, internet news and chat forums. Yes I am missing out not going to games. I miss the atmosphere of the Swans supporters.

Ceri Lewis (38), Swans100 survey

I go to more away matches now as I don't live in Swansea, I live near Bristol so it's easier to go away. Always a committed fan, no matter how often I attend. When I don't attend games I am listening on internet or radio or watching on tv. I visit the 3 main Swans websites daily.

Winston (36), Swans100 survey

We certainly played our part

To Spectators

Don't think your team is the only one that can play a clever game. There are others.

Don't desert your team when they strike a bad match. That's when they want your encouragement most.

Don't blame the referee for your defeats. Take them as men. Don't go to see one team play. It takes two sides to provide your sport. Give them both a share of your cheering.

**Advice to Swansea Town supporters
in The Cambrian, 13 September 1912**

The first annual general meeting of the members of the Swansea Town Supporters Club was held on Monday evening at the Waverley Hotel, Cradock-street, when a large number of supporters were present. Councillor Harry Rogers presided, supported by Messrs. W Davies Sutton (vice-chairman), C. Rossiter (hon. Sec.), and W. G. Evans (financial sec.).

Mr Rossiter reported that the club had had a most successful season, and held 35 committee meetings, five meetings in connection with the assault-at-arms, seven general meetings, and six smoking concerts, and in addition sundry excursions were run, all of which turned out successfully.

Mr W. G. Evans presented the balance-sheet which showed a profit of £75 on the season's working; £65 had been invested in the town club, and £10 was in the bank. He stated that this was very satisfactory for a first season's working. They could boast of the largest supporters' club in Wales with a membership of over 600, and the number of members availing themselves of the 'weekly payment' system was 350. ...

It was decided to assist in the preparation of the ground during the close season, and a great number of supporters offered their services. Mr W. Sutton Davies kindly offered the use of his shop for the purpose of members paying in their subscriptions on Friday nights. It was decided to obtain a quantity of badges in the form of a broach.

South Wales Daily Post, 27 May 1913

SUPPORTERS' CLUB NOTES

BALL COMPETITION—The winning number at the last match was 30338. Tickets are on sale again today, 2d. each.

BOOK THIS DATE—SATURDAY, 23rd MARCH. Special trains have been booked for the Swans versus Bristol Rovers match. FULL DETAILS WILL BE PUBLISHED SHORTLY.

Blazer Badges 3/6, Club Badges 2/-, Ball Point Pens 2/6, can be obtained from the Supporters' Huts at the back of the Main Bank and at Glamorgan Terrace entrance. MEMBERS CAN ALSO BE ENROLLED THERE.

DANCE AT THE BRANGWYN HALL on SATURDAY, 16th MARCH for the HOSPITALS' BROADCAST FUND. Donations to this fund will be welcomed and acknowledged by the Treasurer, Mr. T. B. JONES, 24 Page Street, Swansea.

**Swansea Town v Essen
match programme, 26 January 1957**

SUPPORTERS' CLUB NOTES

TOTE WINNING NUMBERS—Saturday, 29th December—25/29. Tickets 6d. each are on sale again today, from members of the committee, stewards in the West and Centre stands and other sellers. Winning numbers published in the Evening Post every Tuesday.

Please cheer the boys on to victory today. Your vocal encouragement is a great incentive. We wish the team every success and look forward to an attractive game in the next round.

TRIP TO LEEDS, Saturday, 19th January. Leave Swansea Friday midnight. Stay in Leeds Saturday night and leave Sunday mid-day Fare inclusive of coach and hotel accommodation—price £3/0/0. Immediate application essential. Deposit must be paid with booking.

Cushions are for hire in the West and Centre stands, price 6d.

Club Badges 2/3d., Club Pens 2/6d. now available. Membership of the Supporters' Club is only 2/- per season. If you are not already a member please join now.

The match today is being broadcast to the Hospital patients at Morriston, Swansea General, Mount Pleasant and Cefn Coed. This facility is much appreciated by the patients. This scheme is expensive as we have to pay a yearly rental to the G.P.O. for the hire of the private lines from the Vetch field and St. Helen's. Help us to continue this by contributing to the Fund. All donations welcomed and acknowledged. The secretary is Mrs. M. England Jones, 7 Pantygwydr Road, Uplands, Swansea.

Match programme Swans v QPR, 5 January 1963

Which Scheme Suits You Best

All the building bonds on offer have clear advantages and are designed to suit the needs of all our supporters, from the wealthiest to the fan on the terraces.

We are making a conscious effort to cater for all our supporters who wish to help with the Vetch Field redevelopment and at the same time secure for themselves lucrative benefits by investing money in the club.

The £600 Unit (Non Repayable)

These bonds are *not* a loan and can be purchased for £600 each.
Those who buy this particular bond will have the following benefits:-
1. Entitlement to one specific seat per bond for all the Football League matches at no cost for a period of 5 years.
2. The seat will bear the personal name plate of the bondholder.
3. During the 5 year period the bond will be transferable.
4. The first right to the seat (subject to payment) for home cup ties, and a seat for semi-finals and replays on neutral grounds when Swansea City FC is involved.
5. At the conclusion of the fifth year the bondholder will be given the opportunity to enter into a similar scheme for a further five years at a price to be determined.

In addition any subscriber wishing to purchase a Non-Repayable Bond of a higher denomination can do so up to a maximum of 10 years.

The £100 Unit (Repayable)

By purchasing this bond, the holder will have loaned to the Club the sum of £100 interest free for a period of 10 years, repayable from year 6 to year 10 inclusive at 20% per annum of the original capital cost.
Purchasers of £100 bonds will accrue the following benefits:
1. Entitlement to one specific seat per bond.
2. The seat will bear a personal nameplate.
3. For every bond held there will be a 10% discount allowed off the price of a season ticket (or a vice presidents' ticket) appropriate to that seat for the period of the bond (10 years) subject to the season ticket (or vice presidents' ticket) being acquired by 15th June in each year.
4. Over the 10 years the bond will be transferable.
5. A guarantee for a ticket (one per bond and subject to payment) for home cup ties and for semi-finals, finals or replays played at a neutral ground when Swansea City FC is involved.

The £25 Unit (Non Repayable)

Purchasers of £25 building bonds will receive the following benefits:
1. A 10% discount per season ticket off the price of a ground season ticket for the 10 year period subject to the season ticket being acquired before the start of the Football League season each year.
2. The bond will be transferable during the 10 year period.
3. A guarantee of admittance for home cup ties and for semi-finals, finals or replays played at a neutral ground when Swansea City FC is involved. This is subject to payment of the admission price.

We certainly played our part in Swansea City's great season. That is the feeling of our all supporters particularly those who raised the temperature at Preston when victory meant Division One football. Now that all of us have had time for a little back slapping it wouldn't be amiss to look back on the bad old days when gates at the Vetch were barely over 1000. The Supporters Club was reformed in 1976 – Fourth Division memories! The Dragons Club had been helping to fill the gap left by the old Supporters Club but we believed it was time for a proper organisation to start flourishing once more.

Mr. David Cray, his two sons Jonathan and Philip and their grandfather Mr. William Cray photographed with Club Chairman, Malcolm Struel. Jonathan and Philip are the two youngest Building Bond holders to date.   *Photo by Roy Hughes.*

Match programme, 26 April 1980

The five years that have passed have all been exciting. Promotion, tension and wonderful trips away from home where we feel that our vocal efforts did much towards bringing home the points.

John Button, Secretary Swansea City Supports Club, in Swansea City AFC: From Fourth to First, 1978-1981 (1981).

As a keen supporter of the Swans for almost twenty years, I feel that I deserve a return for my loyalty for the hundreds (and probably thousands) of pounds that I have paid into the club at the turnstiles and in the club shop as well as the hundreds of hours spent on boneshaker buses and freezing terraces. I would like to know just how the club is run.

Letter to Swimming in Swansea Bay, 1 (Spring 1992)

Brentford home midweek 1996. Jan Molby scored the winner with a penalty in injury time. I was stood on the east part of the North Bank. I was one of a few who got that part of the bank singing that night, it was normally the end down by the away fans. Molby commented years later how it was like they plugged the fans in as well on night games at the Vetch. I'd like to think I played a small part of that that

We certainly played our part

THANKS SUPPORTERS, SAYS GORDON

The vast increase in crowds this season has caused a busy time behind the scenes at the Vetch Field. Club secretary, Gordon Daniels reports: "I have nothing but praise for the way in which the public have responded to our appeals. Supporters are coming earlier and earlier and this means that congestion at the turnstiles is reduced to a minimum. Every turnstile at the ground has been open for every game this season. In the past, it has not always been easy to get men for this job but they are coming forward splendidly this season."

"The identity pass system for youngsters of 16 and under has been another part of the organisation here which has gone smoothly. Our younger teenage supporters have been coming forward in large numbers to benefit from this plan which reduces the cost of admission. In fact, requests are still coming in for passes. All you need are a passport photograph and evidence of date of birth - we do the rest."

Mr. Daniels also reports that the administration has been helped by the fact that stand tickets these days, especially the centre stand, are in very high demand. This means that most of them have been sold before the match .. so be warned!

The new voice which answers the phone this season belongs to Heulwen Francis who comes from Pontlliw. She has joined the Vetch Field staff to help cope with the extra demands and, judging from the constant flow of incoming calls, must be in charge of one of Swansea's busiest switchboard.

JOHN DAVIES, Chairman of the Supporters' Club, with JOHN BUTTON, Secretary and GEOFF EVANS, Vice-Chairman present a cheque on behalf of the Supporters to Club Chairman MALCOLM STRUEL.

Match programme, 28 October 1980

night. I was hoarse for days after that game, probably close to my swansong as a North Bank chanter.

Stephen James (42), Swans100 survey

Your support will be vital and turning up in numbers at our home games may well be the difference needed to turn a possible draw into a crucial win.

Make no mistake about it, there will be ups and downs over the coming weeks. Some results will go with us, others will go against us, but that's football and that's why we love it.

So, as always, be patient, be supportive. And give Brendan and all the players all the vocal encouragement you can over the coming weeks.

Be proud and remain Swansea 'Til We Die.

Huw Jenkins, Match programme,
Swansea City v Doncaster Rovers, 19 February 2011

Swansea City Football Club

GO FOR GOALS

AND HELP BUILD A TEAM FOR THE FUTURE

Sponsor your Favourite Player or the Whole Team for every goal they score during the 1988-89 season.

The amount can be as much or as little as you like — its your choice.

Not only will you be helping the Swans build for the future, you will also gain automatic entry into the GO FOR GOALS FREE PRIZE DRAW which will take place at the end of the season. Among the prizes on offer will be a continental holiday and season tickets for the Vetch.

There will also be a MONTHLY DRAW giving you the chance of being our guest for the day.

Everybody who makes a pledge to GO FOR GOALS will receive a certificate, a signed photograph and meet their favourite player.

All you need do is fill in the coupon below and return it to:
Tony Russell, Commercial Manager, Swansea City F.C.

GO FOR GOALS

I would like to sponsor .... for every goal
he/they score in 1988/89 Season and pledge the sum of £..........................
per goal which I will pay monthly/quarterly/end of season.
Name .... Tel. No. ....
Address ....

One of the most depressing days of my life

Away at Notts County in the mid 1980s. It was freezing and the fog had come down and I couldn't see our goal at all. All the half was Notts County attacking and we couldn't see a thing. Occasionally we would hear a roar and realise that they had scored. We lost 3 0 and it was one of the most depressing days of my life.

Paul Ashley-Jones (45), Swans100 survey

Generally he is short of stature, anaemic-looking, with a head too big to suggest it contains only brains, a high shrieking voice, reminiscent of a rusty saw in quick staccato action. He is blind to every move initiated by the Swansea Town players, but his attention to a faulty clearance or badly placed pass is microscopic.

Description of some Swansea fans in Sporting News, 1922

With feeling among Swansea Town supporters already running high over the way in which cup-tie tickets have been distributed, there was a remarkable scene outside the Vetch Field this morning.

Between 5,000 and 6,000 people has assembled in a queue from the Glamorgan-terrace entrance to try to get one of the remaining field tickets for the fifth round game with Sunderland on Saturday. Some had

Left:
South Wales Evening Post, 5 February 1952

Change in soccer atmosphere

To the Sports Editor

Sir,—Swansea Town's recent run of success in Cup and League must surely convince those hard-to-please followers that there is some good in the team. Now they are to meet the famous Newcastle United in the fifth round, and are recognised as a vastly improved team.

What are the grousers thinking now? I tire of reading the criticisms of dejected supporters as soon as the team loses a match or two, but unfortunately this tendency to abandon a "sinking ship" is not confined to the ordinary "banker."

Strangely, we have heard little in the last month of the "resignations." Perhaps directors who thought in those terms have also been inspired by the recent run of success. I can recall some lean periods in the history of Swansea Town when some directors footed the bill to tide over difficulties, and every true follower of soccer in the town owes something to those men.

I hear that "resignations" are still a possibility: if that is so, I would suggest that they be accepted and that the "old brigade" carry on as they have done successfully in the past, especially now when a rise in the League is portended and with the prospect of a great cup duel ahead. **"Shareholder."**

queued from 5am.

But five thousand more had queued at other entrances to the ground. No notices had been posted at any entrance to show where supporters should queue.

Despite the fact that some had queued since 7 a.m. it was not until 9.30 that a casual remark by a police officer revealed that no tickets were to be sold at any other entrance other than the one in Glamorgan-terrace,

A regular supporter of Swansea Town bitterly remarked: 'We are disgusted with this lack of organisation on the part of the club.' He added that he did not know whether it would be true to call him 'a regular supporter' in future.

There were many women queuing in the morning.

South Wales Evening Post, 14 February 1955

I would like to express my disgust at the continued apathy of those in control at the Vetch.

I think the time has come when the long suffering supporters should rise and demand action. Obviously the present board of directors have no intention of trying to remedy the present state of affairs by getting new players. I suggest they resign.

No doubt the transfer of men like Allchurch, Cliff Jones and others would bring in huge transfer fees, but what good would that do? It would mean building a practically new team, and men like Allchurch would be impossible to buy.

Surely those in charge must have realised these brilliant footballers would not be content to carry on as they have for so long without a first-class centre-forward or centre-half.

If these men leave Swansea it will be the beginning of the end of 'The Swans' as a first-class team. So let us get something done before it is too late,

Yours,
Another fed up fan
South Wales Evening Post, 4 December 1956

We hear time and time again the old tale of so-and-so being watched, but, of course, never bought. The club have the money; then why don't they spend it and take the Swans up to the First Division not send them there?

Letter to South Wales Evening Post, 10 October 1958

Swansea City had to be satisfied with a point from their game with Northampton Town at the Vetch Field last night under the worst possible conditions which were a test of stamina as well as skill. It was indeed surprising that the teams were able to build up any movements because control must have been a nightmare in the driving wind and rain which persisted almost throughout ... The gate of 1,301 (receipts £353) could well be one of the lowest on record.

South Wales Evening Post, 19 September 1973

They deserve even greater support than we've been giving them. At least one of the chants from the boys at the back of the North Bank "Swansea City are Magic" comes to us all as we watch Curtis and Co. bamboozling the opposition. Why not conjure up some magic of your own, lads and bring your absent friends into the "Magic Circle" at the Vetch. I am sure that once they have been they will be regulars.

Swans v Rochdale match programme, 10 September 1977

The Class of '84

The season 1983-84 holds disastrous memories for Swansea fans. So, sadists as we are, we've decided to feature it!

Swansea City supporters were probably guilty of enjoying a taste of the good life in the early eighties, but for sheer awfulness nothing can compare with the ineptitude displayed during our relegation from division two in 1984. During Swans' storm up the divisions, dismal financial mismanagement and some extraordinarily crass public relations plunged the club into bankruptcy and disrepute. By the time we had suffered relegation from division one, three would-be chairmen, each with local reputations somewhere between Rupert Murdoch and Jack the Ripper, were fighting undignified battles before a disbelieving public. And the players, oh God, the players. A desperately overworked Jimmy Rimmer aside, the team featured those who couldn't play, those who used to play and those whose performances were made available only with a doctors certificate. Ray 'Fatman' Kennedy, having already been stripped of the captaincy was soon showing the sort of form that would take him to London Underground posters. Swansea almost snapped QPR's hands off when offered £100,000 for Beached Whale Jeremy Charles, mediocre son of an accomplished father. Arch jokers in the pack however were international defenders, two local boys made bad, Nigel Stevenson and Dudley Lewis, our very own Abbot and Costello. Stevenson cultivated a feverish resolution to find opponents with passes, but the main question was whether he was paralysed from the waist down or the neck up. Lewis developed the uncanny ability to lose possession only in situations that led to goals and was quickly responsible for creating a good 40% of the oppositions tally. Utility player Chris Marustik, drunkenly moping his way through the year of the blur generally went up in everyones estimations when he followed up a handling stolen goods charge with the honorary drink driving charge. He now runs a Swansea wine bar. The team clicked and burped its way to the foot of the table despite some pretty hot competition off Cambridge and reached Christmas with a sensational 9 points from 21 games. A typical outing was the game against Grimsby in which Swansea dominated, fell behind then lay down and died. Swansea's luck being perfectly illustrated by the fact that Grimsby scored during the five minute period that defender Gary Chivers took over in goal, after Rimmer was injured. Curling his lip icily manager John Toshack proceeded to mete out the pettiest of club disciplines typical of the growing desperation of his crumbling dictatorship were the £500 fines imposed on Alan Curtis and Neil Robinson for urinating during a training session! Emlyn Hughes - he of the boyish grin and arthritic knee - was wheeled in to halt the slide. On his debut at Huddersfield he responded by scoring a match-winning own goal. Worried coach Doug Livermore, wearing the look of a man who knew his intestines were forty yards long, took over the reins and watched as the team coasted to seven defeats in nine games. Toshack reappeared briefly, towing in 'Crazy Git' Wyn Evans and the Masters of Disaster combined their hunt for relegation with a bemusing tour of Malaya. Tosh received his second bums rush in March shortly after nodding a typical goal (against the Swans) in a 6-1 pasting at Hillsborough. Places on the Swansea board were now being distributed free with the morning milk, the reserve team boss Les Chappell was made caretaker. He slammed the team after a diabolical initiation ceremony at Ewood Park and then proceded to reward the dreariest offenders with new contracts. In the Blackburn rout, Dudley turned his back on a pass from his keeper and a Rovers attacker potted home in fits of giggles. They finally bowed out with a sizzling 5-0 defeat at Portsmouth having used a record 33 players over the course of the campaign. I suppose you could cheerfully record the departure of some of the highest paid donkeys ever seen at the club. In many ways matters went from bad to worse afterwards ...Appletons non contract nobodies...John Bond's allstar euthanasia XI...High Court thrills and spills...further relegation after a loo break in division three.

What prospect is there of anyone emulating Swansea's riches to rags story?

Niall O'Brien

Jackmail, 8 (Aug 1989)

One of the most depressing days of my life

'IMPACT' IN JULY

It was common at football grounds in Britain to see the fan skip past the official programme seller and head for the fella standing on the corner flogging the fanzine. One top Scottish manager described 'The Absolute Game', a general fanzine, as "a festering boil on football's bottom". 1988 was the year when the fanzine rose and gave a polite two fingered sign to the quality press and the footballing mafia - the club directors. But where did Wales figure in all this? Until April of last year fanzines were unheard of in the Principality. "I missed my first home match of the season, against Rochdale, in order to get the first issue ready for the following week", recalls the editor of 'Jackmail' the 'Voice of Swansea Supporters' as it proudly declares. And so with a rusty typewriter, some tippex and a bundle of photos nicked from various footy mags, 'Jackmail' stumbled onto the terraces of the Vetch field last September. Here was a platform where Swansea fans could speak their minds.

"I wanted to provide the supporters with a place where they could air their views, previously all comments from the fans have been restricted to the terraces. Fans have always chanted 'We hate Cardiff', but have never had a chance to explain why - now they have somewhere where they can express an opinion on anything from Cardiff City to the quality of coffee on the North Bank." It was this brand of unashamed precocity which was soon to have club chairman Doug Sharpe choking on his after-match Scotch. "I dislike bringing up that old cliche 'More power to the people', but this is basically what it's all about." And the story goes on. Over a year later and 'Jackmail' produces 700 copies every issue, and this has helped to keep supporters from Dublin to Devizes to keep abreast of goings-on in 'Wales Second City'.

One threat of legal action and numerous verbal attacks by the chairman later and 'Jackmail' is in defiant mood on the issue of Doug Sharpe. "Whilst selling 'Jackmail' outside the East Stand last year I was approached by Mr. Sharp himself and told that my magazine was 'Fucking rubbish', and also accused of conning people into thinking I was selling the official programme! The critics are by far outnumbered by the supporters of the mag, though."

So we've established that 'Jackmail' is a much-loved mag, but does it really have a strong case against the chairman? Do his actions really merit the nicknames 'Doug the Thug' and 'Dougie Shark'? "Quite frankly, yes. Many fans want to see the profits made on players sold used to build a better team, and we want the Vetch looking like the first division stadium it was eight years back, not the laughing stock which it is at present. These are just a few requirements. So you see, we aren't just here to point a satirical finger at the board, we also campaign for better facilities. Everyone who contributes to 'Jackmail' has Swansea in his/her heart, whilst Doug Sharpe has this club under his thumb. For instance, if you pipe up and say 'what have you done with the Pascoe sale money, why hasn't the North Bank had a lick of paint?' he'll throw in your face his favourite line 'I saved this club in 1985' It is this reluctance to cater for the fans which is annoying and deeply saddening."

As time goes by, 'Jackmail' may have to remove it's tongue from it's cheek and cast a serious eye upon the future of Swansea. This is 1989, a time when soccer is being dragged through the dirt constantly. Are there any encouraging aspects to have come out of football this season? The Editor of 'Jackmail' recalls Swansea's recent trip to Sheffield United in a game where the home team needed a win for promotion. "How many fans can say that a game which their team lost 5-1 was their best day out? Swansea fans can. At the end of the game, the home fans invaded the pitch and after the ritual mobbing of the players made for the 200 or so Swansea fans. Thousands of Sheffielders, to our surprise, began climbing into the Swans terrace shaking our hands and swopping souvenirs and the whole ground was in unison chanting 'Swansea City'. This is what football is all about and if Colin Moynihan could have seen what happened he would have realised how out of touch he is."

In the wake of Hillsborough and the calls for more 'out-of-town' stadiums, a move from the Vetch field to nearby Morfa is beckoning. "It has been said by some reliable sources that Swansea will move to Morfa when the lease comes up on the Vetch in a few years. Every thing possible will be done in prevention, only once it's impossible will we concede defeat." Strong, passionate words which imply that 'Jackmail' will be losing it's wild, revolutionary image and mellowing with age. "No chance" proclaims Ed, "Look out for some real digs at Terry Yorath in issue 8. You can rest assured that the cynical 'Jackmail' tongue will be wagging for a while yet." Let's hope he's right. Without the likes of 'Jackmail' the football fan would not have a shoulder to cry on, a place to take the piss or praise it's heroes. The fans have lost nearly all their liberties, please don't take the fanzine ●

'Jackmail' is available from:
PO BOX 24, PORT TALBOT, WEST GLAMORGAN SA13 1QN

Jackmail, 8 (Aug 1989)

Attack is the name of the game, it's a style which British football needs in large doses. Declining gates all over the country in recent years show that the public is becoming disenchanted with the way the game is played. The negative pattern of play-it-safe makes football seem such a drudgery.

'Press Box', Match programme, Swans v Liverpool, 2 January 1982

I think the most vivid memory I have, although I don't know why it stands out, is the misery I felt on losing 2-0 to Merthyr in the Welsh Cup 4th Round in 1987-1988. Wet, cold, miserable, lost. Surely a lowest point.

Phil Bethell (53), Swans100 survey

It's a sad fact that our home attendances rarely top the 4000 mark. Sorry Doug, but £3.80 is too much to ask for a place to stand on the North Bank – and the fans reluctance to pay this is reflected in our dismal turn-outs. Way back in '87 we never expected less than 5000 at the Vetch, and the quality of football wasn't as good as it is now – so the only explanation is that people simply can't afford to get in, so the admission prices must be slashed.

Jackmail, 14 (December 1990)

Whilst the racists may be growing in number they will always be abhorred by the vast majority of fans who deplore the whipping up of racial hatred at football matches.

Jackmail, 21 (1994)

We slumped ... we took on the basement's might ... and we failed. Yes we resigned ourselves to the sorry fact that Swansea City could become a permanent fixture in the fourth division.

Jackmail, 3 (August 1988)

It is now ten years to the month since we gained promotion to division one, so our current league position is a bitter pill to swallow. The last eight years have been a bumpy downward ride on the rollercoaster that is football. We've been subject to some embarrassing defeats, and on a few occasions those embarrassing defeats have added up and developed into embarrassing seasons. But even in this eight year long tale of woe there's always been an exciting air of unpredictability at the Vetch Field. A 'not knowing what's around the next corner' feeling, and that gives you hope for the future. It's this that makes you feel, through all the bad times, glad to be a Swansea supporter.

Jack Mail, 16 (June, 1991)

Relegation had become a relative stranger at the Vetch throughout the late seventies and early eighties, no sign of it for quite some time. However, in 1983-84 the bugger bought a season ticket to the Vetch, and seemed to be at most of the away matches, too. I prefer not to recall too much about our slide back down the divisions, it felt like being in a lift with the 'down' button stuck in position. Suffice to say that I confess to losing faith after a mind-numbingly awful 0-2 reverse at Newport County on Saturday, 13th October 1984. The then manager, Colin Appleton, had built a ragbag team of old lags (Tony Kellow, Paul Richardson), fading players (Nigel Stevenson, Chris Marustik), and youngsters being asked to perform beyond their

tender years (Colin Pascoe, Dean Saunders). Newport duly turned us over, pausing only to enable both Richardson and Dudley Lewis to get sent off for throwing a punch and 'foul and abusive language' respectively. It was dismal, and as I left Somerton Park, I not only had to cope with my despair and anger at yet another defeat, I also found myself dodging the 'visiting' Cardiff City psychopaths, determined to give their club a bad name. The whole sorry experience left me in a very reflective mood, and on the train during the journey home, I came to the conclusion that I just couldn't take this any more. Life was hard enough as it was, without Swansea City dragging me down with them week after week. There must be better things to do with my life, mustn't there?

Jonathan Taylor,
'Twenty seven years in a black and white scarf' in Keith Haynes (ed)
Come On Cymru: Football in Wales (1999), pp. 14-5

Regards the club, people in Swansea have no pride in the team. Lack of success made people apathetic, the 80's atmosphere has gone. The astronomical prices ensure this. Still there's 3,500 who will never be disillusioned, and hope for the return of the heady days. Genuine fans.

Love, Peace and Swansea City, 4 (Jan/Feb 1993)

Talking of policing and stewarding, did anybody witness the scenes on the North Bank when we scored against Burnley? Two young boys aged about 12 climbed the fence in celebration, with no thought of invading the pitch, when along came a policeman and instead of asking them to get down or giving them a gentle push, he came along and forearm smashed them from the fence! This is unnecessary as was asking kids to stop sitting on the barriers at the Hull game. They weren't obstructing anybody, and were so little they had to sit on the barriers to see the game!

Love, Peace and Swansea City, 5 (Mar/Apr 1993)

For nigh on fourteen years now I've stood on the North Bank and, like the rest of us, seen the tales of glory and disaster unfold before my eyes. The vast majority of Swans fans have taken the fall from grace with remarkable dignity (perhaps too much dignity). I have always been proud to be a Jack, and although this will probably always remain the case, recent events on the Vetch Field terraces have

One of the most depressing days of my life

made a severely disillusioned fan.

Jackmail, 21 (1994)

Northampton retook the free kick and the ball flew into the net. The other half of Wembley rose to their feet like a wave and let out a huge cheer. I don't think I'd even noticed they were there until then. The Jacks had been so loud that we drowned them out. I certainly hadn't even thought we might lose it. But now I felt physically sick. And then people around me put their arms in the air and started singing 'Take my hand, take my whole life too, for I can't help falling in love with you'. We were still here, we were still proud and we were still Swansea. But I still felt sick and we were still in the bottom division.

Anon (39), Swans100 archive

Recent victories against teams also near the dungeon's trap door have provided some hope but losing to the likes of Rochdale and Torquay is embarrassing. Being down the bottom of League Division Three is humiliating.

Jackanory, 7 (Feb/Mar 1998)

We're never ever going to win the Premier League / I'll doubt we'll even stay in Division 3.

Lyrics to Teen Anthems, Swansea City, late 1990s

The club has never found the power and the freedom of the Internet an easy thing to live with. For reasons known only to football clubs themselves, they seem to think they run best under a regime of mystery and total control. This puts them immediately at odds with a medium such as the Internet where facts, opinion and rumour can be broadcast immediately to the world.
The club's reaction to this has often been to highlight one or two individuals, and through the power of their contacts in the media, try to discredit them as whingers and agitators with hidden agenda. They have found it convenient to class all fans on the Internet under these categories.

Gary Martin in Black Swan, 1 (January 2000)

And so we go marching on to what should be a memorable season. But why do we feel so flat at times? Here we are at last stumbling out of the wilderness in the direction of the warm city lights, but it simply doesn't feel that way. Ask the fan next to you and he or she will probably agree that the buzz of expectation is nowhere like when Molby took us to Wembley or when Frankie nearly gave us promotion and a cup to cherish. A complete stranger arriving in Swansea would never believe that we're virtually unassailable in our quest for promotion; we've beaten the best in the league, put together an incredible run of victories and have a defence that would moisten George Graham's sheets. Despite all this, there's no spark, no passion & at times no empathy.
This can only be put down to two things:
- the quality of Division 3, and
- the way the club is being run.

Black Swan, 4 (2000)

Rotherham in 2000 to win the bottom division. The packed ground, the place going bonkers when Jason Price got brought down for a penalty and then the pitch invasions and the police horses on the pitch. It seemed as if the police had lost control and the whole atmosphere turned sour. Afterwards we wanted to go in the opposite direction to the other Swans fans because we'd parked somewhere odd. The police told us they couldn't guarantee our safety if we went that way. Wearing Swansea shirts we had to walk through a load of cross Rotherham fans. Then afterwards we found out someone had

been killed before the match started. Football isn't worth that.

Anon, Swans 100 Survey

It should have been the party to end all parties. Instead, Swansea's first championship celebration since 1949 turned into a wake.

The death of 42-year-old Terry Coles, a friend of several players, trampled by a police horse, knocked all the joy out of what should have been a champagne afternoon.

Swansea chairman Steve Hamer said: 'I am devastated and the team feel the same. This has ruined what should have been a cherished memory for everyone.'

'A man's life is more important than a game of football'.

Daily Mirror, 8 May 2000.

What a fortnight

I guess I find it hard to understand why there needs to be calls for unity amongst the different groups of supporters because at the end of the day wherever we start our journey to watch the Swans from - we are all 100% Jacks.

Whether we get our news about the club from the Internet, Swansea Sound or Real Radio, Evening Post or Western Mail, HTV, BBC Wales or Teletext - we seek out that info because we follow the Swans - 100% Jacks.

The past two weeks have been an emotional roller coaster, there's been more media interest re the goings on "off the field" at The Vetch then there ever has been over our footballing successes.

Although this can't be compared to some of history's great life and death events there will always be with us a memory of where we were when we heard the news that the "Petty hatchet" had fallen.

There has never been a great "them" and "us" dividing line between Swansea City players and supporters - the kind that you would expect and see at other clubs, but any line there is, has been at it's thinnest in recent days as players, supporters and staff of Swansea City Football Club join together to save the Jacks.

Emotion has been high and no doubts that Tony Petty has become for us "Public Enemy #1".

"Petty Petty Petty - Out Out Out" – "We want Petty Out - we want Petty Out!"

Why? Well, if this fella doesn't go he'll lead us the way of Newport County, Aldershot - in fact there were moments when I

thought that following the fate of Hereford, Scarborough and Doncaster the best of the options we faced - at least we'd have a Swans to watch.

I'm so angry! How could this have happened? I actually introduced the guy to the crowd before the Rochdale game. He didn't seem that excited to be there - I thought he was a bit on the shy side.

This guy has to go - the contempt that he has shown for the players, supporters and tradition of Swansea City Football club mean that there could never be a good relationship between Tony Petty and those who follow this club.

I believe we will win and Tony Petty will tire of the hassle of owning Swansea City Football Club - maybe sooner than we dared think possible.

However, what if we do win - what happens then (and a phone call that I just received makes me think that we will win)?

It will be our last chance! We have to get behind whoever takes this club over (if they are genuine in their desire to take Swansea City forward).

Attendance must improve - in other words if we can get to the game - we must get there!

Maybe like in other football clubs the new owner/Chairman might start to see a profit - fine, as long as this football club is now built on a solid and firm foundation.

The display of support from the supporters of the Swans in recent days has been an example to all.

I firmly believe that whatever reasons are given for Mr Petty saying "Adios" it has been that hostile reaction at the ground, on

One of the most depressing days of my life

Radio phone-ins, on the marches and the Internet that has brought this about.

Now let's keep it going! Let's maintain that unity amongst the fans. Let's all become PR's for the club and get fans to return to watching the Swans.

Maybe we don't go to those swanky "black tie" dinners but August's launch of the Supporters' Trust showed how a much less "posh" do could raise.

By Kevin Johns - 23 October 2001
Published on www.scfc.co.uk

Exeter City's Sean Devine finishing past Neil Cutler in front of the West Terrace in a relegation six pointer over Easter 2003. It sent the Exeter fans behind that goal into delirium. At that point I truly believed that the Swans were destined for Conference Football for the first time in our history. Possibly one of my worst moments in football.

Jack Carter (19), Swans100 survey

The Hull game. Singing the national anthem before the game and having tears in my eyes because of both the emotion and the thought that this really could be it for us.

Huw Mellor (46), Swans100 survey

Personally, from a football perspective, I'll be glad to see the back of 2006. A year that promised so much has delivered so very little... apart from two tin-pot trophies, the heartache of a play off final defeat and a glut of woeful performances from players that are capable of so much better.

Yes, winning the Football League Trophy was nice (especially winning it in Cardiff) and the FAW Trophy provided some welcome easy money. But defeat to Barnsley in that play off final ripped the heart of the fans and poor performances before and after that fateful day have been bitter pills to swallow.

A Touch Far Vetched! December 2006

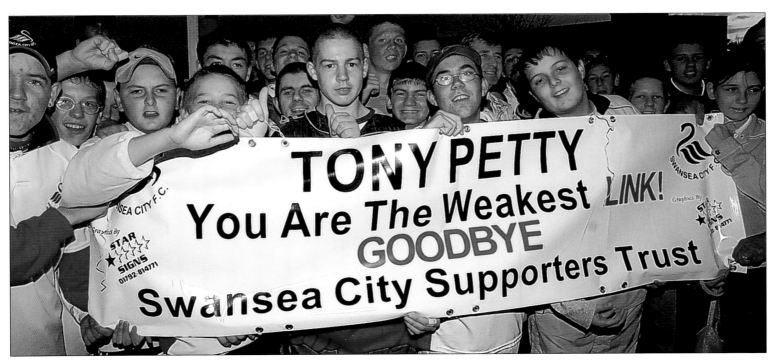

Battle for Britton

The battle has been won but the war is far from over. It was obvious last season that if our beloved club was going to succeed we had to do everything in our power to hold on to our best players. We realised at the outset that this was going to be far from easy.

The Trust, therefore, decided to launch it's most ambitious campaign, "The Battle for Britton". The response from the fans was overwhelming and, on the strength of the pledges made, The Trust were able to offer sufficient financial assistance to enable the club not only to secure the services of Britton and Martinez but also to bring in Trundle, Robinson and Maylett. Imagine a team without these Swansea legends now! The Trust made the decision to continue with "The Battle for Britton" fund and when the nightmare injuries struck our

assistance enabled Brian Flynn to bring in quality loan players such as Wilson, Tate and Neidielo.

We would like, always, to be in the position to assist the club in bringing in players of the highest calibre in our common fight to win promotion and bring even greater success to Swansea City. Brian Flynn has a unique ability of spotting talent. The next Britton, Martinez and Trundle is out there and, when they are spotted, we want to be in the position to bring them to the only team that matters....Swansea.

Make your pledges now! An application Form is included with this Newsletter.

Remember, the next time the boys run out on to the pitch – they TRULY are YOUR team because the pledges you have made turned the dream into a reality!

Macclesfield, Mascots and Martinez
– a recollection of the great escape

It was not the proudest moment of my life, and certainly not the most dignified, but to me there was more than a hint of significance about it as it represented, in one brief altercation, all the tension and pressure of that most memorable of Swans seasons – 2002/3, the year of the great escape. But what was the moment to which I refer? Suffice to say that in my thirty seven years of supporting the Swans, there has only been one occasion when I have, almost, found myself in a full-on fight with an opposing mascot!

As most Swans die-hards will recall, that particular season was one to live long in the memory, and not always for the right reasons. It was a season of frustration, stress and, worst of all, fear of the most dreaded outcome of all – loss of league status. And we had already been through enough in our recent past. There was Petty, the day of the long knives, the near descent into bankruptcy, and the coup to remove Petty. Even in the course of that same season we had seen more ups and downs, mainly downs, than a particularly downward facing roller-coaster. There had been the arrival of the magnificent seven, the creation of team forged from out of contract rejects, ignominious defeat at Stevenage in the Paint thing, the heroic yet ultimately lamentable efforts of Nick Cusack, his glorious removal at Boston after we had gone bottom of the football league, and the appointment Brian Flynn as an unlikely saviour.

We had no idea at the time that these tribulations were in fact forming the platform for the ultimate rise to giddy heights which we have since witnessed – they were the hard yards necessary for the subsequent sprint to glory. In fact, this couldn't be further from our minds at the time, and if you had ventured to suggest to any Swans fan in 2003 that we would be playing premiership football by 2011 they would have considered you to be madder than a Match of the Day pundit on a particularly bonkers Saturday night. Even the halcyon days of Trundle and Robinson were as yet unknown pleasures to come, as we pinned our hopes instead on the goal-scoring exploits of Steve Watkin, Marc Richards and James Thomas!

So by the time the fixture at Moss Rose Macclesfield came along in February 2003, it had begun to dawn on us that Conference football was no longer a vague threat – it was now a harsh reality just around the corner, and the noble efforts of Saint Brian were no means guaranteed to avoid it. Tensions were running high and the scramble for points was becoming more and more desperate, and with Macclesfield also in the relegation running, this was a massive six pointer. My wife and I were the proud parents of a three month old daughter, but for such an important game we were undeterred by this. Said child was clipped into the car seat, driven 150 miles, duly breast-fed in the back of the Focus outside the ground, and strapped onto Mum for the duration of the match. Strangely, our daughter has little recollection of the event, which is probably a good thing.

And so the match unfolded before us, tensions on a knife edge, emotions set to boil over, and a cluster of intrepid Jacks possibly more anxious about the outcome of a match than ever before. It should be said that not everything was entirely hopeless about our struggling side. OK, it may have included the unlikely talents of Keiron Durkin, but also among the Swans ranks was the midfield mastery of one Roberto Martinez, allied to the silky skills of a youthful Leon Britton. How we recall the "Battle for Britton", when we clubbed together to throw our pennies into buckets to scrape together the funds for his wages – only to see him make his premiership debut for our beloved team some nine years later. How many premiership fans, I wonder, can claim such a direct intervention in the fortunes of their team?

But I digress. The Swans began the game marvellously, powered by our enterprising midfield, and played like promotion contenders. We had barely noticed the somewhat subdued presence of Macclesfield's mascot, Roary the Lion, other than a little pre kick off swagger; and when we duly "roared" (geddit?!) into an unfamiliar one nil lead, through the trusty boot of Steve Watkin, Roary was nowhere to be seen, skulking along the touchline I suspect. But sadly, despite our dominance, the game took an unfortunate turn when our own-goal scoring exploits came once again to the fore, gifting the home side an undeserved equaliser on the stroke of half time. Cue mascot – running towards the Swans contingent in a most flagrantly provocative manner, posing and posturing in a way which served only to rub our noses in it big time.

"Unnecessary" I commented to my illustrious companion to my left.

"Bordering on gratuitous" was, I recall, his considered response. It should be said at this point that my co-watcher was no hooligan type – a professor of history at Leicester University no less, whilst I was an executive with a large insurer. Add to the mix the presence of my spouse (herself a deputy head-teacher) and three-month-old in close proximity, and this was no breeding ground for wanton thuggery. I restrained my impulse to mix it with the impertinent lion, and instead concentrated my nervous energy onto my half time pie. But it was no surprise when feelings boiled over seven minutes into the second half, when Jason "Smudger" Smith bundled us back into the lead. The Swans contingent cried out in delight, whilst I, to my eternal shame, heard myself searching out the errant lion by blatantly yelling the words "What's the score now then Roary?" in the general direction of the rather dejected looking mascot. My illustrious companion claims innocence, but I suspect he was inflaming the situation with a well-aimed gesture or two.

On reflection it was not the most mature of outbursts on my part, but I was rather taken aback by the creature's response. So angered was the mascot that he strode purposefully from his location on the touchline, breached the "invisible wall" of the entrance into the family stand (there was no actual wall), positioned himself threateningly a few feet from us, and began to gesticulate towards us in a manner which suggested he wanted an actual fight. Now, I have never really considered whether I am hard enough to have a go at a large furry lion, but I was not about to start then. I found myself surveying the scene for members of the local constabulary, but the best I could find was a St John's ambulance-person. I considered the very real possibility that at her most tender age, my daughter might actually be exposed to fisticuffs (or would that be "pawsicuffs"); but fortunately, after a brief stand-off, the fuzzy aggressor relented and, mercifully, the moment passed.

I thought the game could offer no greater drama than this, but I was wrong. After twenty minutes of relentless pressure from the home side, we were immensely relieved to witness a magnificent clinching goal for the Swans, and what a significant one it was – lashed home from twenty yards by the boot of Martinez. Was that the real turning point of not only our season but our entire recent history? The moment where Martinez, leader elect, laid his claim to the long term throne by setting the tone for the next decade? Perhaps the true king of the jungle was striding around the middle of the park, rather than prowling the touchline spoiling for a scrap – or perhaps I am reading rather too much into that confrontation at

Moss Rose!

The season had many more anxious moments in store – the desperate scraps for points, Richards' priceless winner at Rochdale and, of course, the final day hat-trick for James Thomas which etched him into Swans folklore. But I will always look back to that day at Macclesfield as being the moment which defined the season for me, and possibly my entire Swans history. Never, at any stage, did three points seem more important, never did emotions run so high, and never did a goal have so much significance. As we look back nine years later from our proud premiership perch, I can't help feeling that I have never, before or since, been a more committed fan than I was in that season. I wonder if it all felt the same to Roary the Lion. Was he also desperate for success, clinging to fading hopes for his team's salvation and hoping for a dramatic turn of fortunes? He probably was – and quite seriously, I would love to ask him today!!!

By Peter Charles, Thrapston, Northants – formerly of Mayhill and the North Bank

Wonderful and occasionally sad memories

I have wonderful and occasionally sad memories of my past 65+ years as a true supporter.

Peter Miles (76), Swans100 survey

My grandfather was a town councillor in 1913 and before he died in 1968 he told me of the day the Swans won the cup of Wales for the first time. He talked of massive crowds in Swansea and recalled choruses of singing in the town centre for much of the night. He was not a football man until then, rugby being the main code he preferred, but after the Welsh Cup win he never looked to the rugby ball again.

Jeff Thomas in Keith Haynes & Phil Sumbler (eds), Vetch Field Voices (2000), 76-77

Back in the thirties my father used to take us to the Town field to see the Swansea club side play football. It was a depressing time for industry and we were in a recession, but he brightened up the day. There used to be a man who sold hot potatoes outside the ground and every week I saw him he would wink and say 'A hot potato means a goal for Cyril'.

Clive Owen in Keith Haynes & Phil Sumbler (eds), Vetch Field Voices (2000), 37

Waiting for the gates to open to see the likes of Tommy Lawton, Frank Swift, Ivor Allchurch, Roy Paul etc.

Peter Miles (76), Swans100 survey

To go to the Vetch was exciting – to a small boy it was entering a new world. It would not be unusual to enter the Vetch at least an hour before kick-off to get the unobstructed view from above the entrances on the big bank.

Cliff Davies (71), Swans100 survey

1949 or 50 when we Swansea played Merthyr in the Welsh Cup ... My girlfriend was with me, now my wife, and we were standing at the edge, at the tip of the bank ... The crowd was swaying and on the way out my wife said to me 'Never bring me here again'.

Ieuan Jones, Swans100 interview

In a Welsh Cup match against Merthyr in 1950, the sleepers on the

North Bank went on fire and we all had to run out. We waited until the fire was put out and then the game resumed.

Eileen Morgan (77), Swans100 Survey

It's odd, after the FA Cup semi-final defeat at Villa Park to Preston in '64 my father, a minister in Mid-Wales, did a very strange thing - he swore! He muttered the words 'bugger' and 'damnation' in the same sentence and then just stared at me.

Hywel Thomas in Keith Haynes & Phil Sumbler (eds), Vetch Field Voices (2000), 71

Bobby Charlton rattling a cross bar at the Vetch.

Geoff Whittaker (65), Swans100 survey

Stoke City in 1964 cup run and seeing Stanley Matthews play in the mud which had obviously been watered to slow us down.

Gilbard Honey-Jones (59), Swans100 survey

In retrospect I can remember lots of details of the time - the smells of the awful food and drink, the grimy ground, the lack of 'class' to the entire thing. Nevertheless, for a young boy from near Morriston this was an exciting excursion and an opportunity for escapism. These players (I thought) were above it all - rich, playing sport for a living, the excitement - they had it all. I wanted a life like that. Not the drab unchanging world of so many people on the stands. It was escapism for a young kid. As I got older the whole thing seemed to be more sordid - poor ground, playing boring games in the lower divisions, louts, trouble, cost too high, club couldn't care less about fans etc. Then after I was in London and now in US I look back at the times (and at the team today) with rose tinted glasses. The Swans epitomize boyhood memories and they have become more mythical with the passage of time. People like Ivor Allchurch and Herbie Williams are icons to me now.

Peter R. Jones (57), Swans100 archive

As 14/15 year old teenagers my mate and I often met young females in town on a Saturday morning. Looking for a kiss and a cuddle (and anything else we could get!), we sometime went down the Vetch when a Welsh League match was being played, paid to go in, and went up the top of the double decker stand for a bit of action. We weren't particularly interested in watching Ton Pentre or Abergavenny Thursdays!

Geoffrey Thyer (59), Swans100 survey

The record attendance game against Arsenal, at the Vetch, in the FA Cup; packed in like sardines, all willing the Swans on. Bobby Gould spoiling the day.

Linden Rees (60), Swans100 survey

Many good and bad times which I take on board equally, in fact my loyalty grows when times are bad hence my visits to countless crumbling outposts (well they have their distinctive individuality). I have managed to convert a number of my Brummie work colleagues to the joys of away trips to watch the Swans. However sometimes I think the lure of a night away from the wife holds more attraction than the match itself but maybe I'm being too cynical! As far as I'm concerned I am still as excited by the prospect of a match as ever and as disappointed should we lose, although fortunately I seem to get over a loss more quickly. Here's to many more years watching the Swans which I am sure will involve many more twists and turns but we wouldn't want it any other way -would we?

Nigel Jarman (59), Swans100 survey

My grandfather told me of two anecdotes regards the Swans. He was told by a copper in Liverpool at the end of our 2-1 win in the FA Cup quarter final to "get out of the City quick as there's sure to be trouble and don't stop till you reach Shrewsbury." He also told me that the Swansea fans used to sing I'm forever Blowing Bubbles in the early/mid 1920s and always got mad when he heard West Ham fans singing it. "It's our song" he used to shout at the tv when Match of the Day was on.

David Richards (42), Swans100 survey

Norwich 1965. There were no goals and I could only see by looking between taller adults but the passion for the team was born.

Rob Lewis (56), Swans 100 survey

Fri 25/03/1966 Swans 7 York 2 My hero Herbie Williams smashing in 4 goals, 1 of which broke the net. There was confusion, the ref said that the shot was wide, until he was shown the gaping hole that

Herbie had blasted.

Geoffrey Thyer (59), Swans100 survey

Ivor Allchurch backheeling a goal in the 1-0 win over Grimsby. I was on the terrace beneath the doubledecker that day and was right behind the goal. What skill and cheek.

Rob Samuel (63), Swans100 survey

It has been a real roller coast ride supporting the Swans for over 46 years, the worst point for me was 10 years ago when Petty nearly ruined us but thankfully the fans eventually forced him out. Best moment was getting to the Premier League in May 2011. I was there in the Toshack era but it is so much bigger and better this time and the team we now have are playing the best football I've ever witnessed. My dad died the night we lost to Liverpool in the cup 8-0 in January 1990 which was obviously very sad but also I believe he would have found it quite amusing. I'm sure he would be so proud and delighted if he were alive now to see us doing so well. I can only thank him for taking me to my first ever game at the Vetch in 1965, it was the start of a lifetime of being not only a Swans supporter but a lover of football. I've made many friends through attending games home and away and have travelled thousands of miles supporting my team, as I said it has been a lifetime of ups and downs but my support is always there, win, lose or draw.

Anon (58), Swans100 survey

One of my most enduring memories is of going to Herbie Williams' testimonial match with my grandparents and witnessing the genuine outpouring of love for one of our most loyal servants. I remember Bobby Charlton played in the 2nd half and he hadn't been on long when he did his trademark Charlton routine of picking the ball up about ten yards outside the box, a little shimmy and dropping his shoulder before literally lashing the ball twenty five yards into the top corner. I remember the gasps in the stand and the flashbulbs going off as the ball bounced out at the same time as (I think) Dai Davies hit the ground after vainly diving to save it. Charlton just casually turned and trotted back, taking a few handshakes as he went - what a fabulous footballer he was, and what a tribute to Herbie that he came!

Keith Roberts (48), Swans100 survey

Wonderful and occasionally sad memories

Scoring a penalty against Dave Steward at the Jersey Marine training ground, when Tosh was trainer.

Peter Mallory (58), Swans100 survey

I used to attend Football Combination matches at the Vetch Field when entry was included in season ticket.

Anon (58), Swans100 survey

There are so many but one I'll never forget was we were playing some German side in the Cup Winners' Cup down the Vetch one evening and this German player got heavily tackled on the touchline in front of the North Bank, he rolled around on the pitch and screamed as if he had been shot, you could hear his screams at the back of the North Bank. Next minute some bright Swans fan threw a walking crutch onto the pitch for him. It was so hilarious at the time.

Anon (58), Swans100 survey

Being a fan from the mediocre days of divisions 3 and 4 then the meteoric rise under Toshack, and the subsequent fall from grace. The really dark days under Petty to the magnificent rise from Martinez to Brendan Rodgers. A whole host of emotions and memories along the way. I am lucky that my sons are as passionate as me now and will continue to support the club after my days.

Roy Wells (57), Swans100 survey

I remember discovering, on my return to the car, that I had lost my car keys having been celebrating a goal during an FA Cup game. I returned to the Vetch, which was in darkness and to my surprise they agreed to put the floodlights on for me to return to the North Bank where I found the keys.

Huw Landeg Morris (51), Swans100 survey

I remember fine weather and the smell of grass. Sitting with my grandfather who quietly and patiently explained things to me, the smells of football were thrown at me - the pipe smoke, liniment, pies and peppermints!

Keith Roberts (48), Swans100 survey

Liverpool had already won promotion from the Second Division. They were on their way up to the big time. Bill Shankly was the manager, and I had heard about Ron Yeats, Roger Hunt, and Ian St John from reading football magazines. We won the match 4 - 2. All small boys, such as myself at that time, were given a wooden orange box to stand on so you could see onto the pitch from the North Bank. I belive that small children were allowed to sit on the small wall that ran alongside the pitch as well. (If a ball going out of play hit one of them, it normally resulted in the child being knocked over the wall and into the crowd!)

Geoffrey Thyer (59), Swans100 survey

I have been a massive Swans fan from being very little...I remember in March 2nd (I think) 1978 when I read the Western Mail of my Dad's when it said Toshack was going to be player manager - I couldn't believe it. His first home game was against Watford I think and he scored. My Dad and I had Father and son tickets in the double decker stand - it was a rollercoaster I did not want to get off. I remember getting to the Swansea schools under 12 finals in 1979 playing for Bishop Vaughan versus Cefn Hengoed at the Vetch - I was completely in awe at playing there - We lost 5-1 but got changed in the Home changing room and Alan Curtis was there - Think he was just leaving for Leeds that week. My Dad was there of course. Swans v Chesterfield in 1979 was awesome - I can see Danny Bartly crossing the ball now and Tosh rising like a salmon to head home. My Dad claims he was the first in the ground to cheer and we had the perfect view. Preston 81 was momentous - at 2-1 a Preston player headed the ball goalward and for the life of me I don't know how it didn't go in!! We were on the ropes but it didn't - The most beautiful part of that match was the last goal made by Alan Curtis and Robbie James and scored by Charlo - the 3 players who had played in all Divisions for us. In the 1st Div - away at Anfield with My Dad - We couldn't get into the ground because of the crush as Bill Shankly had died that week and people came to the ground without tickets but just out of respect and mourning...I was scared that day as a 13 year old especially when we went 2-0 up. We went to the Holiday Inn after in Liverpool where the players from both sides went for a drink. Tosh signed my broken arm cast for me. It was Ronnie Whelan's first game- all the Liverpool legends were there - it was awesome. I wasn't there for the Hull game in 2003 - I couldn't be in Swansea and it hurts me not to have been there for our most important game EVER. I needed to be there with my Dad but could not be. The Playoff

Final in 2011 was the best day as a Swans fan...It was the best day of my life I think. All my family there including my wife Jane and 4 kids and Mum and Dad - I had also won the NPOWER 'Face of Swansea' competition and a picture of my youngest son Will and I was all over Wembley / programme , down Wembley way etc - It was just unbelievable - just the most special , golden day EVER.

Steve Meredith (45), Swans100 survey

When the Swans were in the old Division 3 my father got invited to the directors' box for a match v Huddersfield. I got to sit in the guest area but went into the directors' bar after the game. For a 12 year old this was amazing. It was then topped by one of the directors asking me if I wanted to meet the players. Silly question!! He took me down to the changing rooms, and on the way asked who my favourite player was. As someone who played on the wing like me I told him it was Micky Conway. On arrival in the changing rooms (after Swans had won 2-1 I think) he introduced me to the players and told them that Micky Conway was my favourite. Unfortunately he was not there, but Wyndham Evans came over and introduced himself as Micky Conway - a night I'll never forget.

Anthony Hill (49), Swans100 survey.

Watford in March 1978 - moving to the west terrace to be behind the goal for Tosh's first game and being rewarded with him scoring directly in front of me. Chesterfield in May 1979 is a game where I can remember the sound of the crowd being louder than I had experienced before and it was the game I had to ask who Fiona Richmond was! I also remember not being old enough to go on my own to a game against Hartlepool (parents at a wedding) and finding out the Swans had won 8-0. Beating Cardiff 3-2 after going 2 down in 1984 then running like hell to get on the bus home after the final whistle. Hull 2003 for the sheer sense of relief. Darren Pratley's goal from the halfway line against Forest more for the explosion of noise it created than for the goal itself.

Adrian Byrne (45), Swans100 survey

To have been a Swans fan for so many years has been a roller coaster of a journey. There have been great days and terrible days. I feel more optimistic now than ever before that the club is on firm ground and moving in the right direction. Some personal memories

(good and bad): In 1962, seeing Swansea beat Liverpool 4-2 at the Vetch, in what I believe was the last game Liverpool ever played outside of the top division. In 1964 as a 10 year old, getting crushed whilst exiting the Vetch after the 5th round cup replay against Stoke. I owe my life to a stranger who picked me up off the ground and hauled me over the heads of the crowd out into the street. My face was badly cut, and I was frightened of large crowds for years after, but it could have been far worse. Losing to Arsenal 1-0 in the cup in 1969 in front of a 32000 crowd at the Vetch. Many games against Cardiff, including the infamous New Year's Day game. Coming home from honeymoon in 1982, telling my wife that I'd 'just pop out' to get some food for our first meal in our new marital home, and coming back 4 hours later having 'sneaked' a visit to see us play Everton - we lost 3-0 and it was nearly the shortest marriage on record! (We are still together 30 years later and she has finally come to terms with my addiction.) My absolute low from a football standpoint was losing 4-0 at home to Kidderminster in 2002-03 season. The football was dire, and for the first time I felt that there was no way forward. Then, Brian Flynn rode to the rescue and that same season I experienced one of the few absolute highs, beating Hull 4-2 in the final game to keep our place in the league. Whatever highs we may experience in the future, that day will stay with me forever.

Andy Reilly (58), Swans100 survey

February and 5 games no wins. No love lost between Yorath and the fans either.

March and 9 games only 2 wins, Yorath got the boot. Frankie Burrows arrived and as if by magic... we beat Stoke 2-1. Harris scoring a cracker from surprise surprise open play. Roll on April we all thought!

Did we really only draw with Barry? Did we really concede 6 goals at home to Wigan? Did we still get to the Welsh Cup Final and beat Preston and Rotherham in the league? Yes fellow Jacks these momentous events did occur all in the space of 30 days. A draw with Orient meant we wouldn't drop into the mire that Cardiff and Wrexham called home (the 4th Division), but we still needed something extra to prove that we were undoubtedly Wales' finest.

"How about the Welsh Cup?" said Frankie

"We'll take it!" answered the North Bank.

We did, and Cardiff city centre too! On a warm sunny Sunday in May, Dave 'the Judas' Penney and Paul Raynor scored the goals that beat Wrexham, enabled Terry Connor to lift the Cup, gave Sharpe the excuse for his existence and the rolling call that the capital still fears and we all love "JACK ARMY".

And that was it; Swans were back in Europe, the Gulf War broke out the same night as Chelsea played Spurs (coincidence?) "Raynor for England" was held to be the wittiest chant of the year and ominously Shaun Chapple made his senior debut. What a hell of an experience!

Jackanory 8 (Apr-May 1998)

Wonderful and occasionally sad memories

I really got going in 1975 and for about 6 or 7 years leading up to relegation from Div 1 I travelled a lot, usually with official coaches, but sometimes by minibus with friends, occasionally by car and I once hitch-hiked with Elwyn Thomas overnight (via a gay club in Bristol) to watch a defeat at Cambridge Utd. Elwyn blagged a seat on the team bus via George Smith to get us back to Swansea. I must have slept all the way because I remember nothing about it.

Anon (55), Swans100 survey

The craziest random Swans experience: Sat 10th April 1976 v Southport I was 17 years old and my boss was a Liverpudlian who was in his early 30s. After finishing work at lunchtime (10 mins away from the Vetch) my boss said he would treat me to watch the Swans v Southport. When we got there he told me to say nothing & let him do the talking. He then marched me to the players' entrance and told the guy on the gate that he was the Southport trainer, and could he let us through because he needed to give a young player (me) a late fitness test, on the touchline/pitch. (We were both wearing tracksuits/trainers in work that day). The gate guy looked apprehensive at first but let us in and watched, while 'my trainer' had me working out by the wing stand. By the time the guy left us alone I was knackered I can tell you!!! (it was 1pm & the ground was empty). We hid at the back of the wingstand until kick off when we saw the Southport players coach turn up. The closest I came to being a pro footballer... for Southport ffs, lol

Jack Flack (52), Swans100 survey

I remember standing on the railway sleeper behind the goal and the halftime score board used to fascinate me, A 1-1 B 0-0 C 1-0 etc. You had to buy a program to decoded it!

Clive Mitchell (58), Swans100 survey

I do remember Villa at the Vetch in the early 70's, that was a frightener, even with my father for protection, I think they were playing off ground touch with hatchets on the North Bank. Cardiff City home or away was always one that got the hairs on the back on my neck to stand on end. Always remember the 3 all draw where John Buchanan scored a late equaliser, gutted. Crystal Palace at Ninian Park in the cup was another scary one, we were on what was called the Bob Bank and every so often a skirmish would break out

as there were plenty of locals not happy with 20,000 Jacks on their patch, it was one where you had to watch your back. Wembley in 2011 was my greatest day ever and will always stay with me, everything went to plan and I could probably write a chapter on that weekend alone but as the saying goes, what goes on tour, stays on tour. Suffice to say, 'we are premier league'.

Huw Cooze (50), Swans100 survey

Crying with joy in my dad's arms when Swans beat Chesterfield 2-1 under Tosh. It felt as if we had got back to where we should be as a club. Remember people smiling all the way home and they were happier than when we got promoted the previous year.

Tudor, Swans100 survey

Osvaldo Ardilles`s face when Tommy Smith crunched into him almost knocking him over the little wall and into the North Bank right in front of me.

Paul Williams (57), Swans100 survey

Preston. We got the third and the crowd surged forward and I was pinned against a stanchion thinking this is it, I can't breathe...we're going up and I'll be dead and never see us in Division 1!

Huw Mellor (46), Swans100 survey

You can imagine we wanted to be at that game in Preston but due to lack of funds and being on a YTS that money was tight, so we both took it for granted that we would have our ears stuck to the radio. Well due to over 10,000 Swans fans going and some of them using our coaches, it was decided that the both of us would be going on one coach as fitters in case of a break down. To this day I can't remember who granted this or gave us tickets to get in to the game. Well the rest is history. Swans were promoted and Villa won the first division. On the long journey home I still remember going past some Liverpool fans on their coaches who once they noticed it was Swansea City fans started clapping us singing.

David Evans (49), Swans100 survey

TEN THINGS THE EIGHTIES WILL BE REMEMBERED FOR
1. PROMOTION for SWANSEA to the first division.
2. Stuffing LEEDS 5-1 at the Vetch on the opening day of season

1981.

3. Finishing 6th in Division One in our first season in the top flight.
4. Going to Highbury and beating the Arsenal 2-0.
5. Getting locked out of Anfield while the boys drew 2-2.
6. Being on the "The Big Match" on T.V.
7. Seeing the best team ever at the Vetch... ANTE, 'JIMMY,' LATCH etc. etc.
8. Big crowds, good atmosphere, and most of all great football.
9. Returning to Europe.
10. A decline in the game, and for use a rapid return to the 'Land of the Living Dead' – the third division.

"Nobody will ever know..." A Swansea City Fanzine from the South East, no. 1, August 1990.

Colin West getting sent off as soon as he came on at West Brom.

Terry Phillips (44), Swans100 survey

New year's day a number of years ago at Ninian Park and a poor ballboy, even I felt sorry for him. He was rotund to say the least and he had the misfortune to be put at the away end retrieving balls and getting them back to players during the kick about, needless to say he was a little slow in completing this task on a few occasions. This was of course picked upon by a few Swansea fans who would advise him to be a little quicker about it (in no uncertain terms). He appeared to attempt a speed up operation and in front of 2000 or more Swansea fans fell flat on in his face in a very muddy area. As you can imagine the crowd showed little sympathy and a rendition of "one Billy Bunter" went up the poor boy was led away in tears by a Cardiff official. It remains one of the funniest things I ever did see.

Paul Williams (57), Swans100 survey

Preston and Bury away, the sheer amount of Swans supporters at an away match awesome. Had tears in my eyes before Wembley last year for the same reason.

Mike Duffy (52), Swans100 survey

My dad used to signwrite all the advert boards at the Vetch in the 70's and 80's. Remember the Hemling lager and Welsh bitter adverts on the roof of the centre stand? That was him! It was one school holiday

I went to work with him, remember to this day him signwriting a board for "my fathers moustache", bright orange board with black lettering and the handle bar moustache. John Toshack was there, my dad got his diary out and he signed the page best wishes John Toshack. Still have it to this day (papers a bit yellow now). Another time I went with my dad was on a Sunday. Can't remember the board but Colin Appleton (Hummel kit era) had the players in on a Sunday morning after losing the day before. He let me jog around the track with them. Also had Bob Paisley's autograph outside the players' entrance in the 83/84 season. He was down to watch Colin Pascoe and Darren Gale. I represented Swansea Cygnets for 2 years when I was 13/14, captained them in the last year. We used to train every Wednesday at the old Morfa stadium astro turf. My mum dropped me down early that day so she missed the change of plan (no mobile phones in those days). We all jumped in a mini bus with Ron Walton to go to the Vetch for weights and running. After training I told Tommy Hutchison (Dean if you score today I'll give you a mars bar) of my predicament. He gave me a lift back to the Morfa in his red Mercedes and waited with me until my mum got there. All my mates at school were so jealous. All amazing memories! Jack bastard through and through!

Dean Daniel (37), Swans100 survey

Cold, hot drinks, standing at front of old east stand. Loved the sound of the ball hitting the net!

Anon (49), Swans100 survey

Every Swansea City memory makes me feel happy or sad that particular day! I would not ever want that to change! It is the beauty of life and of being a true football fan.

Jim White (36), Swans100 survey

My dad would drive me and my sister to the Vetch - he'd go to the dressing rooms and we'd head over to the shop. We'd get the programmes and go to the East Stand. We could hear the start of the game, then we'd wait 5 minutes, take the money back to the shop and take our places in the East Stand. We had enough wages from the programme sales to buy a pie at half time.

Anon (36), Swans100 survey

Wonderful and occasionally sad memories

My uncle used to run the Caswell Bay hotel in Caswell where a lot of teams would stay during the early 80's, I am told that I was sat on Kenny Dalglish's knee and when he asked who my favourite player was I replied Alan Curtis!

Elliott Greaves (37), Swans100 survey

Andy Legg's spectacular goal against Stoke when Bruce Grobbelar was in goal. Night game. Cold. Crisp. Deep cross from the right byline from Steve Jenkins. First time looping volley smashed over Brucey arching his back like a salmon. What a goal...

J. Borley (34), Swans100 survey

Preston 81 - the trip up, Motorway full of jacks. Preston full of Jacks. The wooden terracing bouncing underneath us.

David Hurst, Swans100 survey

Steve Thornber's hatrick away at West Brom. I lived in the Black Country and all my mates followed the Albion. What a day.

Anthony Dews (35), Swans100 survey

Getting Torpey and Heggs sent off and going 2-1 down before scoring a late equaliser through Basham (?) when down to 9 men. I actually felt so chuffed I wrote Frank Burrows a letter to say how proud I was of the team. He wrote back too.

Anon (33), Swans100 survey

---

15 GOOD REASONS TO REMEMBER LAST SEASON

1. Winning at Ninian Park for the first time in 30 years.
2. Holding the League Champions to a draw in the F.A. Cup.
3. Two great performances in the ECW Cup versus Panathanaikos.
4. The classic "Chariots of Fire" routine on Football Focus.
5. Loan signings - John Salako.
6. Salman burying the ball into the net - Offside!
7. Salako's 2 goal burst at Ashton Gate.
8. The return of Yorath's "crucifixion" pose.
9. Leggy stuffing Steve Nicol at the Vetch.
10. Roger Freestone splitting his track-suit bottoms at Walsall.
11. Chrissy Coleman almost on the fence at Reading after scoring.
12. Terrace celebrations at Leyton Orient - 2-0 away.
13. The return of Alan Curtis.
14. Steve Thornber's glancing header at Brentford.
15. Cardiff's (deserved) relegation!

Nobody will ever know, 1 (August 1990)

I forgot we'd changed sides at half time and cheered a lot when they scored what I thought was an own goal. Everyone glared at me and a few comments were made!

Anon (33), Swans100 survey

Lots of banter with Cyril... remember when crowd chanted Cyril do a Beckham which he duly obliged in front of the English away fans (this was shortly after Beckham was sent off in the 1998 World Cup). Fantastic stuff!!

Ian Taylor (35), Swans100 survey

Trundle scoring to put us 2 - 1 up against Preston in the 4th round of the Cup. We had been 0 - 1 down and Preston had outclassed us throughout. A Robbo free kick had levelled things and Trundle put us 2 - 1 up for an unlikely win. I vividly remember screaming with delight into a complete stranger's face!

Stuart Middleton (30), Swans100 survey

Memories in Verse

September the second, sixty-nine,
Was the first time I went down,
To the Old Vetch Field to watch our team,
Then called Swansea Town.

My father said he'd take me,
As close as he could get,
He sat me on a barrier,
Right behind the net.

Now he wasn't keen on soccer,
But I was football mad,
And watching the Swans was brilliant,
Especially with my dad.

That night we lost to Swindon Town:
Three-one was the score,
But that special Vetch Field atmosphere,
Left me wanting more.

I've seen us lose to Darlington,
I've seen us lose to Crewe,
But I've seen us beat the Arsenal,
Liverpool and Man U.

I've seen Robbie James score a 30-yard goal,
It bent as it flew in,
I've seen Jimmy Habziabdic,
But nothing rhymes with him.

From Bentley, Gregg and Harry Griff,
Through Toshack, Hollins and Flynn,
I've stood on the North Bank,
Willing them to win.

Way back in the nineteen seventies,
At the time of the three-day week,
Miners on strike and power cuts,
It really was so bleak.

There was no night-time football,
Due to the power cuts,
The Swans were losing money,
It drove the chairman nuts.

But the clever man came up with a plan
To bring in the extra quid:
He told the Post, "There's a game mid-week!
How? I'll tell you later"
Then he got on the phone to a local firm
And he hired a generator!

So I stood on the North Bank,
With my pasty in my hand,
To watch the only night-time football,
To be seen across the land.

From the start we were on the back-foot,
Our opponents that much quicker,
But the chairman's mind was elsewhere,
As the lights began to flicker.

The players went back to the dressing room,
And then it started to rain,
It was totally dark all over the park,
And they never came out again!

This story is true, because I was there,
Just another memory,
Of countless visits to the Old Vetch Field:
Way down by the sea.

Terry Rogers

A home game at the Vetch in the late 1990's/early 2000's, half time and in the middle of a packed concourse someone set off fireworks within the crowds - Yeovil home 2005, the first time the Liberty was really loud - watching Freestone taking and scoring a penalty at The Vetch - the noise of fans hitting seats off their fixtures after the last home games - walking down the Garbaldi lane as a youngster on the way to games - Chester home (think it was around 1996) they had been relegated, Monster Munch were doing a promo at the Vetch and I remember packets being everywhere on the terrace - Hull home 1999 when the game got delayed due to the rain. Finally kicked off late, the pitch was flooded, fans were running on. Mayhem of a day. - Oxford home (again, must be around 1996) 3 mates as real youngsters were talking to an Oxford fan a few hours before the game. He gave us money to get in, we were still short so tried to gamble it down at The Marina amusement arcade but lost it all and saw no game that day! - West Ham and Derby at home in one season in the FA Cup. - Getting to what must have been an Auto Windscreens game against I think Bristol City with my father in the 1990s. Had to go in the East Terrace as we were late. Got to the end of the game and expected extra time as it was 0-0. Everyone started to leave. Turned out we missed an early goal, we lost and no one had said a word/reacted all game. Found out through teletext when we got home.

Lewis (27), Swans100 survey

I met Jan Molby in the old club shop. I had a broken arm and he signed my cast. I was so happy and was almost in tears when they took my cast off and didn't cut out his signature like they promised!

Jack Taylor (22), Swans100 survey

My son was given a pair of Ashley Williams's boots last year after he got hit in the face by the ball while Ashley was clearing it against Norwich. The way the club and players treated my five year old son after the incident was fabulous and showed that the club's attitude to its fans is first class.

Colin Jones (42), Swans100 survey

I also met Brendan Rodgers in unusual circumstances. My friends and I were in Aspers Casino a few days after we had beaten Reading in the Play-Off Final and saw Rodgers having a drink with his friends.

Wonderful and occasionally sad memories

I approached him, shook his hand and thanked him for what he had achieved. He was very grateful.

Daniel Brown (20), Swans100 survey

I have only attended one game. I worked as a youth worker in a particularly deprived part of Swansea. Some of the young people I worked with were disadvantaged in multiple ways, excluded from schools, faced intergenerational unemployment and low prospects of work. There was also a lot of bullying between different families and within families. I had noticed they loved to play football, usually kicking the football around with each person representing their own team, with one goalie. I decided to take what they already loved and create a football team, to develop a sense of team spirit and hopefully try to end the bullying. We set up weekly training and even entered a few contests and did quite well. I wrote to the Mayor's office and asked if I could take this new team of young people to the Liberty to watch a game. We were approved and had 16 places to attend a game watching from the Lord Mayor's box. It was a great day and Swansea even managed to pull off a win; some of the young people even got autographs from the players. For a little while, those young people thought I was the best ever.

Sarah Jones (47), Swans100 survey

Probably at Cardiff...either when the stupid catering people left a palette full of burger rolls outside and a huge food fight started up (!!!!) or when police charged at us and the fence they'd pinned us against collapsed, seriously thought I was going to die from being crushed. On the field.... West Ham in the FA cup, brilliant day out.

Clare Ridley (37), Swans100 survey

The last game of the season against Hull City. Went with tears in my eyes thinking it maybe our last ever game but came out with tears of joy and no voice.

Eileen Morgan (77), Swans100 survey

1991, Swans away at the top of the table Brentford, having just beaten Bradford 6-4, Gilligan or Williams or someone put us 2-0 up. Being totally pissed I go totally mental, insane in fact. Anyway, we lost 3-2 but some days after the game I somehow got hold of the Brentford video. So sitting down watching it with some mates, Swans

score the second, camera pans straight on to yours truly. At the time I was a student and into wearing a big old winter coat. So in the cold light of day I'm watching myself doing stupid drunken celebratory dance with this scruffy coat flapping everywhere, while the commentator completely takes the piss. Never again.

Richard Jones in Jackanory, 7 (Feb/Mar 1998)

Wembley 1997. Having been to the majority of games that season home and away, I missed the final as I had an exam that afternoon.

John Williams in Jackanory, 8 (Apr/May 1998)

I won the half time flyer at the Vetch! Went on the pitch to collect my money and Kevin Johns jokingly said my ticket wasn't the right number and I almost died of shame right where I was standing. And

he wouldn't let me back on the North Bank with an envelope full of cash. Bless him for looking after the females!

Clare Ridley (37), Swans100 survey

I first attended in a pretty depressing era, with the Swans almost going 'bust', languishing in Division Four, with half the North Bank sectioned off. Even so, it was exciting and fun. I enjoyed the company, and the witticisms of some fans. The abuse was less welcome. I remember it being fairly low-key, and I sort of preferred it when expectations were lower. It's more fun to have a grumble than to win all the time, and it was distinctly uncommercial compared to today. I enjoyed the cosiness of that time. It was a bit more of a minority interest then, and you had to make a point of following the Swans. Today, with Sky TV and mass media, it's rammed down your throat too much. I prefer to be part of a discerning few rather than something with mass appeal, and the late 1980s were certainly for the die-hards.

Although my level of support has fluctuated over the years, I doubt I will ever cease to be a Swans supporter. I have seen enough ups and downs to be philosophical about it, and it is not my life, but it is nice to have a common interest with many friends. I think that I have become far more of a proud Welshman and a Swansea person over the years, and I am sure that following the Swans and the Whites has helped. The highlight of my supporting has to be either the Play Off Semi Final against Nottingham Forest or the Final itself. Both were fantastic days. In a way, I enjoy it slightly less now, as our aim is likely to be to survive in the Premiership, whereas winning promotion was more exciting. I wonder if, if we do stay up, fans will drift away a bit as games become more a case of attrition than having any realistic chance of winning something. I see empty seats at clubs like Wolves, Wigan, Blackburn etc, and wonder if the magic wears off when survival is the only aim. Thankfully, the Swans' style of play is far more attractive than any of those clubs, and I hope it remains so.

Anon (44), Swans100 survey

I work part time for the Liberty Stadium in the response on the away end. I also work part time at Wembley stadium as a quad supervisor. Well I was working the Swans end when we played Reading in the play offs last May, seems like yesterday. Whenever I work the

stadiums you have got to show that you're impartial to all fans, whether its football, rugby or NFL.

Anyway when the Swans were 3-0 up and the Swans fans singing and the stadium rocking all I wanted to do was celebrate with the fans, but as stated above couldn't. The second half started and Reading got 2 early goals in no time, so from being 3-0 up to then 3-2 the Swans fans started to really get right behind the team.

I started to walk to the disabled platform on my level to ask some fans to be seated when the Swans got a penalty. Up came Scott Sinclair. I thought to myself if Scott scores I will celebrate, so what I done was I asked the two male fans to pretend to grab me and start jumping up and down if Scott scored. Well he slotted the ball in to the back of the net, the boys grabbed me and we all erupted. In the end the boys were trying to get me to leave them go.

David Evans (49), Swans100 archive

My favourite home game has to be Burnley home. This is because me and my friends dressed up as smurfs – SMURF ARMY! This got everyone talking and is still being talked about today.

Becca Williams (19), Swans100 survey

The Nottingham Forest play off semi - final game. It was an evening match and I had a R.E. GCSE exam the next morning, it was a fantastic night, full of excitement and we won and made it to the final. Luckily I achieved a A* in the exam, I think the win gave me motivation.

Georgia Watts (15), Swans100 survey

In late March 2011, Carmarthen held a fans forum with Swansea. Brendan Rodgers, Alan Tate and Stephen Dobbie attended. The event was organized by my Father who is a massive supporter of both clubs. So Dad asked me to help steward the car park and show people where to park. Dad left for the loo, and in that short space of time, Rodgers and the players turned up, with Tatey in his flash car. And I had to greet them, I was shaking like a leaf meeting my heroes but it was a brilliant experience.

Owain Ashley-Jones (16), Swans100 survey

I remember 'cos I was there!

It was the evening of 11th May 1979 and the last game of the 1978/79 season – a sell-out match at the Vetch – Swansea v Chesterfield. I was in my last year at Pentrehafod School and had managed to atttend every home and away match that season.

At all the home matches during the season I, and several of my friends, earned pocket money by selling Swans programmes and for each programme sold – earned 1p!! As the Chesterfield match was a sell-out, I easily managed to sell all my programmes that evening well before the start of the match which meant I would be able to get into the ground earlier than usual and see the whole of the game. Well, that was the plan. However, I had not considered what happened next.

Rushing to the main gate with my pal Wayne Morgan from Gendros, who had also been fortunate to sell all his programmes, we were confronted by one of the older stewards on duty who said, 'Sorry, lads – no way are you getting into the ground this afternoon without a ticket. The ground is completely full.'

Devastation!

Even though I explained that I had been to ALL home and away matches that season, had sold programmes all season and had not needed a ticket previously, there was absolutely no way that he was willing to let us in to the ground that day no matter how much we begged and pleaded with him.   Needless to say we continued arguing for some time, getting more and more irate with the steward.

Okay – what do we do now?   There was no way we were going to miss the last match of the season. ABSOLUTELY no way!

Quick thinking was the order of the day! Desperate diversion tactics were definitely required if we had any hope of seeing the match that afternoon. We managed to draw the attention of the steward to a (non-existent) fight taking place and as soon as his attention was diverted, Wayne and I both jumped over the gate and ran at top speed towards the ground. Unsurprisingly, it was no time at all before we were being pursued by the steward!

The next course of action was to split up and for both of us to run in different directions. This worked and we both thoroughly enjoyed the match with a 2-1 win albeit in different parts of the ground!

However, this was not to be the end of my adventures that day. As already explained, as it was the last game of the season, a pitch invasion by fans took place. Whilst this was taking place I decided to take the opportunity to sneak in to the Swans dressing room and to 'acquire' Alan Waddle's jersey.

Luckily, no-one was in the dressing room but just as I was about to escape the dressing room with the prized jersey, who should appear and confront me but Terry Medwin! An explanation was needed! I related my story to Terry Medwin about having managed to attend all the matches for the 1977/78 season and how desperate I was to have Alan Waddle's jersey as a souvenir. Fortunately for me another really good friend Lee Merrells appeared in the changing rooms at that point and, as Lee had signed his contract that day, Lee eventually persuaded Terry Medwin to let me have the Alan Waddle jersey which I still possess.

Lee and I are still the best of mates and are both still as passionate, if not more so, about the Swans as we were then – as anyone who knows us will confirm.

So all's well that ends well!!!

Martin Morgan

The Swans saved my life

The legendary Liverpool manager Bill Shankly once made a quip about football being more important than life or death; but for Swans' fan Paul Griffiths the club made a big difference to his life, and may even have saved it!

Paul suffered an adverse reaction to a vaccine when he was 7, leaving him brain-damaged. The best treatment for him to survive and have any chance of a fulfilling life was to be had in America, but the family needed £2,000 to make the trip – a huge sum in 1977 for an ordinary family. One of the fundraising events was a match between the Swans' first team and Pembroke Borough, and this took place on 19th July 1977 in Pembroke Dock.

The Swansea team included Mel Charles and Harry Griffiths, and they won 6-1, Pembroke Boro' replying through their 15-year-old centre forward. Tickets for the game cost 30p, and about £200 was raised. How much was spent in the clubhouse afterwards is anybody's guess, but everyone had a very good time according to Paul's mum Joyce: apparently the star of the "après jeux" was John Charles – entertaining the throng with song, in English and Italian! Those were the days.

Paul has had a connection with Swansea City since then, and his carer Amanda now takes him to the Liberty where he has a season ticket. He has met many of the players, and loves nothing more than a beer before the game and a good game with plenty of shouting!

Paul was recently able to repay some of his debt to the club, raising £468 by growing a Movember moustache last year for charity – his cash was part of the £1,500 donated by Pembrokeshire Jacks to the Marie Curie Cancer Care charity, and Paul was pictured handing over the cheque to Brendan Rodgers at the stadium.

This story is just one example of the powerful bonds a club like Swansea has with its fans and the community in general – the Swans may not have saved many lives, but they have certainly touched a good many, and mostly for the better!

Right: Paul pictured inside Wembley, May 2011

How d' the Swans get on?

I must have been about seven, when my Dad came home and asked the family a single question, 'How d'the Swans get on?' There was a short silence then Ninna, my grandmother, piped up, 'they won 6 -1 and Jack Fowler scored five.' I was delighted but Dad ignored her. Then my Mam gave him a cup of tea but made no reference to the question. That left Matthew and me to respond. I thought about it, looked to Matthew for inspiration but he just stared back at me (he was after all only a cat). I was baffled but that was the end of the matter as Dad settled down to drink his tea.

This happened every other week and seemed to go on for ever. I just had no idea how to find the answer.

Then... Durrumdurrumdurrumpetydum. Durrumdurrumdurrumpetydum. Durrumdumdumdumdumpdum. SPORTS REPORT on the Wireless, 5 o'clock Saturday. THE FOOTBALL RESULTS.

Next time Dad came home late on Saturday afternoon, I was ready for him. 'We beat Doncaster Rovers 2-1'. There was a hint of a smile when he drank his tea. That evening, I had a great tea. Even when I found out that he only ever asked about the Swans after he had already been to the match, it was still a great tea.

As time went on, I asked him about the matches, and he told me about what had happened and all about Ivor Allchurch and Cliff Jones, of Terry Medwin and Johnnie King, Harry Griffths and all the others. I couldn't get enough of it and my imagination was on overload. I desperately wanted to see them play.

But, I had to wait a little longer. Dad and his wicked sense of humour hadn't finished with me yet. He asked the question when the Swans weren't even playing. This time, the famous result from 1924 took a little longer but, eventually, Jack Fowler's achievement rang out loud and clear and, this time we all ignored it. Mam poured a cup of tea and retired to the kitchen. I turned to confront Matthew. After all, with his background in football - he came to live with us on Cup Final Day in 1953 and his name really was Stanley Matthews – he just had to know something. But he blanked me and walked off into the kitchen to discuss with Mam what he was going to have to eat. Dad drunk his tea.

Some Saturdays, we all went to Aunty Nora's house in Paxton Street. She was one of Ninna's sisters and her house seemed to contain the whole family. Seven other great aunties and uncles, cousins, husbands and wives, friends, neighbours, workmates and, usually, a couple of people no-one had ever seen before. When we got there, the small terraced house was jam-packed with people and the miracle of feeding the 5000 was already underway, as wave upon wave of cups of tea flowed through the house. There were dozens of conversations, lots of laughter and a fog of smoke from cigarettes and pipes. Then they started to go in dribs and drabs, twos and threes said their goodbyes and off they went to the match. 'Can I come?' 'Can I come?' I went from uncle to uncle. 'You'd better ask your father'. 'Can I come?' 'When you're a bit older, it won't be long, I'll see you after the match'

Hence I was relegated to the sub's bench with the non-players, non-supporters and non-interested. Anyway, I used to get a glass of pop and most of these non-supporters were great aunties and they really were great aunties and I had a fine time.

After an eternity, they came back. Everyone talking about the match and I would flit amongst the groups and listen to what I could hear about Tom Kiley or Charlo or Davo...

One day, I was sitting in Auntie Norah's waiting for my pop, when Dad said 'If you're coming, you'd better get your coat on' and, immediately, I was outside in my coat waiting for Dad. Soon, I was walking past the jail with all the other supporters, going to the match and chuffed to bits. Then we were there, on the terraces behind the goal at the Town End. I could see the top of the double decker and lots of close-ups of big damp overcoats but nothing else. I thought that I would never see the Swans.

After a long time I heard a roar from the crowd and I was picked up and transferred man to man to the front by the railings right behind the goalposts. I was in amongst some other boys who seemed much bigger and had obviously been there before. I could see the Swans in front of me around the penalty area and they scored a dozen goals with several balls and no opposition from the other team who were down the other side of the pitch, also scoring lots of goals. It was like three goals and in but without changing the goalie.

The ref. blew his whistle, tossed up, the teams switched over, the game started and I was there watching the Swans down the Vetch.

I cannot remember much about the game itself. But I do remember feeling a huge anticipation at the start, just actually being there, the atmosphere, the spectacle, the speed that everything that happened and I just felt so good. This was my top experience in 8 years. I still got fragments of that feeling in other times down the Vetch and occasionally at the Liberty but the full monty did not come again until Wembley in 2011.

After my debut as a Swans fan, I remember going to the match occasionally but not often. Sometimes I'd go to the front but more frequently I stayed about 10 rows from the front with my family. On those occasions I was put behind a group of 'short' people who suddenly grew and threw their arms up when something exciting happened and, again, I was watching the top of the Double-Decker.

However, I got to know who the players were and soon decided on my favourites. As the years went by, I went to different parts of the Vetch searching for a place where vertically-challenged people were able to see. If you got in the Enclosure an hour before kick-off, you could get to the front, look over the wall and see everything all through the match – even better if you could find a box to stand on

During most of the fifties and sixties, my Dad had a season ticket in the Double- Decker and he used to sit next to my uncle Tom. For ten years from the mid fifties, I was the nominated substitute to have the ticket if Dad could not go. In the ten years I only managed a couple of appearances - my Dad was very keen on the Swans.

My visual memories are few but I do remember Terry Medwin scoring with a header right in front of us and Cliff Jones missing a penalty and Cliff didn't miss many penalties. But I clearly remember one of the times when Dad could not go. He had a gum disease and the treatment was to take all his teeth out. Even I, as an 11 year old, thought that it was a bit drastic. But there did not appear to be any alternative. So I got the ticket. He was scheduled to have half his teeth out on the Saturday morning of the match and my fear was that he would make a remarkable recovery within an hour and claim his ticket back. I really should have had more sympathy but I was concerned about the ticket.

Anyway, come the day I held the ticket tightly in my hand, caught the 58 bus and got off at the Tenby. Then I streamed down Richardson Street with hundreds of other fans. Uncle Tommy lived at the bottom of the street, just a corner kick away from the Vetch. No time for a cup of tea, and we were in the wooden cathedral of the Double-Decker in no time. Tom had a similar sense of humour to my Dad and, during the match, he said to me with a dead-pan expression on his face, 'Your Old Man would be all right with them out there, they haven't got any bite in front of goal' and everybody

seemed to agree and stamp their feet to make the rumble of the Double-Decker.

Dad told me about the team of 1955/56. The Swans had been top of the Second Division and were on course to get promotion to the First Division for the first time. Centre Half, Tom Kiley, got injured in mid-season and the Swans did not replace him. They lost matches and momentum and were, comfortably, not promoted. He couldn't forgive the Swans' board for depriving him of seeing them in the First Division.

As the decade wore on, the team of '55 started to break up and I don't recall them getting near to promotion again. I saw some of the big teams of that era playing in cup matches and friendlies. Arsenal and Burnley, who were top of the First Division at the time, and Manchester United and Hibernian played friendlies.

In the early sixties, when I had grown enough to see at least half the pitch, I started going to the North Bank. The mid-fifties squad had gone by then, apart from Ivor returning in mid-decade. But there were dozens of new Swans who took their places over the years. Many of them inspired me to come back again to watch them. Names from the sixties spring to mind, especially the local boys, Herbie Williams, Brian Hughes, Barry Jones, Brian Evans, Barry Hole and Dai Gwyther.

About this time, it was expected that we go to Aunty Rosa's (great aunt and grandmother's sister number three) for a cup of tea before the match. This event was smaller than the one at Paxton Street in the early fifties. There with about 30 people attending and they were a slightly different squad of relations but still, a good sprinkling of the originals from the fifties. Rosa lived half way down William Street and her garden backed on to the terraces behind the goal at the Town End of the ground. There was a ten-foot wall with a ladder up it and the Vetch's six-foot, corrugated iron fence on top of the wall. Some of the family used to climb up the ladder, stand on a box on top of the wall and watch the match peering over the fence while holding on to it for dear life.

The first time I went to William Street, one of my uncles told me he was at a recent pre-match gathering at the house, when somebody knocked at the front door. He answered it and there were two men standing there. They pushed him out of the way, ran through the house and out the back. Then, they climbed up the ladder, over the fence and were never seen again. A few weeks later a different uncle told me the same story but it was him who opened the door. I heard of several different hands on the door during that season and as so many people had told me the same story, it must have been true.

Back to the North Bank. In the fourth round of the 1964 FA Cup, the Swans had drawn their away match with, First Division, Sheffield United and the replay was at the Vetch on a Tuesday evening. The ground was packed and the atmosphere was noisy and exuberant. It was a great match, and with all the North Bank kicking every ball, it wasn't surprising that we won and all went home happy. Then we drew Stoke City in the next round. Another First Division team and another replay at the Vetch. It happened again. Wonderful atmosphere, brilliant match and we were all cheering and shouting until we were hoarse. Actually, I don't know if they were good matches but the excitement was really something else.

We got Liverpool, away, in the sixth round and I didn't go but I watched Noel Dwyer's finest hour on the TV highlights. Who could stop us now? We had beaten the cream of the country. Wembley here we come!

So, Tom, Dad and I set off to an incredibly wet Villa Park and the semi-final against Preston. They were below us in the league and we had already beaten them earlier in the season. The other two semi-final teams were First Division teams playing each other. This was our year. We took our places, under the stand, behind the goal and out of the pouring rain.

It was a great occasion, except the Swans were playing in sort of

pinky, orange shirts. As I remember it, the game was pretty even in the first half until Jimmy McLoughlin scored just before half-time. Lookin' good for the second half. We seemed to be holding them comfortably until that fluke goal by Singleton who scored from 150 yards out with Noel Dwyer standing on the penalty spot. Then there was the soft penalty when Alex Dawson 'went down easily in the box' and there was no way back. We were out of the Cup. What a disappointment. What a way to lose. Somehow, all the talk about coming back next year didn't convince. What's with all this rain in Birmingham? It was a tedious journey home and I couldn't have been more miserable.

But hope springs eternal. The man, who everybody that was older than me told me was the best, was coming back to the Swans. It was the mid sixties, Ivor wasn't the Golden Boy any more; he looked older. I had been too young to appreciate him when I was a kid in the fifties, was it too late to appreciate him now 10 years later when he was coming to the end of his career? Not a bit of it. The first time I saw him he scored a goal from 25 yards which just went in like a rocket. The way he passed the ball, the way he ran with it, the way he read the game and conducted the team like an Orchestra. Those guys, who told me about him, they were right. I got to the matches earlier after that day, I didn't want to miss a second of him.

In late 1965, I moved to London and was unable to find anybody who could tell me how the Swans got on. Mam came to the rescue by sending me the Sporting Post. I devoured it every Tuesday and kept on looking, without success, for another Swans fan. It was such a barren place for Jacks.

Then just when I thought that I'd never find anybody, I met someone who restored my faith in humanity. In 1968, I went on an FA Coaching Course. I was in my early twenties and completely out of my depth being mixed in with professional coaches and old 'pros' who were looking to move into coaching at the end of their playing careers. I met a guy called John Dick. He was a Scottish international inside forward who played for West Ham in the fifties and early sixties. I remembered him playing. When he found out that I was from Swansea, he made a bee-line for me and told me that Ivor Allchurch was the best player he had played against in his whole career. All was well with the world.

Bill Johns

What a perfect day

Greatest day ever was being at Wembley with my son of 11. What a perfect day.

Anthony Tyrell (45), Swans100 survey

The winning of the Welsh Cup by the Swansea Association team has incidentally had the effect of disclosing the large proportions already reached by the local supporters of the dribbling code and the intensity of the enthusiasm. Thousands of people waited in the dribbling rain for the home-coming of the players, and a huge procession accompanied the latter from the Rhondda and Swansea Bay Railway to the Hotel, where the time-honoured custom of "filling the cup" was observed.' **South Wales Daily Post, 25 April 1913**

When the referee blew his whistle for the cessation of the game there were scenes of great jubilation. The crowd jumped over the railings and rushed towards the Swansea players, whom they shook by the hands and congratulated upon the success. Duffy was carried shoulder high to the pavilion where a dense crowd congregated, and patted the players on the back as they went back to the dressing room. Cheer after cheer was raised for the Swans, and one of the spectators called out to Bullock, telling the Swansea skipper that the Cup ought to be presented to Swansea straight away after their magnificent victory. It would be unfair to single out any Swansea player for special mention, for each and every one did his level best. All contributed equally towards bringing about the desired result. But for the fact that there is a war on, the Swans' success would be emblazoned forth to all quarters of the world, and their praises would be loudly sung all over the country. Circumstances demand that we shall not attach as much importance to the game as in normal times, but still, 'twas a glorious victory.

Swansea Town beat league champions Blackburn in the FA Cup South Wales Daily Post, 11 January 1915

Outside in Gordon-terrace, a crowd of several thousands wedged themselves between the gaol walls and the gardens opposite, and overflowed into the alley leading to the stands, and waited for three quarters of an hour to see the Swans clamber into their charabanc and celebrate the victory by heading a procession through the town. Lamp-posts, windows, walls, everything of vantage was requisitioned to see the victorious Swans make their bow to the town, and when they did arrive there was another mad rush to hug and cheer, so that it was with the utmost difficulty that Mr. Owen Evans and his directorate got their dishevelled team into the charabanc.

When everything seemed ready for a start it was suddenly learned that Sykes was missing. The diminutive skipper had followed in the wake of Mr. Watts Jones' burly figure, but he was cut off in the alley and had to run the gauntlet of congratulations and handshakes from hundreds of adoring admirers. He was pushed into his seat at last, and the St. John Ambulance Band struck up a spirited march and the procession moved off – at two miles an hour. The crowds followed with some semblance of order and cheered all the way through Oxford-street, Castle-street, High-street and Alexandra road. Traffic was held up most of the way, whilst at the Empire the club's charabanc was deluged with streamers thrown by the Empire staff.

Report of victory procession after Swans win the Division 3(S), South Wales Daily Post, 4 May 1925

The Cup-tie was on and rain or no rain, enthusiasts from the populous outer districts, who had all the week promised themselves the treat of seeing the match were determined upon not being disappointed.

The G.W.R. ran nearly dozen special trains, all of which arrived between 12.0 and 1.30. From North, South, East and West spectators came to town in their hundreds. Work was forgotten for the day; they had thoughts only for the match, and it was evident that with such a large and enthusiastic district following the local supporters would have to be early in the queue, if they were to be sure of good places.

About a thousand well-wrapped men, ready to weather the heaviest downpour, waited patiently outside the Vetch Field for the gates to open, and during the short time they formed a queue – the gates were opened at 1 o'clock instead of at 1.15 p.m. as advertised – they were serenaded by a number of street musicians, banjoists and a male quartet predominating.

By 1.20 p.m. the turnstiles were clicking merrily, and from then onwards there was a steady stream into the ground. Many wore a miniature swan in their hats.

South Wales Daily Post, 30 January 1926

The final whistle at the Vetch Field on Saturday was the signal for the most amazing outburst of enthusiasm Welsh soccer has ever known.

It was a roar of relief as well as joy. A dense mass of almost hysterical supporters – shouting, cheering, brandishing flags, rattles, sticks, and even leeks, yelled in unison for the heroes of the afternoons. Several women were in tears with joy.

Swans v Arsenal, 1926

Memories of a great occasion nearly 25 years ago, when the Swans of those days lined up against Exeter to decide a great promotion issue, were recalled this afternoon when the present-day representatives of the club opposed Newport County again in search of championship honours. The enthusiasm at the Vetch Field had to be seen to be appreciated.

All morning thousands of supporters had awaited the great day. Several hours before the start there were big queues at all entrances and at 2 o'clock these had grown to such proportions that it was obvious that many thousands would never see this great struggle with Welsh rivals, Newport County. ... The match had also aroused tremendous interest outside Swansea and from Newport alone it was estimated that 8,000 people had come to the Vetch Field.

With Swansea and Newport supporters augmented by a great crowd from the other Welsh Valleys, the Vetch Field was sorely taxed and a capacity crowd of something over 30,000 was, of course, assured. ... Some considerable time before the game was due to start the closing of all gates leading to the ground was ordered. Several thousands of disappointed followers were left outside.

In the long interval preceding the start there were many cases of fainting and the ambulance men were kept very busy.

South Wales Evening Post, 18 April 1949

Chesterfield 1978, over 22,000. My father and I in the South Enclosure behind the floodlight where the terrace rises. Couldn't move it was so packed all old Sandfields guys with flat caps, Capstan and Embassy Regals hanging out of mouths, pipe smoke floating up. The noise, the sheer quiet at going 1-0 down and the explosive roar when Toshack scored the winner. Then every man and boy on the pitch at the end, my Dad and I included celebrating promotion to the Second Division.

David Richards (42), Swans100 survey

It was probably the Swans' most memorable game, even allowing for

recent success and the Toshack era. It was the 1964 Semi Final at Villa Park. I remember the great lines of coaches going up Rhigos Bank, being just 45 mins from Wembley when THE CUP was THE great prize in football, the incredible tension during the second half, and the tearful old men at the end of the game.

David Lewis (67), Swans100 survey

John Toshack's debut against Watford. On about the half way line, he turned the defender inside out with a body swerve.

Anon (58), Swans100 survey.

Seeing Arthur Rowley's Leicester City top of the League getting beat 6-1. 4-0 half time. Great Day out.

Norman Mathias (72), Swans100 survey

When Charlo scored it was relief all round!
I've seen many, many games in my 40 odd years following the Swans, none more intense than Preston in 1981. We left the Millers Arms in Ynystawe early in a convoy of six cars, but by the time we reached the M4 just a mile away the convoy had split up.

Despite passing hordes of the Jack Army making their way to Deepdale, we never saw any of our lot again until we hit a pub on the outskirts of Preston. It had not been planned and without the aid of mobile phones it was quite uncanny that all six cars stopped in the same pub. Great minds think alike.

The game itself passed me by although I seem to remember a group of about 50 Blackburn Rovers supporters to our left who had come over to support their Lancashire neighbours hoping for a Preston victory in order for Blackburn to pip us at the post. Why they weren't at Bristol Rovers supporting their own team was beyond me.

They had something to cheer when Preston pulled one back and news filtered through that Blackburn were winning at Eastville but we were still 2-1 up at this stage as I took leave and went to the toilet.

From my position behind the goal it took quite a while to push through the crowd. The toilets were located to the rear of the stand. There were many grown men there pacing nervously like expectant dads in a maternity ward. They were unable to watch the end of the game. Everyone knew that if Preston scored Blackburn would be promoted and not us.

What a perfect day

I got back to my place just in time to see Jeremy Charles score our third goal and seal our place in history. That was the signal for all those 'expectant dads' to rush back to the stands to join in the celebrations. Happy days...

Huw Cooze

My dad drove us up to Preston; we left so early, it must have been six o'clock in the morning. I remember stopping at a service station, which was a real treat for us. As we got closer to Preston there seemed to be thousands and thousands of Swansea City fans on buses and cars. My dad said he had never seen anything like it before; I was ten at the time, and neither had I. We squeezed into the enclosure behind the goal and it was absolutely deafening. There were people with wigs and painted faces, gangs of lads with attitudes, coach parties of families and all to see Swansea try and gain promotion to the First Division. When we did, my dad cried and cried. He was hanging off the fence at the side with his fist clenched, he looked so proud and happy. My brother lifted me onto his shoulders and we danced around the terraces singing 'Johnny Toshack's black and white army'. It was a very happy moment for me as a Swans fan, and now I am older I still get a tear in my eye when I think of my Dad and what it meant to him.

James Thomas, in Keith Haynes & Phil Sumbler (eds), Vetch Field Voices (2000), 23-5.

Beating Leeds 5-1 in Division 1 in 1981. Was with my father and older sister, with me sat on top of a crush barrier on the North Bank, baking in the boiling sun and being overawed by the numbers of Swans fans pouring into the ground. Then, each time we scored, the chant of "Super Swans, Super Swans, Super Swans" got louder with each goal we scored. And then came CURT'S GOAL...I'M GETTING GOOSEBUMPS JUST THINKING ABOUT IT NOW!!

Robert Dixon Miles (42), Swans100 survey

My first visit to watch the Swans away was the 1994 Autoglass Trophy final against Huddersfield Town. I travelled up on a coach with my Dad and local football team and the other boys' parents. The atmosphere was great. It was brilliant to watch a football match at the Old Wembley. **Carl Smith (30), Swans100 survey**

Autoglass final win at Wembley. To witness Swansea at the great Wembley which I thought will never happen, but to win as well via a penalty shoot out was a dream come true. Super John Conforth lifting that trophy was out of this world!!!

Matt Parry (40), Swans100 survey

West Ham 1999. I was in a world of my own. Dazed and in heaven absolutely ecstatic. So happy and shocked that it seems I was only semi-conscious.

'Amber' (29), Swans100 archive

5,000 Swans fans going to Bury on the verge of promotion to league 1. Adrian Forbes scoring after a minute and a pitch invasion. Willy Gueret getting arrested after the game during the celebrations. An amazing day.

Ben Ace (21), Swans100 survey

Adrian Forbes smashing the ball past Glyn Garner after 25 seconds at Bury, and the utter chaos which followed as many of the 5,000 travelling Jacks spilled onto the pitch to celebrate with him. The goal that sent us on the way to where we are today.

Jack Carter (19), Swans100 survey

Wembley Play off. The way Swansea played in the first half was unbelievable. 3-0 half time. Story book stuff. Pinch yourself, yes it is true. Game over not likely but it all worked out right in the end.

Norman Mathias (72), Swans100 survey

Wembley 2011 - beating Reading to reach the Premier League. The sea of black and white as we walked out of the tube station, everybody with smiles on their faces, the heart stopping moment when Reading scored. The tension, the rapturous applause. Very emotional for us as a family as our daughter was in hospital at the time, so we had put a photo of her on our Swans flag so she was with us in spirit. Tears of sadness, and joy.

Cath Dyer (46), Swans100 survey

Seeing the ground for the first time was an eye-opener, and going in to half-time leading 3-0 was like a dream. Perhaps most vivid was seeing Sinclair scoring the fourth goal, and knowing that the Swans were going to join the Premiership. **Anon (44), Swans100 survey**

When you look at the fixtures and see Swansea v Man Utd and then beating Arsenal it defies belief!! Long live the Swans!!!

Ian Taylor (35), Swans100 survey

The atmosphere at Villa Park when we won our first away game in the Premiership. Brilliant day

Matthew Harrison (23), Swans100 survey

I follow the team because since entering the Premier League, there are more conversations about the team, at work, university and on Facebook. It's now an important part of Swansea culture. I am now asked how the move to the premiership has affected Swansea by friends from other parts of the country. Friends from elsewhere seem to want to know more about Swansea; it seems to have put Swansea back on the UK map.

Sarah Jones (47), Swans100 survey

2011 has probably been the proudest year yet as a Swansea fan. People all over the country know and respect my club. Last season, the play offs, the final, all amazing. This season - amazing. I still can't quite believe we are meeting the giants of the British game in league matches. It's surreal. Now, in 2012, our centenary year, I hope to be even more proud. So far so good!!

Richard Davies (40), Swans100 survey

These are fantastic times to be a Swans supporter. Most of us have put up with a lot of dross, down to genuinely dark days like the Petty era. But, to see where we are just 8 and a bit years on is amazing. I often think about myself after the Exeter game when it really looked like we were going down, and I think what he would have thought if someone had told him that in under 10 years we'd be in the Premier league, competing with and even beating the best. All while still being locally and fan owned. It genuinely warms the heart. For me, the most important thing is the football we play. I'll always go down, no matter what division we're in but I feel Swansea have an identity to our play, going back way before I was born and typified by players like Alan Curtis. We'll never be the biggest club but we definitely have flair! STID

Anon (33), Swans100 survey

My playground

I was born and brought up in the Sandfields area of Swansea, Western Street to be precise. The Vetch was the centre of the area and dominated the Sandfields. Even on non match days. In the early 70s even at a very young age we could go anywhere to play from Singleton Park, the beach to the docks. There was so much more freedom back then. And at the centre of our world was the Vetch. We would play football at the back of the west stand just by the TA centre. We used to call it the Arsenal.

But it was inside the Vetch was the real adventure. Why play football outside The Vetch when we knew every nook and cranny in the walls and fences of that old beautiful ugly stadium. We could get in and out of every stand through old fencing, gaps in walls, loose stonework which we would put back so nobody would know we had been in the ground.

We would get on the pitch and have a kick around or take penalties at each other in the goals. Or we would just sit in the stands and be the only ones in the ground. Or so we thought. Eventually someone would come out of one the stands and shout those immortal words (Oi you lot get out of here). We would be off in a shot with someone chasing us through the deserted stands laughing our heads off. We never once caused any damage and never ever got caught.

On match days it was the same we would use our little bolt holes to get into the west stand or get under the fence at the back of the east bank up into someone's back garden and climb into the old east bank up onto those old railway sleeper steps, sometimes the house owners would give us a bunk up their garden walls to get into the ground. The North Bank was a bit more difficult to get into. A few times because we were so small at the time (7/8/9 years old) we could get on the floor and sneak in by the turnstiles through the fans who were paying legs. A bit more dangerous way was to climb the fence by the power station (I KNOW VERY STUPID) and climb onto the roof of the toilet block and down into the ground, far more easier at night games.

It was one of these night games that a memory would stick in my mind for a long time. We were waiting for a chance to climb the fence at the back of the north bank when an older boy came along and tried to get in the ground before us he climbed the fence and more or less straight away a copper shouted at him to get down he slipped and fell to the ground he started to cry and hold his hand. The copper came over and asked if he was ok and he saw blood coming from his hand. When the policeman took a look he saw that the top part of the boy's finger was missing. He wrapped the boy's hand with a bandage or something like that and started to shine his torch on the ground to find the top of the finger. He then shone the torch at the top of the fence and there it was lodged between two of the three prongs at the top of the fence, he plucked the tip from the fence and wrapped it up and gave it to a St Johns ambulance man who had now arrived. I never used that way to sneak in again, and never did find out if the boy's finger tip had been sewn back on.

A few years later we got into and out a few times when some rock band had a concert there we kept picking up full unopened cans of beer and hiding them outside until someone must have found them and took them (cheek of it). I did not realise at the time that that band on the stage were one of the biggest in the world and would become one of my favourite groups of all time THE WHO.

Those early years of sneaking in led me to a lifetime love of Swansea City and The Vetch and although it was sad to say goodbye to the old stadium it was for the right reasons. On the last ever game at the Vetch when the final whistle blew I was there on the pitch and I was very sad to see the old ground being torn to pieces, men women children tearing up the seats and the pitch for mementos. I could understand why they were doing it. And I do not have any problem with it. Me, I just stood there and thought and smiled about those early days of my life, about a bunch of scrappy kids having a laugh being chased for having a kick about in.......MY PLAYGROUND.

Andrew Fall – aged 47

"Why I Love Swansea City"

I love the Swans and have been to see them a few times this season with my mum and friends and really enjoy it (even when they loose).

I am also a member of the Cygnets.

I really like Brendan Rodgers and think he is the best Manager ever, I really hope he decides to stay with us and not move on to another club as I would be really sad. I sent him a letter before Easter saying this.

My favourite players are Michel Vorm, Scott Sinclair and Leon Britton, but I think all the team are great.

My family have followed the Swans for quite a few years. My Nan used to go down "The Vetch" about 50 years ago with her friends (I think it was to look at the players legs more than to watch the game from what she says). My uncle used to go to see them when John Toshack was the Manager. My Nan used to take my Uncle to Marios Café in Union Street, Swansea where the players used to go after training for a coffee and a toasted tea-cake. They used to regularly see Alan Curtis – who is still involved with the Swans today.

My mum had a season ticket for a few years she thinks the last season was 1999-2000 or maybe the previous season, when John Hollins was Manager. She used to stand on the "Northbank", her favourite players were Stuart Roberts, Richie Abbleby, Matthew Bound and Roger Freestone. Mum used to go down the old Swans shop with my Nan and they say that quite often the Players would be in the shop, so they got to meet quite a few of them.

I really hope the Swans do well next season, score loads of goals, play well and stay in the Premiership – but even if they don't I will still support them.

WHO ARE WE?

JACK ARMY!!!!

By Nia Hughes   Age 8
Ysgol Login Fach, Waunarlwydd, Swansea.

a century of supporting the swans

'If you take the badge off it can be a Swans kit just the same as a Leeds kit.' My poor Mam has spent ages getting me a white football shirt and a Leeds United badge and now the day after my birthday here was my Dad telling me I shouldn't wear the badge. I wasn't for telling. Dad was never keen on me or anyone else from Swansea supporting any other team. 'This is our team, our town, what connection have we got with Leeds?' Within 6 months the badge was gone and it was a Swans kit, Dad had started taking me to the Vetch, and I was hooked. Cheers Dad.

Clwyd Primary School in Penlan, which I attended was a different matter altogether. There football was banned, as was using the school playing fields after school for football, talking about football and taking your football stickers to school to swap. The Swans were definitely not a welcome subject. The school only did two sports, rugby and cricket, thanks in the main to one of the teachers at the school, Alan Williams, who later went on to be head of a school in Mumbles. He was a fantastic teacher, but I vividly remember after one assembly him calling me out in front of the class because I had been spotted at the Vetch, a cardinal sin in his view. 'Who saw me there?' I asked anything but innocently. It didn't matter who had seen me but I must never do it again. 'Will Mr Roberts (another teacher) get the same warning as well, because he was standing just behind me!' I was made to stand in the corridor outside the classroom for the first lesson but my support for the Swans was never brought up again.

From Clwyd I went to Manselton (Colditz) and Pentrehafod Schools where rugby was definitely not the main sport and nearly everyone supported the Swans apart from the unfortunate Maaaaaaaaaaaaaaaaaaaars Baaaaaaaaaaaaaaaaar, whose family had moved down from Cardiff City's eastern valley hinterland. Strangely, despite being a really good kid he was not the most popular in school. I continued playing rugby until a chance came to play for the school football team when the first choice goalkeeper broke his leg. I was rubbish I have to admit and let them down on many occasions with my hapless rugby style keeping (two penalties in one game was my record). My final game for the school was against Dynevor when with Steve Potter like timing I came for a cross, missed the ball and was headed into the net by the Dynevor centre forward. The next thing I remember was waking up in a teacher's car, being driven home, with the instruction 'You'd better go down the hospital'. I still don't know why he didn't take me there himself. Claims Direct would have had a field day back then! My parents were shopping in town so, after admiring my morning's work in the mirror (two black eyes and a nose pointing a different way to when I'd woken up), changing into my Swans gear, black and white hooped pullover and scarf tied round my wrist, I called on some Swans supporting mates and we made our way to Singleton Hospital, where I was X-rayed and told that I had broken my nose. They took what I thought was unusual interest in how I had done it etc etc. They went away to 'get the medicines from the pharmacist'. Close to an hour later we were in danger of missing kick off and one of my mates was convinced they were calling the police because we had Swans kit on. So we legged it, just made kick off and the Swans beat Brentford 2-1, Curt and Robbie the scorers I think. Thirty five years later, I still can't breathe properly out of my left nostril.

PLEASE KEEP OFF THE PITCH!

Dreams were made at the Vetch

Enjoyable times, never to be forgotten. Dreams were made at the Vetch.

Andrew Jones (42), Swans100 survey

The ground has been transformed at a big expense and the playing area is nice and flat, but there is scarcely any turf. Improvement, however, will come in time. A splendid pavilion has been erected for the players, whilst an embankment has been erected all round so as to give the spectators a splendid opportunity of seeing all the play.

Description of the Vetch at Swansea Town's first match
Cambrian, 13 September 1912

On the first occasion that it was open to the public, the new grandstand was very much needed. Heavy showers of rain fell before the kick-off, and the covered stand was soon filled. Despite the unfavourable weather, the cheap side was rapidly occupied, and the interval of waiting for the teams to field was wiled away by the band discoursing ragtime. The teams were given a warm welcome when they came out, and at that time there were about 5,000 spectators present.

The opening of a new stand at the Vetch, Swans v Barry
Cambrian, 19 September 1913

Just before the teams fielded appeals were sent out on the loud speakers to ask spectators to pack together as there were thousands outside the ground trying to gain admission. ... The more daring spectators had climbed the steel girders on the cheap side of the ground, and had a clear view, although from extremely uncomfortable conditions.

Swansea Town v Bury, FA Cup
South Wales Evening Post, 1 February 1934

The crowd behind the Wind-Street goal came forward and the barrier supporting them collapsed, dozens of spectators falling onto the pitch behind the goal.

Police and ambulance men quickly ran to the spot. Eventually the game contuinued with a human barrier behind Gillfillan. No one was injured.

Swansea Town v Portsmouth
South Wales Evening Post, 17 February 1934

I was living down near the Vetch Field. We were football mad, and especially near the start of the season, sometimes we used to climb over the wall and have a kickabout on the pitch. The pitch was brand new this time, ready for the start of the season. So the next night, we thought we would do this again, and climbed over the back again – we were only about 12 then, you know. And when we got onto the Vetch to kick the ball about, there was about one hundred sheep on the pitch! They must have brought them on, they reckoned sheep could eat the grass, and bring it down to the level that was needed, you know. So all the boys was running around, jumping over sheep and playing about.

Roy Griffiths (73), Swans100 archive

A move will be made very soon by Swansea Town supporters' club to put into operation a scheme for providing covered accommodation of the main bank at the Vetch Field.

South Wales Evening Post, 13 June 1958

Vetch floodlights are now a must

Lights on every ground would enable the league to insist on a standard kick-off – say 3.15 – throughout the season.

That would certainly be a step forward, for many fans have to rush their lunch to get to a ground for 2.15 or 2.30 and then the game finishes in semi-darkness ... When I spoke to Mr Trevor Morris, the manager, on the matter this week, his immediate reaction was that "We must have lights. In a year's time we shall probably be the only team in the first and second division without them.

"We might well be left in the dark," he added jocularly.

South Wales Evening Post, 13 February 1960

Every town gets the football ground it deserves. ... at Swansea the buildings look to be extemporized as hasty defence against the overhanging mountains or the encroaching sea...

Percy Young, 'The Humour of Soccer', in Leslie Frewin (ed), The
Saturday Men: A Book of International Football (1967)

HTH Poor. Wasn't done up until the 1940's. There was no cover for the North Bank and it was terraced in rotten sleepers. The East Bank was the same. The players tunnel was situated at the centre of the South Stand. Under the clock.

IGR The North Bank was still awful, all ashes and no wall at the back. You could just run down the ash slope to the other side. No pylons then so the team played home on Thursday afternoons. DGR The East Bank was still there, awful to look at but it added character when full. No fences even then and I used to watch the Swans from the old South terrace, where it came round behind the corner pylon.

Three generations of the same family remember the Vetch in Love, Peace and Swansea City, 5 (March/April 1993)

[In the 1950s you] could stand next to an opposing supporter complete with rattle etc. and there would be no animosity.

Love, Peace and Swansea City, 5 (March/April 1993)

The East Bank

The old small bank had a very special atmosphere which was different from the rest of the Vetch. Like the 'Casino' and 'Pier' dance-halls of old, it was what the estate agents call 'compact'. That meant for those stood there, that there was a friendly warm feeling about it. Not warm you understand in the climatic sense, but rather in its ambience. And partly because of that it became the regular spot for hundreds of Swans fans. A spot from which you could almost feel to be part of the game which you were watching. After all, those gladiators in white were almost within touching distance when the tide of the game lapped at the bottom of the bank.

Memories come flooding back. I remember Norman Lockhart taking a corner there one day. He was so near to me that I could see that he had cut himself shaving that morning. Were my heroes human after all? And I remember Raich Carter falling over a photographer behind the goal there and grinning at a comment from the crowd. That, of course, was during the match which was watched by half the schoolboy population of Swansea, all of whom had 'cut' school to see the famous Derby County. For us Dynevor boys there was a special attraction, for the captain and right back of the visitors was an old boy, Jack Nicholas. That put us one-up for a long time over the red-coated horde from up the hill. Somehow or other I escaped retribution the following morning when the others around me suffered various punishments. I can only hope that having owned up this way, I'll not provoke a retrospective hundred lines.

The old bank had many facets. The old half-time board used to

Dreams were made at the Vetch

stand there and those who manipulated the numbers had, so it was said, a wonderful view. Despite all my best efforts I was never able to establish whether that was true - though that smug look on the faces of the chosen few up there suggested it was. The bank was, of course, open to the elements and remained so to the end. Thus 'small bankers' tended to be pretty hardy folk long after those who populated the 'Tanner Bank' had forgotten how to deal with the elements. It was said, too, that the small bank was a Sandfields reserve (maybe that's why it was so friendly). However, the story went with the idea that each of Swansea's districts favoured part of the ground. Derwen Fawr and Sketty, of course, in the stand; Cwmbwrla, Waun Wen and St. Thomas on the big bank; Manselton and Brynmill under the double decker, and so on. And, while the hypothesis wouldn't stand up to too close a scrutiny, there was something in it.

Match programme, Swans v West Ham United, 10 January 1981

The Vetch Field renovation process has been steadily progressing so far and congratulations are in order for those responsible for dealing with the West side of the ground. No one can call the Vetch scruffy any more, and, sentimentalists excluded, very few will have been sorry to see the old Double Decker come tumbling down. In its day, it boasted the best view in the ground but since its closure in 1985 as a fire hazard it's proved a safety hazard for Sandfields residents (not to mention away fans!) and a waste of space. Now the new, slightly lower all white roof is a boost to the ground.

Jack Mail, 14 (December 1990).

The Vetch was great. Standing on the North Bank, eating a cold pasty and cold tea!!!! We had our same spot every game in the corner near the East stand side.

Ian Taylor (35), Swans100 survey

Ambition: To have sex on the pitch and then slide on my knees in front of the North Bank when I'm finished!

Andy Bowen in Jackanory, 11 (February/March 1999)

Since the first match that I ever saw at the Vetch (8-0 against Hartlepool back in 1978), I've seen many changes at our beloved home; players and managers have come and gone, first division football, Jimmy Gilligan being cheered by the North Bank faithful,

the Double-Decker becoming a Single-Decker. None of these changes compare, however, with the evolution(?) of the humble Vetch Field pastie.

"Nobody will ever know..."
A Swansea City fanzine from the South East, 2 (November 1990)

They've painted the steps in the Centre Stand a nice yellow colour! A stand which has the great honour of being the only multi-coloured seated stand in the world! When a seat breaks in there the most difficult thing to do is to find a replacement that's colour does not match anything around it! The East Stand is getting that way now but with different shades of grey seats! It's a bloody shambles isn't it!

Jackanory, 7 (February/March 1998)

The single most vivid [memory I have] is going to a night game at the Vetch and walking up the ramp to the North bank seeing the foodlights on, onto the pitch, fantastic.

Mark Samuel (43), Swans100 survey

I remember the days of hospitality at the Vetch with cold beef from the packet being warmed up by the gravy! My customers didn't know what to do!

Jim White (36), Swans100 survey

I do miss the atmosphere of standing on a terrace. Now I take my family, the Liberty Stadium is a better place to visit. I dreaded my young sons asking to go to the toilet at the Vetch!

Adrian Byrne (45), Swans100 survey

Darkness at the Vetch

It was a place you didn't want to be. Not of your own free will anyway. I don't know whether away fans would have wanted to be in there. But I know most of us Jacks didn't. A hostile place, unfriendly to those passing through. Or anything being passed, really. It must have been something in the air. It looked so unassuming from the outside as old men and flat caps shuffled in, youngsters in oversized, football manager jackets with wispy moustaches pritt-sticked to their top lips, and the occasional child contemplating the abyss, the darkness before them. It was a rite of passage to adulthood some say. I know it made a man of me.

I was about thirteen when I first went in there. Terrified at first, I was. Standing shoulder to shoulder with grown men and bewildered, wide-eyed youths like myself as the cold air billowed in through the entrance and flaked the peeling, black painted brickwork. The sounds of crackling, 90s electro-pop pierced and pained the clean sea air above us. But that was a million miles away, now. The air inside here was thick. And it had a queer, otherworldly stench, somewhere between retirement and rigor mortis. Nearby, but out of sight, the air was impregnated with the waft of one hundred degree Celsius pasties, real burgers without the foil bags and hot, insipid Bovril. I wanted to be over there, I did. The hustle shuffle of excited fans anticipating the game or second half, oblivious to my first time standing in here. And things were different in here. Mumbled conversations from denim jacketed forty-year olds with love & hate tattoos on their teeth and a few rotten or missing knuckles. One growled that the away manager was an English count - at least I think that's what he said - and I wondered innocently why an aristocrat would want to manage Torquay. Then words faded out and our feet shuffled away with the mild tinges of disinfectant and bodily wastes. I had nowhere to dry my hands but the slimy walls...

I, with those brave ones, who couldn't hold it in any longer and had to pass through there, shall never forget.

The horror. The horror of the North Bank toilets.

J. Borley

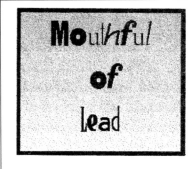

Why Our Toilets Are Special

by Prof. C.A. Manaboutadog

Swansea has always been home to architectural curiosities. From the Hanging Bastards of Dyfatty, to the neo-baroque Georgian facade of the Union Street Spud-U-Like, the city's buildings have a diversity all of their own.

The Vetch is no different. Swans supporters have their very own unique heritage in the form of the North Bank urinals. Built in 1645 by a chain gang of Nubian murderers, it has stood the test of time and continually offered itself as a primitive shrine for the discerning slack-bladdered Jack who demands the very basic in urinary facilities.

There are plans to achieve listed status to preserve the unique 3mm terracotta drainage system which spews back 80% of human waste over all & sundry; and lottery funding to make a themed section where Peter Day will be employed in period costume to direct adrenaline junkies into the '7th Wave' - an exciting ride on the yellow foaming surf which propels one violently towards the hamburger stall.

New Exciting Ride

Exciting times. Swans fans should respect the history - not moan about their camels smelling of piss.

Mouthful of Lead

http://www.btinternet.com/~A.S.Thomas/SCFC.html

Jackanory, 8 (Apr-May 1998)

A Friday night in early May 1979

It was a Friday night in early May 1979 and the final home game of the season. I was nine years old and going down the Vetch for only the second time in my life. I had a strong family connection with the club with Barrie Hole being my uncle, Carl Slee a distant relative and my mother the best friend of Cliffy Jones's sister and Swans regular to boot. City was in the blood.

The occasion was as big as it could get, the Swans were up for promotion. Put simply City had to win, if they did Division Two football could be on its way. Division Two meant Chelsea, Newcastle, Sunderland, Blackburn Rovers and West Ham; it would be a return to the heights of years gone by after a decade in the wilderness.

Along with 22,000 other hopeful souls, my father and I made our way through the Sandfields streets towards the Vetch. The North Bank was already in full voice singing booming around the Sandfields and the queues to get in were already 30 long. We promptly rushed round to the West Terrace but that too was already full by the time we got there, so on this occasion we ended up in a packed South Enclosure, where it rose up behind the floodlight pylon. Everyone was there for what they hoped would be promotion. Somehow I can't recall much apprehension, it felt more like everyone was buzzing, waiting for the confirmation for the expected win and therefore the ensuing triumph. Daft I know, but that's what I, as an eight year old, thought at the time; everyone there seemed totally confident the Swans would clinch promotion.

Not having grown that much over four foot my Dad forced me to the front of the rickety terracing bypassing flagons of ale and cider, vapours of cockles with vinegar and paper confetti, all in order to drape my black and white scarf over the wall. From this vantage point, I witnessed amongst surges, (yes surges in the South Enclosure) Chesterfield score and the Vetch turn into an instant funeral parlor. However, Waddle and Toshack's goals, the winner a superb header in the second half, secured Swansea's promotion to the Second Division for the first time in 14 years. I jumped up and down like a hyperactive Zebedee at the winner and I remember turning round to see the biggest smile I'd ever seen on my father's face. The good times were back and his boy was in on it all.

Amid the all jubilation in the enclosure flat caps, motif less black and white scarves and the iconic seventies bobble hats went flying in the air and gave cue to tons of rust falling off the roof in a Newton like reply. Everyone on the terrace eventually turned their attention to the pitch, already half of it was engulfed by invaders from the North Bank complete with Up the Swans banners, Noddy Holder haircuts and in Don Morgan's case a flagon or two in hand. To prove they had no monopoly rights on celebrations, the East and West terraces duly emptied and it was party time on the Vetch itself. I was never one to miss an invasion, so after begging the old man senseless, we eventually ended up on the pitch ten minutes later. It was here to the left of the centre spot in front of the Grandstand we heard the official announcement Swindon Town had lost and in the ensuing mayhem I spent a full five minutes recreating Toshack's winner in the wrong penalty area. As the champagne flowed in the Directors Box and 'Super Swans' reverberated around Swansea Bay, we headed for Western Street to bring the family the news. We got there to find that they'd left for Clydach for a big family knees up. As we drove off I remember all the cars hooting by the lights at Dyfatty, scarves draped out of windows and people shouting and cheering. It was like all those celebrations you see on TV when a Mediterranean or South American country has won the World Cup, except this was not Buenos Aries or Naples, this was South Wales and people weren't singing ' Champione, Champione,' they were singing "Swansea, Swansea City."

On arriving in Clydach we came out of the car all smiles and singing, my grandfather Trev and great Uncle Bunt responded with a chorus of 'Bubbles.' It was then that I learned from these old hardcore Jacks the history of the song and how Swans fans in the early 1920s had sung it at the Vetch at an FA Cup tie against West Ham and again in the replay at Upton Park and how the Londoners then took it for their own. Knowing little about Hammers fans or Swansea Town I let this detail brush over me, I was all ready to tell them of the exploits of Messrs Toshack and Waddle. After a party of sorts we all travelled in convoy back into town – in the Sandfields it was lock up time, but I swear there were as many on the street outside the Panty that night than I've ever seen since in my life and all due to the Swans. Going to school the following Monday I was adamant I would be wearing my scarf all day. Fat chance. However, when asked to write about what I did that weekend I was in my element. I got 9 out of 10 - gold star. The match account is still kept with the programme ready for the next generation to discover.

David Richards, 41

The old club shop

"Do you remember the old club shop?" Oh Yes, more than 7 people in there, jam packed #jackmemories

Neil, Twitter

It was classic and iconic - forget your modern day superstores. Was it Myra who worked there, the old girl? #clubshopisahouse

Jacs y Gogledd, Twitter

Yeah but no matter how many was in there, good old Myra sorted the tickets out no fuss #fablady

Robert Day, Twitter

Wow those were the days! Buying tickets, programmes and a few replica shirts in the little old box room! #goodtimes

Jason Evans, Twitter

Did 6th form work experience in the 'commercial dept'. There was a huge mushroom up in a corner of the back room ceiling!

Nick Clark, Twitter

I phoned up once for tickets to the fourth round of the F.A. cup against Derby and Myra asked me to ring back in fifteen minutes as she was having lunch. Priceless...

Phil Williams, www.swans100.org.uk

I remember feeling totally intimidated by Myra and Joyce when I would be brave enough to buy tickets from them. I would also spend time in the week browsing through the limited stock in the hope of getting a glance at the Legendary Alan Curtis when he did the Football in the Community role from there – looked silly staring at those rulers for hours on end though!!

Nigel Davies, www.swans100.org.uk

Myra & Joyce I have to thank those two lovely ladies. I have spent quite a few years abroad in the Army and every other week I used to receive in the post a programme from the latest game. At the end of the season I personally delivered a thank you card it meant so much getting up to date news on the Swans before the age of the internet.

Matt Parry, www.swans100.org.uk

I have such fond memories of the club shop dating back to the early 1990's. Living in Gloucester in those days I used to make the most of every visit and would come home with all manner of memorabilia including many programmes.

On one occasion when Myra discovered how far I had travelled she became very concerned that I shouldn't wear my scarf when I changed trains in Cardiff (I was only 13 at the time)! This really epitomises the club shop. It felt like being in someone's front room and the staff always gave you a warm welcome. Whenever I enter the Superstore at the Liberty I can't help cast my mind back to those days, it certainly highlights how far the club has come.

David Viner, www.swans100.org.uk

Here are ten good reasons why you should buy a club replica kit:

1. You will look great in it.
2. Your girlfriend, boyfriend, uncle, grandad etc. will look great in it.
3. You can look (and play ?) like the new star signing.
4. Our wives and kids need the money.
5. Some visiting talent scout may make you an offer you can't refuse.
6. All your mates are buying it.
7. Your mum will think you look lovely in it.
8. Your favourite colour is White.
9. The team likes to see that you support them.
10. They have been ordered specially for you — so don't disappoint us.

From the Club Shop and good local Sports Shops

LET US SHOW THE TEAM THAT WE SUPPORT THEM: Admiral

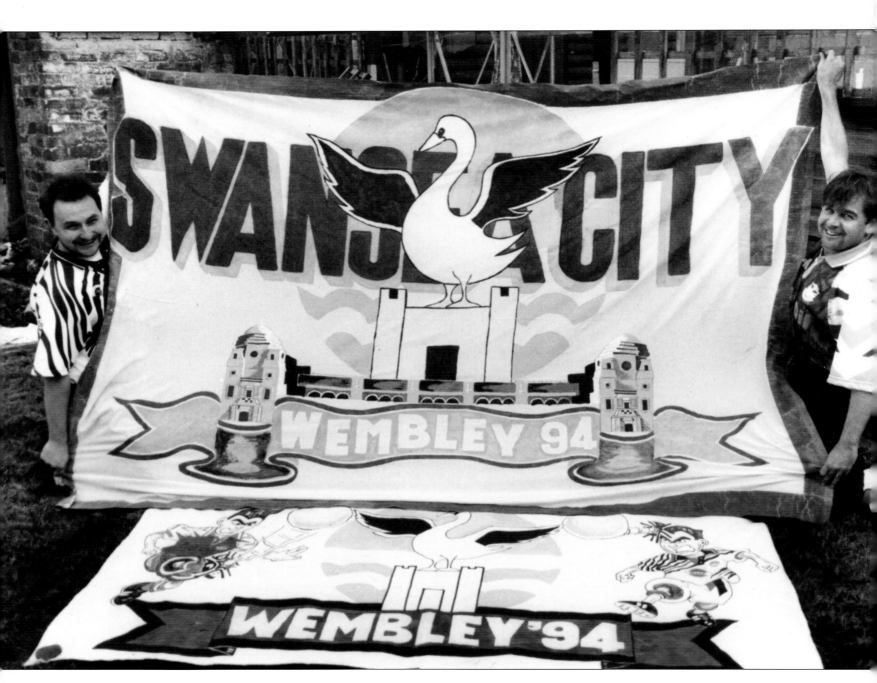

Three generations watched on

The tin can rattles as it bounces down the concrete steps of the North Bank. I had scored a 'goal' on my first visit to the Vetch Field!

As a child of 7 or 8 the attraction of seeing my first football match had lost its appeal after 20 minutes or so. My Dad was enthralled, as I was to become in later life but at this age the subtleties of the game were lost on me. Although in those days subtlety wasn't a feature of the Swans play and no one would have conceived then that they would one day be compared to the mighty Barcelona!

Looking around the North Bank, there were lots of empty spaces in those days, I saw another boy about my age also kicking a can along the steps. A game quickly ensued but like the Match itself I never knew the name of my opponent or the final score.

Over 40 years have passed since my first visit and like my father before me I have taken my children to watch my beloved Swans. My son was only 6 months old when he made his debut at the Vetch but he has not become a fan. My daughter follows in the steps of her father and grandparents in being a loyal fan from an early age. The photo of her standing in front of the Vetch sign on her last visit before the move to the Liberty ranks alongside the pictures of the magic day at Wembley.

The short 25 mile journey of my youth from Hirwaun, has been replaced by a 300 mile round journey from Farnham in Surrey for the last 17 years. But still we come, not put off by the dark days of relegation or receivership. We were there for the Hull game and have spent many cold and winless nights on the terraces.

My one regret is of not making the trip to Preston to follow Tosh's boys but I beg forgiveness of the footballing gods as I had to stay behind to await exam results that day and I was there to welcome the boys back home! But the old Division 1 was a great experience and a trip to Anfield in the week Shankly died was followed by a trip to Old Trafford.

Friends have been made and lost along the way. Both my parents followed the Swans for years but are sadly no longer with us. John, Alan and Mike on the North Bank, Haydn and Ronnie in the East Terrace at the Liberty, are amongst many we have shared the highs and lows with.

Pre match rituals continue with a coffee and Kit Kat amongst them. But the coffee now comes from a machine and is delivered in cups with lids and health and safety concerns. No more polystyrene cups from the North Bank café with milk in large plastic bottles standing on tables in the rain. No tin cans anymore and no longer the smell of burgers wafting around the North Bank.

The urinals no longer smell and are not painted black, which often reflected our mood after a poor game. Now it is the hygienic facilities hidden in the bowels of the ground. TVs to watch as we stand in the dry but there is more of a crush than there used to be at the Vetch or is it just my imagination of a beloved ground lost.

The pre/post match drink and/or visit to the shops are harder to achieve at Morfa. Parking is a nightmare now and road closures prolong the post-match departure. No more parking opposite the prison, waving to the inmates and then a quick exit down the Mumbles Road.

I've travelled to games when a doctor's paper for my ailments would easily have been obtained, especially as our local GP was also a fan! I've queued for tickets around the Vetch and also around the Liberty. We've gone from the low tech club shop, with the quaint old ladies behind the counter, to the high tech computerised ticket office.

So four decades, three generations, two stadiums and lots of memories remain. Some great highs with promotions, cup victories and some great players. Who can ever forget Tommy Smith scoring two goals in a match and one direct from a corner, or Tommy Hutchison gliding past players in front of the North Bank? But even the darks days of receivership, relegation and the Hull match give us great memories. Other clubs' supporters will never understand us, as we have seen more than the average fan of Arsenal, Chelsea or those of the so called elite.

So after 100 years I salute the Swans, their Directors, Managers, Players, support staff and most importantly my fellow fans. For it is you who have helped made my experience great. While the Swans may not in Shankly's words be more than life and death, surely our experiences are echoed in Alex Ferguson's words, "football, bloody hell."

So as we enter the Second Millennium at the top table of football, let's give praise to the homely spirit and core values that still remain at our club and hope they continue for another 100 years.

Christopher Drew

A more upmarket experience

Now it is a more professional, upmarket experience, with a wonderful level of skill.

Peter Miles (76), Swans100 survey

In the beginning I thought we'd lost so much of the wonderful atmosphere at the Vetch but now it's really taken off at the Liberty. The facilities are so much better at the Liberty.

Eileen Morgan (77), Swans100 Survey

[The Liberty is] Much better. Good view from all areas of the ground and most importantly the seats are well spaced.

Colin Short (75), Swans100 survey

[The Liberty's] better – due to the improved facilities, although the atmosphere at the Vetch and close proximity to the game being played will long be remembered.

Brian John (73), Swans100 survey

Loved the Vetch. Saw some great games and great Players. Liberty is brilliant. Great atmosphere.

Norman Mathias (72), Swans100 survey

Cleaner, better loos, more space etc but lacks the crush, adrenalin and raw passion of the Vetch. Maybe the east is different but the west is constrained but hey I'm, nearly 60 so maybe that's the way it should be.

Nigel Jarman (59), Swans100 survey

Couldn't beat the Vetch for atmopshere. Now we play in a clinical drab cold stadium, where health and safety rules all, and stewards often act like sergeant majors. e.g. Trying to exit from the East Stand at the end of the game, and being told that you cannot use the South Stand exits, even though they are clear is typical of this.

Geoffrey Thyer (59), Swans100 survey

I used to love the Vetch field but knew that we needed to move to enable the team to progress on and off the field and so it proved. The Liberty has much better facilities and the atmosphere has greatly improved as we've risen up the leagues.

Initially I found it strange but am now used to the Liberty and in

some ways prefer going there now. It certainly has encouraged more families to attend which is surely a good thing for the future.

Anon (58), Swans100 survey

Recollections of my old experiences on the 'North Bank' were terrific but they are probably being viewed with rose tinted spectacles. The current facility at the Liberty is where the game is at today.

Paul Williams (57), Swans100 survey

Whilst I thoroughly enjoyed standing on the North Bank all those years ago the new stadium clearly has much better facilities and crowd control. It is much more family orientated with a feeling of safety. I appreciated being able to have my own seat and camaraderie with those around me. As the Liberty is close to my home it is a much less stressful routine. I have a parking permit so know I always have somewhere safe to leave the car. I can always anticipate an enjoyable experience owing to the good organisation, the bonhomie of the crowd and the more than adequate facilities.

Alan Hughes (56), Swans100 survey

I love the atmosphere around the Stadium and the way you can see everyone heading in one direction.

Peter Dawson (55), Swans100 survey

The Vetch was easier to get to - we still need better bus services to the Liberty on match days. But the approach and the bars are more spacious, seats are more comfortable with better views, and regularly having 20,000 others to sing Hymns & Arias with is incredible. My memories of the Vetch are being cramped but hugely excited with 30,000 crowds for Villa, Arsenal, Cardiff cup games etc. Otherwise a dingy, damp, miserable place with little to shout about in terms of football entertainment most of the time, if we're honest.

Tim Douglas (54), Swans100 survey

I think there are pros and cons to both grounds, and in summary my answer is that they are very different. The Vetch: I could see the ground from my house, walk there in 10 minutes. Often there was a queue to get in, so arriving early was important to get a good place to stand. The buzz building up in the North Bank as the ground filled up was really exciting. The Vetch facilities were poor (the toilets!), but I have never gone to football games to eat and drink. The great thing was you could stand on the terraces. Little could be more exciting than the mass hysteria of a mob of 10,000 Jacks in the North Bank when a home goal went in! The Liberty; have to drive to get there, but no queue as I have only attended with season-ticket holders, one of who could not be there that day. The pitch views are fantastic, and the atmosphere is good despite the sitting down. The quality of the football is also fantastic - not something that could be said of many years at the Vetch. I think the real test and comparison would come if the Swans were playing at the Liberty in League 2 in front of 3,500 fans. So - nostalgia tells me the Vetch was better, but head tells me they are too different to compare directly.

Phil Bethell (53), Swans100 survey

The North Bank at the Vetch was a more social event. The Liberty is more comfortable.

Phil Roberts (50), Swans100 survey

The overall experience at the Liberty is better when the atmosphere is bouncing it's a fantastic place to be. Nobody could miss standing in the urine trench at the North Bank.

Martin Bowen (49), Swans100 survey

Liberty is hard to get to, have to drive instead of the train. I miss matchday walk through Town, lost touch with old mates I had stood with for years which is sad. Nice to have a seat, miss standing. Nice to be able to leave your seat, miss the fight back up to where you were standing. Great views at the Liberty, looking through a pillar at the Vetch. Don't miss the North Bank Toilets. Vetch atmosphere was hostile, miss that but Liberty has a good atmosphere since the drummer arrived.

Simon Stranaghan (48), Swans100 survey

The Liberty is better. Modern Times brings progress and this has improved everything in my opinion (as you would expect it to). Facilities, family focus, comfort, bigger crowds, more showbiz!

Keith Roberts (48), Swans100 survey

I loved the Vetch it was OURS.I loved the smell of the turf and the liniment, tobacco & booze, 3 inches of piss on the floor of the bogs,

the swearing, shouting, singing & fighting. The Liberty's only ok in a bland 21st century, Sky TV obsessed way. I hate the fans in front of me constantly on their smartphones, texting, chatting & playing bloody games when they should be getting behind the team. I can't stand vacant eyed kids slopping down overpriced shitty junk food and pawing at Dad (or worse Mum) to go and get them fizzy drinks. The view's good though.

Steve Close (47), Swans100 survey

The overall match-day experience is better at the Liberty as it is a better stadium with better facilities & the atmosphere has been improving season on season - especially the renditions of Hymns & Arias this season & in the Playoff game against Forest! That said, The Vetch was The Vetch! Up close & personal, intimidating, loud & proud! I can still remember the feeling of awe & pride walking through the tunnel onto the North Bank & seeing the pitch in front of me & the noise from behind. Shivers down my spine even now!

Rob Jenkins (46), Swans100 survey

We used to arrive at the Vetch very close to kick-off, sometimes so close the game would kick-off as we reached our seats. Different story at the Liberty, we usually arrive a good hour and a half before kick-off I can't say why although my dad always wants to look around B&Q, so maybe that has something to do with it!!

Stephen Howell (45), Swans100 survey

Liberty is much better, due to the capacity being much higher and much louder.

Andrew Grove (43), Swans100 survey

I will always love the atmosphere from the North Bank, close to the pitch, noisy, fanatical. The Liberty is getting there, but as I will always say, the Vetch will always be the real home of Swansea City, the Liberty Stadium is where the Swans play football.

Andy Robinson (43), Swans100 survey

It's different. Not necessarily worse, just different. It's a more sanitised experience at the Liberty, cleaner, family friendly. There was a raw edge at the Vetch, something unsettling for visitors, more organic. The atmosphere has definitely improved markedly at the

A more upmarket experience

Liberty over the last 18 months and that can be tracked back directly to the arrival of 'the drummer' in the East Stand. I find that quite sad really, in that it seems fans have had to be shown how to enjoy themselves and back the team almost, and can't think for themselves. However, it does seem that this may just be 21st century football in the UK generally as it seems most Premier League crowds lack that natural passion and the Liberty is actually one of the liveliest, if not the liveliest.

Peter (40), Swans100 survey

I loved the Vetch, but the facilities were truly appalling. People paint a picture of the roaring North Bank, and at times that was very true. But I have also been there with less than 2000 in the ground, in the rain, watching us play Darlington. The Liberty can appear soulless (go see an Ospreys game) but with the team doing so well, and crowds flocking, it's an excellent place to watch modern sport.

Richard Davies (40), Swans100 survey

The matchday experience is not what it was - queuing for ten minutes for a plastic pint doesn't appeal to me. The Liberty experience is much more corporate. Overpriced beer/food etc. You shouldn't serve French fries at a football match.

Pete Jones (39), Swans100 survey

I miss the Vetch for its atmosphere and general "feel", but I love the Liberty, facilities are better and atmosphere can sometimes be electric. It's still relatively new. In years to come it will be our true home and fortress!

Clare Ridley (37), Swans100 survey

It's worse. Can't stand with your mates, doesn't feel like the club I loved as much. Feels like I'm cheating on my slightly backward underachieving Mrs with her better looking, high flying sister.

Luke Thomas (33), Swans100 survey

I miss the bookies near the ground that would take my 2:45 bet after I have heard the teams for that day. I miss the ground being in the town centre and having a choice of pubs to drink in.

The new stadium has grown on me as I hated it at first. I feel now after some great days there that it is our home now with a growing history. I still miss the Vetch but I realised that the new stadium is necessary to evolve as a football club. I miss standing on a terrace the most and think safe standing should be trialled at the Liberty.

Scott Thomas (33), Swans100 survey

I find it different. Initially, I always rated the experience as worse, but over time I have appreciated that the Liberty experience is very good. It is something very different to the Vetch, which I loved. I think some of us forget some of the staggeringly awful performances at the Vetch and the archaic facilities in a warm glow of nostalgia. It was great but it was well past its time and I'd never go back. The Liberty is neither better nor worse but very, very different, as is football compared to the 80's and 90's.

I no longer stay in the pub until 2.55 and then stagger into the ground in a semi-catatonic state. I now normally drive to the match and socialise in the ground or at the pub with a soft drink. I get to the ground earlier and to my seat earlier than the little bit of terrace I claimed as my own for so many years. My feelings of going to games have changed due to this change, in that it is no longer some season-long drinking competition but a chance to see top quality football and teams in a good facility, a function of the club's improvement since the move to the Liberty.

Leighton Evans (32), Swans100 survey

I think people look at the Vetch with tinted specs on.

Matt Read (31), Swans100 survey

It was a step back in experience, but a massive step forward for the club as a whole.

John Richards (31), Swans100 survey

Attending the Vetch was far easier in terms of leaving the house and arriving in time for kick-off due to its location. At the Liberty the match-day traffic means that journeys to the stadium must be planned well in advance!

Gareth Francis (25), Swans100 survey

I hold a nostalgic view of the Vetch due to spending the majority of my childhood standing on the North bank. I do however find the

match day experience better at the Liberty as it's nice to mill around the stadium before kick off speaking to different people. Although as far as ease of access goes it was a better experience at the Vetch as there was no waiting around for hours after the match ended to get a bus into town and also the freedom of standing all game meant that if there was someone standing nearby who spoilt the game with comments etc you could move something that cannot be easily done in the confines of an all seated area.

Laura Williams (24), Swans100 survey

The Vetch obviously had that old ground character, and you could feel the history within its walls. It was great to be close to the pitch, and to know that when you shouted at the linesman they could hear

every word. The Liberty however is better in many other ways. The facilities are obviously great, and there isn't a bad view in the ground. We wouldn't be where we are now without the Liberty. So, overall, the Vetch had more character, but the Liberty probably gives a better matchday experience.

Gareth Howe (23), Swans100 survey

I'm a traditionalist and not really a big fan of the new modern soulless bowl stadiums, so I was far more fond of the match experience at the Vetch and the electric atmosphere that can't be replicated at the Liberty without a terrace.

Rhys Buckney (22), Swans100 survey

A more upmarket experience

I find the match-day experience at the Liberty is worse than the Vetch. I feel it doesn't have the same special feel as going to the Vetch and smelling the burger vans and hearing Daydream Believer playing with the North Bank singing. Being at the Vetch was just simply more entertaining than the Liberty (the quality of football is much better these days though).

I will always miss the cheeseburgers from The Vetch. They should be bought back instead of the microwavable ones at the Liberty.

Rhys John (21), Swans100 survey

The move from Sandfields to Landore meant a longer journey for us to get home from Mumbles, and also a change in pre/post match watering holes to somewhere nearer the new ground. It has also meant that I can no longer simply watch the game from whatever position of the stand I like. I have not seen a lot of people who stood around me on the North Bank for years. I feel that The Liberty Stadium at times has a much more sterile feel about it, this is not helped by Stewards who at times seem determined to ruin any atmosphere.

I find the match day experience at the Liberty Stadium worse overall than The Vetch Field. There was something special about walking up the ramp to the North Bank and being hit by the glow of the floodlights on a Friday night match. It was brilliant being able to roll up at the ground at 10 to 3 on a Saturday afternoon, paying £5 on the gate and grabbing your usual spot on the terrace. The atmosphere, for example at the Swans 3-2 win over Oxford on a Friday night in the near relegation season was something I do not think could ever be replicated. However, the Liberty Stadium has offered a more family-friendly experience. It has attracted new fans to the club, which was needed in order for us to expand. The new ground is not without its own charm, there are several pubs such as The Railway & The Coopers which have carried on the tradition of pre-match refreshment offered in the Sandfields.

Jack Carter (19), Swans100 survey

It may be nostalgia but as a child the Vetch Field was magical. It held the ethos of Swansea as a city, working-class, quirky, the floodlights were beautiful, as is our coastline and scenery. The Liberty severely lacks that, though it has improved - particularly towards the end of last season when the atmosphere was fantastic. If you consider match day experience with regards to safety, practicality, cleanliness, facilities etc., then Liberty is definitely better.

Anon (18), Swans100 survey

[The idea] of making every team in the country convert to having an all seater stadium. What next? I hear you cry. Will every ground in 10 years time be made to have executive boxes that you have to hire each game, a month in advance? Just so that you can sit in the dry, in the warm, with food at the ready and a television with Teletext available. Yes, it sounds nice doesn't it, but football supporters, REAL football supporters know that this would not be part of the game we all know and love. We want the terraces, terraces are football. Everyone has grown up with them and have their own place to stand, their own territory. If you're a regular, you'll see the same faces around the place you find to stand and you'll see those faces week after week. That all adds to make the ground feel like home. You're comfortable in your surroundings because you're familiar with the faces and the atmosphere they create. Get rid of the terraces and you will lose a very great passion that comes hand in hand with football. The comradeship, the laughter, the exchanging of views, the coming together of a group of people on a Saturday afternoon and regardless of race, religion, size, age or any disability you can be strong together knowing that you all want the same thing. You all want your team to win and in that, everyone is equal. We need to keep the terraces.

Rhonda W. Voice of the Vetch fanzine, vol. 2, 1990

It has often been repeated by fans and owners alike that it's no good playing 3rd Division football in a swanky stadium seating 25,000. The Vetch in its current state can accommodate the atmosphere of a fatalistic 4,000+ and still make it sound like a fortress of dread for the visitor. But a new state of the art complex will simply enhace the penury of the lower divisions and reduce the game as a spectacle.

Black Swan, 1 (January 2000)

I wouldn't have it any other way

2012 will mark the 34th year of my love affair with Swansea City. 34 years? That's two life-sentences. First a long stretch served at HMP Vetch Field and now happily institutionalised at the Liberty Open Prison. That's right, 34 years with the same bird. And I wouldn't have it any other way.

My journey with the Swans began in 1978, at a school games lesson at Ashleigh Road. I remember being assigned to put down a marker for a game of rounders and as I did, a big greasy football strayed from the big boys who were practicing nearby. I gingerly side-footed it back and looked up to see a veritable giant of a man in a kagoul say "thanks, kid." It was John Toshack. I was utterly spellbound, and it was the first day of the rest of my life.

I went home that afternoon and demanded a Swansea City shirt. My older brother obliged and I was soon eagerly pulling on this itchy polyester abomination. It didn't half chafe, but it didn't matter. What did matter was the Bukta motif and the jet-black vinyl Swansea City Football Club crest, which already started to crack as I pulled it over my skinny torso. I then did what any right-minded nipper would do; I ran to the mirror, arms aloft, pretending I was Tosh himself.

It was a full three years before my true baptism: Liverpool at home in the F.A. Cup third round. You have to remember what an utterly brilliant time 1981 was to be an eight year-old Swansea City fan. For a football-fanatic raised on 'Roy of the Rovers', the on-field exploits of Tosh and co had become more exciting and fantastical than anything a comic-book would dare create. And here I was - a young cygnet about to truly get my wings and break my Vetch Field duck. (I'll spare you any more avian-related puns before someone cries "fowl!". Ooh, sorry.) Anyway, it was all set up; and what an occasion it promised to be!

Well, we lost four-nil but naturally I was hooked. Ian Rush bagged a couple, and even Alan Hansen got on the score-sheet. There are unconfirmed reports that it may even have been the first time he used the term "woeful" to describe the defending. The day had started so positively: I remember walking from the Quadrant to the Vetch, intoxicated by the noise that was emanating from the fabled North Bank. There are flats there now but it used to be a barren wasteland where flocks of blokes with moustaches and black-and-white bar scarves walked, almost religiously to the Vetch Field. I couldn't get enough of it. The noise was unlike anything I'd ever heard, before or indeed since, and I would go on to replicate that

roar, quite bizarrely when you think about it, as I'd flick Dzemal Hadziabdic up the left flank with an oversized Subbuteo football. I had three teams: Swansea City, Brazil and Argentina, who doubled as West Brom if you squinted a bit. Naturally, we lifted the World Cup on a four-weekly basis. I was unstoppable.

I've since gone on to witness things during the late 1980's that no man should witness at a football match but I can honestly say it's never, ever been boring. Athens to Anfield (er...8-0). Macclesfield to Monaco (er...8-0 – we were nothing if not consistent). It's all been in there, as I'm sure all readers will concur. When I remark how Angel Rangel in the blue away kit from the 2007/08 season bears an uncanny resemblance to Dudley Lewis at Deepdale I know I should get a life. But do you know what? I don't want one outside of this magnificent football club. Wives and girlfriends have come and gone and all the while the only constant seems to have been a messy backbeat of 'Take Me to the Vetch Field'.

One of my quirkier recollections comes from the dark days of the 1984/85 season when I was called into service as an emergency ball-boy for a clash with Preston at the Vetch in the old Division Three. I'd been stood on the North Bank when four or five bobble-hatted ball-boys approached me, explaining they were "a man down" and could I step into his boots? Of course I was only too happy to help and here was a chance to watch a game from a unique perspective. The only problem was the absent ball-boy hadn't left any boots to fill, and so I would spend the ninety-minutes slipping and sliding up the wing in my leather tasselled-loafers; which when paired with the old Patrick tracksuit and obligatory bobble-hat looked a right sight. My footwear may have been better suited to a regional heat of 'Junior Come Dancing' but I gamely patrolled the gravel track along the Centre Stand and enjoyed a rare Swans win – by four goals to one, no less – and was rewarded with a match-day programme and a pat on the head from Alan Waddle.

So, what a journey it's been my life with Swansea City, and something tells me this is probably only half the story. All that remains for me to say is, with the same naïve wide-eyed fervour that I did all those years ago as a six year-old boy in that scratchy Bukta shirt....COME ON YOU SWANS!

Pete Jones, 39, London (nee Baglan)

My football team

My football team, Swansea City FC. As I personally have just edged over the quarter of a century mark, the Swans are about to pass the full one hundred. Whilst I've been a regular attendee and a proud Jack all the way, my experience has been a little different to that of many others.

Choosing to support the Swans was simple enough; with all of my immediate family originating from Swansea, my Dad brought me up that way. However, with my Dad and his side of the family being more for the Whites of Swansea RFC, it's testament to the Swans' exciting escapades that my Dad now joins me as a season ticket holder for the beautiful game. Along with him, I've been going down to matches and keenly following the club through the years with cousins, uncles, aunties, friends and I've even managed to get my Grandma along to a game or two.

Where my journey differs in comparison to many others is that I was unfortunately born outside Swansea and have spent only a few years of my life so far living there. Mostly I've resided where I live now, near Newport. So lots of Newport County fans in my regular life you might ask? Barely a handful, try Cardiff City. So you could say I grew up as a minority fan; meeting another Swans fan in my area would probably be as likely as bumping into the next Leon Britton or Nathan Dyer at the current Stoke City football academy.

To some this might make their support waver. There were no fellow Jacks immediately around me apart from my parents at home. Bear in mind as I grew up it was the Bluebirds who spent most of my school years as the more successful half of our rivalry. Whilst Sam Hammam prophesized about how Cardiff were to be the next Manchester United, the Swans continued to bounce between the bottom two divisions. But on non uniform day at school, you wouldn't see me shy away from turning up in my Swans shirt. At 14 years old I made up the dizzying count of one walking around Caldicot School in my Barcelona-colours, Evening Post-sponsored Swans replica away top (ironic we played in Barca colours then when you consider who the current crop get compared to now, maybe a return to that away strip soon would be appropriate?).

As I've already mentioned, my Dad and I can both claim to be happy owners of a season ticket each, but we haven't always been so dedicated. In my younger years trips to the Vetch each season could usually be totalled up on one hand, with trips to St Helen's totalled up on the other. The big turning point which took us both from the bracket of casual fans to the more hardcore Swans-mad fans we are today was when we nearly lost our club altogether.

The 2002-2003 season won't be remembered in quite the same way as the 2010-2011 one, as surviving relegation from the Football League contrasts to winning promotion to the Premier League. However, it was the former that brought on board more fans to ultimately make the latter possible. I might as well have been a season ticket holder the number of times I ended up going down to throw my support at the cause. Especially so after Christmas that year when the situation was looking really bleak, leading onto the tense and unbearable last three months of the season. Come the end of it and not only were the Swans safe from relegation and to continue pushing away from the lingering threat of liquidation, but my support had transformed from casual to regular attendance at home games.

And so the journey of the club was written, from rags to riches. From being David and coming up against fellow Davids every week, gradually getting ourselves more David v Goliath fixtures as we rose through the leagues to the most glamorous of all. We're not involved in David vs David or David vs Goliath anymore; in the Premier League we're David vs Goliath's bigger, richer and more intimidating brother.

To have been involved in this unique ride up close is something I feel privileged to have been a part of. To remember the club as it was at the Vetch in those early days of my support and look at how it is now, they're two different clubs essentially. You could pick out any number of clubs from today's League One to the Conference who are of a similar status now to how we were then. The Vetch will always be fondly remembered (and I still miss it today) but it was a ground suited to a lower league club. We had no money, went through managers faster than Michael Chopra goes through betting slips, had a tiny little box room for a club shop with not much in it, and a much smaller fan base than the present. In comparison now our widely hailed financial prudence sits alongside an overall club and footballing culture, managers are headhunted to supplement, whilst our modern merchandise-filled club shop caters for the ever-growing fan base. From struggling to get a few thousand through the turnstiles at the Vetch, these days we have a waiting list for season tickets in a twenty thousand seater stadium. The transformation has been incredible and I'm lucky to have been here all the way through.

So we can all count ourselves fortunate to have been part of such a remarkable rise. Not many get to experience relatively fast progression from the bottom league to the top league, but we've had it twice in thirty five years. The top looks that bit more impressive when you've seen it from the bottom too. So here's to the next one hundred years and whatever ups and downs it brings, however many times. I've certainly enjoyed it so far and look forward to the adventures that lie ahead. There's no hardship in wearing my Swans replica shirts now, then again there never has been or ever will be. League Two or Premiership, Swansea 'til I die.

Owen Carter

But seriously Miss... why Swansea?

On the 6th April 2012 I attended my first Swansea City Premier League game at the Liberty stadium. Honestly, that does not make me a 'plastic' fan, out for the glory days of this Swanselona team that is heralded across the world – if only by Facebook and Twitter these days! On this day unfortunately our consistent possession and passing style did not bring us the result I'd have hoped for as we lost 2-0 to Newcastle United – arguably one of the most famous and well supported teams in the English League, although we quite honestly outplayed them and let them only have two shots on goal – we can all see where those went.

It's usually taken a lot of explaining how an Essex girl became a Swansea City fan. In fact the Newcastle story correlates nicely with that same day nineteen years previously when I was briefly shown the light in the shape of a first date with a Swansea City fan who lived in Peterborough. Over a couple of pints in a country pub he told me all about the delights of Toshack, Curtis, James, et al. I had been brought up a West Ham fan who, when Swans fans were enjoying the above legends, was still taking great delight in having beaten Arsenal in the FA Cup and returning to the first flight ourselves. The possibility of a Play-off run was explained to me although I confess I was still a little confused.

This new romance of ours was further cemented on Tuesday 14th September 1993 when I was given my first opportunity to watch live league football – I'd always been told it as a child it was too expensive to take me to watch West Ham so lower league football seemed a dream. We set off from where we worked in Peterborough and drove to the local University City of Cambridge. We followed the car parking signs and found ourselves on a local Common with a few dozen other vehicles. I think parking was free and then we set off to find the Abbey Stadium. I had wrapped up warm it being an evening game and found some sturdy warm boots to wear – just as well as most of the walk involved dodging cow pats from the random bovine creatures that I presume were the car park wardens! We then had to cross a small ditch via a couple of planks of wood before making our way to the small turnstiles to pay the little man with his cash box and ticket counter. (Yes honestly you didn't need to mortgage your house and have 1001 Jackarmy points to get a ticket in those days!)

It was still early days in our relationship and Peter was still keen to impress so I was treated to a visit to the outdoor snack bar inside the ground to pick up a legendary Cambridge United bacon butty and

hot chocolate before choosing our standing position on the terrace near to one of the corners. I looked around to suss out the home fans ... only to find them few in number and quite a way away, and taking no notice of us at all. I'd guess by the time the game kicked off there were about 2,000 fans in the stadium – approximately 100 in the Swansea 'end'.

I honestly don't remember a great deal about the game– in fact we still disagree to this day about the fact I am positive the score line was 2-1 but both my now husband and all the stats pages on the web say it was 2-0. I don't remember many of our players - although I have a vivid image of Andy Cook running down the wing and I think this perhaps led to the start of my Swansea infatuation. I don't remember Gary Johnson managing the opposition or even our celebrated Frankie Burrows – although I do remember the 'Barmy Army' chant that now belongs to our own Brendan Rodgers. BUT I know I was completely hooked and I've never looked back from that day.

At this point in life I was a primary school teacher in Peterborough and I soon found there was nothing to relieve the pressures of teaching, quite so much as a trip to a lower division football ground on a Saturday to shout and chant at 11 men representing MY team. I know I was not born in Swansea and could only claim to be half Welsh through my mother, I lived the 'wrong' side of the Severn Bridge and so forth but that team became mine. Of course that first full season became special with the trip to the Old Wembley and a cup win in the shape of Super Johnny Cornforth and the Autoglass Trophy. I wondered whether supporting this team meant that lifting trophies at Wembley would become routine! League status was not as impressive as we finished that season in mid table mediocrity of 13th with 60 points – but I was gripped!

On a Monday morning I was always questioned by my charges as to how Swansea had done at the weekend and over the years I have brimmed with pride at being able to tell 5-10 year olds regularly about the exploits of MY Swans. There is now a whole bunch of people in East Anglia and Northamptonshire looking out for what was to become a little Welsh team languishing in the lower leagues results each week – usually to think up ways to give me a hard time about how badly they had done! None of this has ever put me off though – I have become a Jack through and through. I even had the honour of hosting the team for a warm up session on my school field before a Peterborough game in the Hollins era – so proud.

Many memories – most of the favourite are at lower league grounds where if you shout loud enough at your players they will reply (sorry Tony Bird!) There was many a dodgy pie or pasty, pint in a local pub before the game, terraces being gritted whilst game is being played, knocking on the turnstiles to ask to be let in, apologies from the manager after a 7-1 stuffing, banter with the opposition subs as they warm up ... and really you don't want to go there in regards to the state of ladies loos (award to Rotherham there definitely). Many friends have been made – and no matter what walk of life you come from having a common identity in the shape of Jack army gives you something to be proud of together.

Two other dates stick in my memory on a personal level – in February 1997 having lost 3-2 at Brighton, Peter felt so sorry for me he finally proposed – at the end of the pier next to the large plastic dinosaur! We set a date 18 months hence only to discover the fixtures worked against us as we were due to play at Cambridge again – kick off at exactly the same time as the wedding. Despite trying to work out if the team could pick us up on the way through we lost again 2-1 (really this time) to the mighty U's.

And then of course we come to the last few years and the Mighty Jacks creeping back up the leagues and suddenly people are less curious and surprised to find a Swansea fan living in Northamptonshire as I do now. The banners in the car do not get noticed any more as we have

joined the 'big boys' and people know our players' names. We get to fewer games – difficulty in getting tickets, rising costs and the small matter of family commitments. But these days we can watch more games on the television – would never have happened in the Cusack era!

We will be celebrating our centenary year in the top flight of football – who knows what will come after that. But one thing I do know is no matter how high or low we are in the football tier I will still be cheering on MY Swansea boys – thank you Jacks!

Still not sure who scored that phantom goal at the original Cambridge game though!

Bethan Charles

Due to living away from Swansea, and Bridgend being a Cardiff town, finding fellow Jacks is a hard task. Being one of about 3 Swansea fans in my whole school year group of about 200 pupils (no exaggeration!), seeing Swansea reach the Premier League has its perks, especially as all my close friends are Cardiff City Season ticket holders. Always loved watching the Swans on the tv or at the ground. I have seen the Swans play in all four divisions, something few fans across Britain can say.

Anon (16), Swans100 survey

'30,000 Come to Swansea'
Arrangements to cope with 30,000 visitors to the Cup match were made by the G.W.R. and L. M. and S. Railways. Nineteen special trains were run.

Nothing could indicate better the grip of the Cup-tie fever on

Swansea. Beginning on Friday night, football enthusiasts poured into Swansea literally from all parts of the British Isles.

The rush reached its climax shortly after midday on Saturday, when a solid stream of visitors poured through the streets down to the Vetch Field from the stations and 'bus termini.
FROM IRELAND
The first arrivals were a party of Irishmen from Dublin who reached High-street station on Friday evening. They have followed the winning team in the F.A. Cup for the past four years, so one of them told a 'Daily Post' reporter. An omen?

They were the advance guard. Lancashire, Yorkshire, Cornwall, and London all sent parties, a big crowd coming from the North.
WELSH ENTHUASIASTS
But it was essentially a Welsh day. North Wales and South Wales poured enthusiasts into the town. Ten special trains came on the

Supporters Club News – Aberdare Branch

It is unfortunate that our first contribution to this publication from the Aberdare Branch should be brought about by anger, following the F.A. Cup tie against Crystal Palace at the Vetch, our coach was hit by a large stone thrown from alongside the Jersey Marine Road as we were leaving Swansea.

Obviously the side window shattered, showering several of our people with broken glass. Luckily no-one received serious injury, although a few people did have scrapes and bruises.

The probable reason for the attack was that we were 'mistaken' for a group of Palace supporters. However, this is not really the point! A serious accident could have occurred, causing injury to innocent people or Swansea City Supporters. As it was, Swans fans were directly hurt and angered.

Now, the possible result for our branch is that we may lose the contract for our coach to Swansea and elsewhere.

Swansea has always had a good behaviour record in the past, but a certain section seems to believe that success has to be supported by violence. This should not be so. Liverpool, who have been the most successful club in the last decade, have had no such trouble. Let us in Swansea welcome away fans and beat them the best way possible — by supporting our team to victory. Only true support will win, not violence!

In conclusion I am sorry to say the story does not end there, as on the previous Tuesday (Cardiff City game) at the exact same spot, the identical thing happened, only this time the stone only marked the window of the bus. The incident after the Crystal Palace game was placed in the hands of the police, who were called by the driver.

Match programme 29 February 1980

G.W.R. line bringing followers from all parts of the coalfield.

Two special trains from London crowded to the last inch of corridor space brought down a cheering mass of Arsenal backers, wearing their colours defiantly.

On the L.M.S. six special trains were run from Pontardulais, as well as ordinary Saturday service – all crowded to the doors. There was a special from Llandovery, and another from Craven Arms, which brought a big crowd from Llandrindod.

Three specials were put on to cope with the crowds from the Brynamman, Ystalyfera district, and the ordinary trains carried additional coaches.

SWANS' COLOURS EVERYWHERE

The Swans' colours were everywhere, the white outnumbered the Arsenal red by fifty to one. For five minutes on Saturday morning every single person passing the 'Daily Post' offices sported the Swans' colours.

On a crowded special excursion from Newport which reached High-street about 11 o'clock the colours were sold en route by an enterprising vendor travelling from Newport.

On a West Wales excursion – also crowded – the central feature was a large retriever who was almost hidden under a wonderful display of Swans' colours. And when he got into High-street the crowd cheered as though Fowler was passing!

It was the biggest, jolliest, most enthusiastic crowd that has ever been drawn to Swansea. Many large flags with the words 'Play up, the Swans' were to be seen.

Report on Swansea Town v Arsenal
in the South Wales Daily Post, 6 March 1926

The Swansea club were my life in the fifties and have been ever since. We used to travel by train to The Vetch Field from East Wales, through all the industry of the day. Hundreds of us all packed on the 11.20 train to Swansea from Newport. There was never any hint of trouble and Swansea were very well supported in the Cardiff area.

Lloyd Thomas in Keith Haynes & Phil Sumbler (eds)
Vetch Field Voices (2000), 29

There had been occasions when I half wished that I had opted for something more conventional within the narrow terms defined by Bridgnorth schoolboys. At any time supporting the Swans would

Steel Town Swans

Can we once and for all, writes **David Corcoran**, nail the myth that Port Talbot is predominately a Scum City town.

The fact is, Swansea City has a large and very loyal following in the steel town. Yes it is true there are some sad buggers who prefer to suffer and support our bitter rivals but that doesn't mean that Port Talbot is a lost cause. In the distant past, it was fashionable to be a Scum supporter because they happened to play in a higher division. Of course since the late 70's , the Swans apart from one season have always been above the old enemy. This has ensured a lot of Port Talbot's younger football fans took to following the Super Swans and have remained loyal ever since. However even before the Swans meteoric rise up divisions there was still a dedicated band of supporters from Port Talbot who regularly attended the Vetch during the dark days of re-election in the early seventies.

Over the years, supporters from Port Talbot have been instrumental in furthering the cause of Swansea City. *Jackanory* is the latest in a series of Swans fanzines but let's not forget the very first, entitled *Jackmail*, was produced by a Port Talbot boy. Of the current web sites on the Internet dedicated to the Swans, one A Mouthful Of Lead featured in the last issue of *Jackanory* is run by a Port Talbot Swans fan. The present Chairman of FOSFCA comes from that beautiful town across the bay and the group I belong to namely THE PORT TALBOT SWANS have been involved in kit and match sponsorship.

However it isn't just the fans that make Port Talbot a Swans town but also the players that have come from there. Colin Pascoe, Michael Hughes, Huw Morgan, Darren Gale have all worn the white jersey with pride. Of the current side, Kris O'Leary is another from the seaside town. Certainly, Port Talbot boys play for the Swans and not since Rod Thomas and Alan Durban in the early 70's has a Port Talbot lad disgraced the town by playing for the Scum.

Despite Swansea being the nearest professional football club and undoubtedly the best, some Port Talbot residents still profess to being Scum followers. However few go to watch the boys in blue on a regular basis, whereas the Swans followers are regular attendants at the Vetch. In fact I would suggest that Swans fans from outside the city are far more loyal than those who actually live in Swansea.

So next time you condemn Port Talbot as being a Scum stronghold just think on and remember all the loyal Swans fans that live there.

In Shrewsbury this season, there was a pub (with knock on the door entry), which contained 10-12 Port Talbot Swans fans all aged between 18 and 24.

Myths

What about the other nearby towns of Neath and Llanelli ? Has support for Cardiff City died in these towns ? Does support for the Swans predominate? Write and let us know.

Jackanory, 8 (Apr-May 1998)

have been seen as deviant behaviour: in the sixties and seventies it was an open invitation to derision. The chemistry master's comparison between my third-year performance in his subject and

Living away from Swansea

the Swans' position in the Third Division was intended as a compliment to neither.

But in my family supporting the Swans is an incurable genetic disorder contracted by my grandfather in the 1920s and passed through the male line. ...

Huw Richards, 'The gospel according to St John the Alchemist: Swansea City 1978/9', In Nick Hornby (ed), My Favourite Year (1993)

Harry Welsh used to organise a bus, every other Saturday, from Carmarthen. There was nearly a full load every time. That was 1953 to 1959.

Ieuan Jones, Swans100 archive

By this time [1970], a black-and-white scarf adorned my neck, and the ridicule of my peers at school was something I accepted as part of the course. This was, after all, Llanelli, one of the homes of Welsh rugby, so supporting a football team was bad enough, let alone the fact that that football team wasn't Manchester United.

Jonathan Taylor, 'Twenty seven years in a black and white scarf', in Keith Haynes (ed), Come On Cymru: Football in Wales (1999), p.7

I first saw Swansea in the 'heady' First Division days of the early 80's. Being only 12, I was a huge Liverpool fan and hated Man Utd and disliked Swansea (I hated any team that wasn't Liverpool). My Dad, who is a huge rugby fan and didn't care much for football, got tickets for both the Vetch games against Man Utd and Liverpool. My first game was home to Man Utd and the Swans won 2-0. The excitement was in-describable. I knew more of the Man Utd team than the Swans...and I didn't like both teams although I hated Man Utd. Gordon McQueen, I'll always remember him, he got so much stick at corners as I was stood in the East Terrace, couldn't see a bloody thing.

But I loved it. I wanted more. Noise; swearing; pasties; seeing the game on Match of the Day; famous faces; the joy of winning.

For the Liverpool game the Swans also won 2-0, but this broke my heart, so I hated Swansea even more!! But all this changed in 83-84 when we were heading back to the lower divisions as quickly as we'd left them. I guess I supported them because they were the closest professional club to home and most of the locals supported Cardiff. Believe me being a Port Talbot boy and a Swans fan wasn't

something you shouted about too loudly. So I wanted to be different, plus the bus fare was cheaper!! Since then I've been hooked.

Neil Jones, Swans100 archive

A mention for the Cwmbran Jacks who shine like a beacon in the barren wastelands of the East Wales. They were in evidence on the recent trip, to York, along with crews from Bridgend and Pontypridd. All were in fine fettle and made themselves heard.

Better than Sex fanzine 1993

I became a supporter of Swansea City in the 1978/79 season. Although I was born and brought up in Newport but thankfully my Dad was from Gorseinon and he took me and my twin brother to see John Toshack's Swansea rather than Newport County. We were both hooked on the Vetch Field atmosphere and every time we went "home" to visit family and friends a trip to the Vetch during the promotion years from the Fourth Division to the top of the old First was a must.

Stephen Hughes (46), Swans100 survey

Growing up as a Liverpool fan, living 45 mins from the Vetch meant I was never taken to see the Swans as a child. Totally fell in love with the club though from the first time my stepdad took me to see a live football game. The atmosphere was unbelievable in a different way to the way I had experienced before, with men screaming, singing and shouting; it really opened my eyes to the world around me, and made me experience a different sort of person and behaviour to the people I'd experienced in my sheltered, rural upbringing.

Tom Giffard (20), Swans100 survey

As I live in a Cardiff area, I have banter with their fans. I am the only Swans fan in my school and proud.

Georgia Watts (15), Swans100 survey

So where were you in the early hours of Wednesday 22nd October 2003? Ok, so as inquiries go it isn't quite up there with 'when Kennedy was shot/Obama was elected/Bayo skied that penalty in the playoff final', but for me it is just as vivid a memory.

The answer is 'asleep in the Holiday Inn, Brisbane, Australia'. At least that was true until about 5.45 am when ... PING....off went the mobile phone on the bedside table. Cursing whoever back in the UK had forgotten my location and the time difference, I picked up the offending instrument and beheld the following message 'O2 SWA GOAL : D3 : Swansea 0, Cambridge 1 (Kitson 1 min)'. The cursing grew in both volume and scope, incorporating O2, Dave Kitson and most of all myself for not switching the phone off. Nor was the news at breakfast time any more cheering : 'O2 SWA FINAL : D3 : Swansea 0, Cambridge 2 (Kitson 2)'.

Such is the lot of the long-distance Swans fan. You don't live in, or even near, Swansea. You're not even from there, but a second-generation product of the Swansea diaspora. A lot of people leave Swansea, not because they want to (few do), but in search of work. They take the city and the Swans with them, and pass them on as genetic inheritance. Some of us were even born in England, although since this heritage is shared with Leon Britton, Ashley Williams, Nathan Dyer and about 45 per cent of Swans players since the club began, it is nothing to be ashamed of.

Unless you have the time, money, energy and single-minded focus needed for a long (in my case 400 miles) return journey every other weekend, it means that you don't get to nearly as many matches as you'd like and most of those are away. This means a great deal of travelling hopefully and much disappointment on arrival (latest personal approximate count – 109 different away grounds and defeats on 85 of them). So you can frequently make the Max Boyce boast of 'I was there'. But more often you weren't, and this inevitably colours experience.

It is dominated by a single question – 'what's the score ?' - and its supplementary 'how do I find out?' Nothing is more basic. If Maslow had conducted his research on human motivation with sports fans, his Hierarchy of Needs would undoubtedly be topped by 'needing to know'.

Finding out has admittedly got much easier thanks to technology – the Internet and mobile telephony – and status, meaning the Swans are on telly much more. Future generations will probably be able to fit a microchip that makes them a virtual presence at Swans matches, complete with a soundtrack of anti-Cardiff chants and a hologram of the chap in front blocking your view by pointlessly pointing at opposing fans a safe 50 metres away.

Their imperative, though will be the same as the fans in Neath and Port Talbot who mobbed sellers of the first postwar Sporting Post. It made me an enthusiastic BBC World Series listener when I found as a student that they had a late night sports programme, ending the overnight wait for the results box in the morning papers. It accounts for the peculiar frustrations associated with the regrettably located motorway bridge – Scunthorpe United 2 Swansea City bzzz – that cuts the signal at the strategic moment of the latecomers' reading and the truly maddening melange of disturbances in the ionosphere, French talkshows and distorted opera that accompanies Radio Wales broadcasts anywhere east of Offa's Dyke. And then there was Teletext, with our result always the last through - and the more it mattered, the later it came.

You have to know. Not wanting to would mean that you did not care any more. The moment I knew that my 90-year-old grandfather, a West Countryman with a passion for cricket, was going to die was when he was no longer interested in how Somerset got on.

The need, of course, becomes more acute if you are expecting good news. That Cambridge game was in the glad confident morning that followed the near-death experience of Tony Petty and the Great Escape of 2003. We were playing well again, with Lee Trundle and Andy Robinson offering a fresh dimension in attack. It was only a couple of weeks since I'd been rebuked in a Marseilles museum (want to be really rebuked ? Offend a French functionary) for my instinctive, insufficiently stifled reaction to tidings of a fourth goal against Mansfield. Perhaps I should go to Marseilles more often – the next visit, in 2007, found me unsure whether I was more disbelieving of England's Rugby World Cup quarter-final defeat of the fancied Australians or the text-messaged news of the Swans winning 5-0 at League One leaders Orient.

And while the phone is intrusive and antisocial, at least it is quick, clear and cuts the waiting. Visiting Italy in 1978 meant waiting for day-old British newspapers. Bad enough, but still worse when a rail strike cut the supply on the day when news was expected of the League Cup replay at Spurs. An agonising 24 hours punctuated by friends asking how my reaction squared with previously noisy sympathy for striking trade unionists at least had a happy ending - a dishevelled youth dancing triumphantly around the main square in Capri brandishing a bottle of dubious beer in one hand and the day-before-yesterday's Daily Mirror in the other.

But for any Swans fan over 25, the days of apprehension have far outweighed those of anticipation. Yet, while you feared what the news would be, you still had to know. I really didn't want to listen to the radio commentary of the FA Cup replay at Liverpool in 1990, particularly during one spell when any Duckworth-Lewis projection of the final score would have been in the region of 21-0. In the end 8-0 seemed merciful. It was agony. But to have switched off would have felt like betrayal, deserting your team in a time of adversity. And of course it would have introduced the further horror of not knowing.

Not least, of course, of the problems of not knowing is that it introduces the imagination. This is one area in which radio's excitable commentators and an unavoidable lack of precise information can be peculiarly agonising. I am reliably told by friends who were at the penultimate match of the 2002-3 season, the 2-1 win at Rochdale with league status on the line, that they could imagine nothing much worse than the final 10 minutes. I in turn find it hard to imagine anything more excruciating than spending the same time in a post-Challenge Cup final queue of rugby league fans outside Cardiff station with a radio pressed to my ear and the Radio Wales commentary team having hysterics every time Rochdale crossed the halfway line.

Work has been one of the most consistent reasons for not being there. It means that Swans memories are unavoidably enmeshed with those of other sporting events. It was rugby league that time in Cardiff, rugby union in Marseilles and Brisbane, and cricket in 1999 when the Swans reached the semi-final of the (then) Division Three playoffs against Scunthorpe. The evening of the return leg found me driving through a biblical deluge between World Cup games in Northampton and Cardiff, wrestling with the car radio as frequencies faded and realising that if the match went into extra-time, the only way I could be sure of finding food (I was starving, very tired and booked into a hotel with no room service and no food outlets nearby) was stopping off while the match was still going on. The solution was obvious. Missing the end of normal time was unthinkable. So was missing the end of extra time and the possibility of penalties. The only option was the first 15 minutes of extra time, which is how I returned to my car at Severn Bridge services to discover that during my brief absence the Swans' competitive status had shifted like a manic hokey-cokey – in, out, in, then finally and definitively out – as three goals were scored, followed by a massed brawl and a sending off.

But that was probably preferable to what happened at the same stage of the season five years earlier. Then I became perhaps the only ever visitor to Prague to wish that I'd been in West Bromwich instead, and had to wait an hour to get hold of a phone, get a line and contact relatives who had been at the match in order to find that yet another Swans promotion bid had foundered at the penultimate stage.

So much for Jerzy Kosinski, Hal Ashby and Peter Sellers. It is Not Being There that is half the battle, and perhaps the tougher half. But maybe you had to be there to really appreciate it.

Huw Richards

I ordered the tickets on the Swans website for the second leg of the playoff semi final against Forest and I already started to get butterflies in anticipation of this game – a game that could get us to Wembley with a chance of playing in the Premiership with £90 mill coming our way....yes us, Swansea City....I couldn't believe it. We were heroes in the first leg at the City ground getting a 0-0 draw after Neil Taylor had been sent off in the first minute and I just knew we were going to beat them at the Liberty because of that result.....As I went to turn off the computer I just noticed a link to say ' Shirt competition'.....At first I ignored it then just pressed the link as I cast a very suspicious eye over this NPOWER competition asking fans to send in a description of their favourite football shirt stories that meant something to them. I just thought sod it I'll tell them mine in a maximum 40 words ! I briefly wrote about the birth of my twins in 1997, Megan and Will. Will was born by normal delivery, and was handed to me, whilst Meg had to be whisked off to enter into the world by Caesarean section...whilst I was left with Will on my own in the room I wrapped him in my Swans shirt I had brought along. I also did this with Meg after she came out of the special care baby unit some weeks later........

A week or so later whilst on the road working I get a call from Mollie our eldest girl to say that NPOWER had been on and wanted to speak with me.....without thinking I said 'tell them politely to go away as we were with British Gas and I have just changed suppliers'.....I get a call back some moments later by a very polite lady from NPOWER and as I was just about to utter something polite to get rid of her she said she was Head of Marketing from the energy giant ! eh.....what the hell did she want ? 'Is that Steve Meredith?'.....'You have been shortlisted with another Swans fan along with 2 Forest fans to win a shed load of prizes and the chance to be 'The Face of Swansea City if they reach the final'......! 'what does that mean I asked her?'.....'just come to the Liberty at 2.00pm on the day of the playoff 2nd leg for a photoshoot.........? Photoshoot......OMG!' ....I went home and told my wife Jane who screamed with laughter and panic.

The morning of Monday 16th May I set off with Will (whom NPOWER had asked to come along also) very early as we live in St Helens near Liverpool and set off for that 4 hour journey once again down the M6 – M5-M50- M4 to my hometown with emotions running wild. This is a journey I have made hundreds and hundreds of times for most home games and to spend time with my family but this time it was a chance to get to Wembley and maybe be the 'Face of Swansea' but we had to win the game first and there was another fellow Jack Army fan called Mike also shortlisted.

All four fans (2 from Forest and us 2 Swans) (and Will) chatted prior to having our photos taken in the tactics room before the biggest game in years for us. The other fans were real football fans through and through, it was obvious and that made us all feel great that we were sharing this day....the people taking the photos asked if I could put the old shirt I wrote about on.......Well, there was no way I could get that on....I was weighing in at 15 stone these days and would have looked ridiculous in it... they threw the shirt to Will who donned it instead....but they said to me you have to wear a current Swans shirt....but I did not have one with me...In fact I haven't got one.....Then a lady named Dawn said...'Don't worry I'll get one from the first team changing room !!...She came back with Fabio Borini's shirt...threw it at me and said get that on......Well it was a medium and skin tight....There were ripples everywhere and I was sucking in air as if my life depended on it.....It was fruitless I looked like a an adult seal !! Will and I had our photos taken....flashes everywhere , white umbrellas, with the well coifed photographer saying 'Give it more' etc., etc....who the hell did we think we were !!!!!!

When Darren Pratley ran away up to the half way line my lungs just could not scream anymore...they had given up...but as that ball hit the net in injury time I grabbed my father as we screamed together louder than we have ever screamed because we were there....there was no coming back for forest.....Even being with him at Preston in 1981 it was magical when Charlo belted in the third but the excitement that night at the Liberty was phenomenal and seemed more raw...........We were off to Wembley.....I couldn't care less about the photos.....what bloody photos ? !

The next day We had travelled back to St Helens and I had a call again from NPOWER to say that our photos were chosen to represent Swansea City at Wembley plus we had won another season ticket and complimentary tickets and other things.......I couldn't believe all this.........

I asked the lady what they would do with the photos and she explained that the a photo of Will and me in Swans shirts would hang from Wembley....60 foot by 30 foot !!!! and all down Wembley way and in the Wembley tunnel / programme etc. etc. etc.......Please wake me up from this dream I said.....but all I wanted was for us to beat Reading.......We were asked to come down a couple of days later to have some clips with BBC Wales / Sky and press........Now this was getting ridiculous and I'm now getting way too show biz....but sod it !! 15 mins of fame and all that.....On BBC Wales news they had me coming out of the ticket office with the playoff cup but had Leighton James speaking before me and my all time Swans hero Alan Curtis speaking after me......What was going on ?.....Please wake me up.....It's becoming a joke now !! I bought the Evening post that week and it said 'The Face of Swansea' and 'Poster Boys'...The sponsors know how to milk it mind.

Very early on May 30th we set off from the North West. My wife Jane and all 4 of our Kids who are all huge Swans fans and everyone in this part of the world knows them as massive Swans fans – we really do fly the flag in this hotbed area of football greatness , in between Liverpool and Manchester....we tuned into Owen Money and then Mal Pope on Radio Wales and they were brilliant all morning with wall to wall Swans and great music.......we sang all the way down to the big smoke. Without a word of a lie we were about 2 miles from Wembley and our eldest son Tom said ...Oh my god Dad, I can see you and Will from here its massive.....There we were draped all over this famous ground. At the ground fellow Swans fans were coming up to me saying....that's you son ! – I just couldn't believe it !!!!

What a game, what a result, what a day ! There have been some amazing moments I can remember as a 44 year old Swans fan but that day with all my family around including my Mum and Dad in Wembley was the best.....The rollercoaster of winning it and almost losing it and finally getting there was draining but awesome. To top off this memorable experience for me there was a massive Swans and Reading shirt held up by an inflatable with my name on it....I hadn't even noticed it as I clapped as hard as I could for the soldiers coming around the pitch.....I felt a fraud as I knew these were the people who deserved to be held up and celebrated.....They should have chosen one of those boys to give the tickets and everything to, not me.

I gave the sponsors tickets NPOWER gave me on the day to others and bought tickets right behind the goals to be with my fellow Jacks........I will never ever forget that day and those few weeks.....EVER.

Steve Meredith

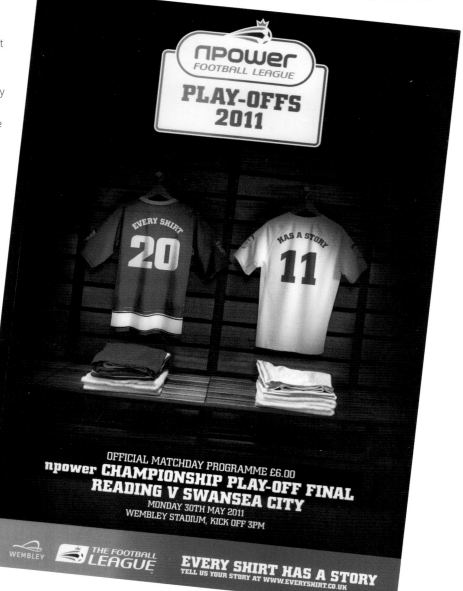

Always wear the home shirt

Always wear the home shirt, or something else which is white if it's in the wash!

Jack Taylor (22), Swans100 survey

A couple of Swansea Valley men came to Swansea prepared for sunshine and had no overcoats. They were soaked through before they got to Castle-street, and their unfortunate fate was the subject for much comment.

However, their Swans' colours were not drooping.

South Wales Daily Post, 30 January 1926

Hat/scarves/And if you could afford it a wooden rattle. Times were hard post war.

Peter Miles (76), Swans100 survey

I always had a rattle in my hand to cheer the Swans on.

Stephen Bresnan (62), Swans100 survey

I remember as a kid in the early 70's saving up my hard-earned pennies (the ones I resisted spending on allbright bitter or skol lager) to purchase a prized black and white silk scarf which would be proudly displayed around my left wrist or on my trouser waistband. I know this activity would seem very naff now to the modern North Banker but in those days it was like making a big statement, you know "This is me, I'm Swansea, I'M PROUD". It was a tribal thing, akin to Bloods and Crips. Everyone knew from a mile what gang you were in.

Jacks Eye, 2 (December 2000)

Christmas is rapidly approaching and if you are stumped in the present you want for your 'Swans' crazy husband, son or boyfriend or even girlfriend, we have sweatshirts with the Swans insignia in navy, both with hood and without hood. The price without hood is £4.95 and with hood £7.50.

Match programme, Swans v Crewe Alexander, 12 November 1977

Still got my 1981 Swansea jumper which I wore to every game, also wore it to Wembley final play off. Had photo taken with Leighton James and David Giles. And also wore it to the first game at the Liberty [and] in the Premiership.

Norman Mathias (72), Swans100 survey

QUESTION – When is a Jack not a Jack?
ANSWER – When he/she wears a football shirt not depicting the Swans badge.
It has come to the notice of many Jacks that when shirts are worn on the North Bank, or on any other part of the Vetch, many are not of the white, yellow or black/white hooped variety. The colours of Spurs, Arsenal, Leeds, Rangers, Celtic, and many other top sides have been spotted on the Bank over a period of time.

To show your loyalty to the club, and to also put much needed money into the club, it is important that a Swansea City short is worn, whether it be the present Spall design or perhaps an Adidas, Patrick, Hummel or Admiral from previous seasons. If you decide to wear the Bukta shirt from the late seventies, then make sure it's

VISIT THE SWANS SHOP FOR YOUR

**XMAS Gifts Galore
For the Whole Family**

Swansea City Pullovers £8.00	Swansea City Grip Bags £4.90
Swansea City Annual £2.50	Swansea City Pens. £0.25
Swansea City Jacquared Scarves. . .	Swansea City Rossettes £0.30
. . . . £2.60	Swansea City Football Jerseys . . . . .
Swansea City Jacquared Bobble	. . . . £4.00
Hats to match £1.70	Swansea City Song Record . . . £0.90
Swansea City Bal Scarves £1.70	Selection of First Division Pennants
Swansea City Black & White Bobble	. . . . £0.55
Hats £1.10	Swansea City Coloured Team Photo
Swansea City Super Swans Scarf. . .	. . . . £0.70
. . . . £1.80	Swansea City Players Individual
New Swans Mugs with Crest . . . £0.70	Photos £0.45
also First Division Mugs £0.70	Swansea City Players Coloured
Swansea City Towels £3.00	Lapel Photos. £0.45
Swansea City Belts £0.60	Swansea City Car Stickers (New
Swansea City Patches (5 varieties)	Crest) Coloured. £0.50
. . . . £0.50	Swansea City Black & White Car
Swansea City Lapel Badges . . . £0.50	Stickers . . . .
Swansea City Key Rings£0.50	Swansea City Blazer Badges. . . £1.30
Swansea City Pilot Caps. £2.10	Swansea City Car Motifs. £0.65
Swansea City Pennants in PVC. . . . 55	Swansea City Commemorative Wall
Swansea City Beaney Hats . . . £1.10	Plaques in Copper £7.00
Swansea City Flags £1.00	Swansea City Sports Boards. . . £1.00
Swansea City Ties £3.25	Limited Supply:
Swansea City Shoulder Bags. . .£4.20	Swansea City Match Box Holder
	with Players Photo. £0.70

Match programme 8 December 1979

My first Swansea shirt was a stylish 1978 Bukta item which had a crinkly trim running down the arms with lines of Bukta badges. I pulled that shirt on for school games lessons as a six year old, and sad to say, I'm damned if I know where that shirt is now. I loved its big black collars which typified the groovy moods of '78, and its rubbery badge a plain and simple floating Swan. (I wonder how many people prefer the floating Swan to today's both-wings-out Swan? Answers on a postcard please). The away strip of that era was a distinctive yellow shirt with distinctive red and blue diagonal stripe cutting across the chest, most people will associate this design with Crystal Palace. Another predominant feature of this shirt was its extremely tight v-neck collar, which, when worn by burly Jacks like Alan Waddle or Pat Lally, could seriously affect the respiratory system. This was a popular shirt though, and if the commercial department had it's head screwed on then they could cash in with a re-issue of this shirt.

Jackmail, 16 (1991)

been washed before you leave the house!

Can you imagine walking onto the Stretford End at Old Trafford and seeing some United fans wearing the grotesque Liverpool shirt or spotting Chelsea fans wearing Tottenham shorts, etc. It's just not done is it? We are after all a professional football club and if we think are to think of ourselves as loyal Jacks then a Swans shirt must be donned. So next time you see anyone standing on the Bank wearing any shirt other than a Swans top (Wales is obviously acceptable), have a quiet word with them.

Swimming in Swansea Bay, 1 (Spring 1992)

At the moment, the Vetch is a daunting place to visit – the North Bank's chanting can and does intimidate the opposition but when a large minority of that support sees the Swans as their 2nd choice team by wearing other clubs clothing – I accuse them of being 'Glory Boys' – only at the club when we're winning or it suits their purpose

and worse than that verging on the hypocritical – you're either Welsh or a Jack or not! Don't slag England if you follow English Premier League teams – that just plain DUMB!

Jackanory, 11 (Feb/Mar 1999)

I always have something Swansea related on and exactly what depends on how "lucky" it is. If we get win then I wear the same thing next time. I have an orange away shirt that I never wear and my son has a home shirt that he always wears.

Paul Ashley-Jones (45), Swans100 survey

I will always wear black & white and never wear any colour that the opposing team could wear.

Andy Grainger (36), Swans100 survey

I always wear my watch, if I forget to wear it, we usually lose. Also, I wore my lucky Fred Perry polo shirt for certain games at the end of last season, Sheff United, Forest home in the play offs and the Wembley final. We have won every game I've worn it, including 3 in the Prem this season.

Stuart Middleton (30), Swans100

Love, Peace and Swansea City fanzine, issue 6 May 1993

Football and fashion

M ansel Street: "Who's that Tw*t in the big black hat?"... we sang enquiringly. The seated audience shifted in their seats. 'Dixon, Dixon'. We answered our own question.... melodically of course.

Walter Road: We asked the first question again.

Even more shifting amongst the audience.

Then, we identified him.

'Dixon of Dock Green'

By the time we were in the Uplands, we had, tunefully, lauded his dedication to the job 'by day' and praised his very obvious love for his wife 'by night'.

The audience continued to shift in their seats. They knew they were in for a catalogue of the North Bank's finest ditties and they could do little about it.

Now I say audience, but in truth one could hardly say that our co-occupants on the Rees and Williams Bus Company (Tycroes) coach (departing St Mary's Church at 5.30pm) were exactly 'willing' participants. More accurately, they were a mix of mothers with children, elderly couples weary from a day 'in town' and encumbered by C&A shopping bags, the odd courting couple perhaps and sometimes a few other Swans fans.

Unfortunately being youthful and somewhat callow of course, we were oblivious to the sensibilities of these people because, after all, 'WE were the Ammanford Contingent of the North Bank Boys' and WE were going to sing all the way back to Ammanford!!

And sing we generally did.

We knew 'em all. There was 'Herbie oo-oo', 'Lenny (Lenny) Allchurch on the wing', the cheeky little offering that was 'Dixon of Dock Green' and of course the (almost) semi lament that linked poor Molly Malone to our beloved Swans.

There were more of course, and they too were rendered with gusto to our captive audience as the bus made its journey via A roads (no M4 section in those days) through Fforestfach, Penllergaer, Bont (Pontardulais to the uninitiated btw), Fforest, Tycroes and onwards to Ammanford.

Respite for some came early because they lived somewhere 'en route' and were able to get off!

Others were less fortunate. They actually lived in Ammanford and although we couldn't see the despair on their faces as yet another 'Herbie oo-oo' rang around the bus, I'm pretty sure, (now

that I'm older and blessed with a slightly Meldrew-esque view of youth) that 'despair' is probably the right word to use here.

But, we didn't really care of course and apart from the odd journey where the driver ("driver, driver, give us a song") got out of his seat at some stop and threatened us with an early exit (usually somewhere particularly bleak like the stretch of road between Fforest and Llanon for example) we found ourselves back in Ammanford, jubilant, hoarse and somewhat unpopular with those that arrived with us.

They were heady days though for us North Bank Boys as we graduated slowly, both as Swans fans and (ever so slightly) as confident teenagers. Pete and I had been following since '68, Roger, being younger was a more recent conscript and it was only now as we got to the 71-72 season that we started to band together with others for those excursions to see the Swans.

They were great times truth be told. Britain was changing, music was vibrant and football fashion had its own identity as younger fans started to find a collective identity through dress. We were no different and we too embraced the fashion that was to dominate the terraces for a few years.

There was a bit of a stumbling block though - we lived in the Amman Valley. At the best of times it could never be remotely considered as a hub of fashion and its rugby bias generally meant that football was seen as something of a 'minor sport'. Merging football and fashion was therefore certain to bring ridicule upon one's head, but that didn't stop us of course and off we went anyway, to embrace what was also to be widely viewed as a 'hooligan' culture.

Swansea was our lifeline here, both in terms of football and fashion and it was to shops like Phil Pritchard's in Shoppers Walk that we were drawn in search of the clothing that would help define us more on the terrace at Swansea and would similarly set us apart from the hairy hippie loon fest that was prevalent in Ammanford at the time.

And so it was Ben Sherman shirts, Levi Sta Prest trousers, half mast Levi jeans, Brutus faders, Harrington jackets, Crombie overcoats, tassled loafers, bright socks and, of course, a pair of Doc Martens.

All were amassed, gradually and with some fiscal parental persuasion over time and with it came that sense of identity that youth craves from generation to generation.

Football and fashion

It was truly brilliant, I won't lie, and almost 'overnight' I do believe that we started something (admittedly small) in the semi-sleepy hollow of footfall 'fan-ship' (if there is such a word) that we perceived Ammanford to be at that time.

We were different and whilst not all of our little group embraced the fashion, going to matches in Swansea, (we weren't away travellers at all) became even better because you saw people similarly dressed in the city and it was even better when it came to being at The Vetch and in amongst the boys on the North Bank.

In a local sense we started to stand out in the town and Saturday night dances at the Civic Hall became reasons to parade, almost peacock like in the cult finery of our choice.

I can recall journeys back from some games at the Vetch (singing was obligatory of course) merging with a 'session' at the local Con club (we even got 'our Roger' recruited as a member to make it easier for us to be signed in!) and then an evening at the aforementioned Civic Hall 'in all our glory'.

And, that glory was often two tone Sta prest trousers, gingham check/buttoned down collar Ben Sherman shirt, a Harrington jacket and, a pair of highly polished Martens. On the belt loop or around the wrist would be the scarf - the colours that confirmed us as Swans supporters.

No one else dressed like this at that particular time (although this did gradually change slightly over the next year or so) and we were most definitely at odds with our tie dye, moccasin 'n afghan coat wearing peers of the time. Generally this posed no problem but as is the case with Saturday night dances in rural towns all over the world, alcohol often brought out the worst in people and many assumed that if you dressed like a 'hooligan' (by the way, we weren't by any stretch of the imagination), you were one and were therefore good for a fight.

These occasions therefore found us often at odds with the other clientele and an evening out would involve a lot of tactical manoeuvring (difficult in a smallish dance hall), staying in the bar (our favourite tactic) or making sure that one of the very large bouncers knew 'the score' and could keep a beady eye on the other protagonists.

Sometimes, none of these tactics worked and the inevitable scuffling (it was usually no more) would take place. We always survived of course and looking back, I now just see it as part of that 'right of passage' that people mention when talking of youth. It did us no harm. Compared to what sometimes happens these days, it was nothing. Indeed, it was probably educative!!

And so it was, fashion interwoven with football, at least for the next couple of years.

'72-73 was a decent year as we moved, ever so slightly to a 'smoother' look. Oxford bags from My Father's Moustache and brogues, still mixed in with the Harrington and crombie, still looking good, at least in our eyes. Things were changing of course. We were getting older but our short lived dalliance with 'hooligan fashion' had already satisfied that need that youth has, at a particular time, for identity and belonging.

Like most people, we moved on. Along came the Claims Adjuster, the solicitor and the Taxi Business Proprietor. Along came (in no particular order) work, marriage, children, divorce, responsibility. Along came 'older' age.

Thankfully, 40 years on, those days of 'fashion and football' seem as fresh in the mind, as enjoyable, as ever. The fashion was 'then' and it was intertwined with our fervour for the Swans.

And as for the Swans, well they don't get mentioned much because they were always there anyway. Fashion is transient, WILL always be the 'then', but a love of your club is never so, just lifelong. It was then, it is now.

Pete and I remain firm friends. We sit next to each other in the West Stand. Our children, adults themselves, sit with us, all Jacks, through and through. STID as we say. Roger keeps a watching brief. No need for fashion these days but damn it, it was great when it happened................

And by the way,............ I STILL own a pair of Martens. They're so bloody comfortable!!

Paul Morris

Those of you that recall our beloved Vetch Field will back me up here, every time you entered the ground it was an experience. Maybe not for the coming game but what had gone before - real history bled from the walls and those piss-stained floors and terraces. The energy and the love for a team in white shirts, irrespective of the person wearing that jersey. To me it didn't matter who they were, just that they gave as much for that shirt as I would have, should I have had the opportunity. I am not a hero-worshipper of men who play football - what I am and have been for many years is a Swansea City supporter, a supporter of the team and not the individuals that have been loaned for a period of time a football strip so valuable that some would lay their lives down for it. This I suppose is where the 'wonder' of entering the ground of any team is felt. The eleven players on either side are only a part of what it is to be a supporter of Association Football. They play their part, often demoralising their own club's fans, never delivering the final masterpiece having worked so hard to canvass their ideas in many-coloured formations. Young men handed a gift, many not appreciating what they have until it is too late, but that is life itself, that is football as I know it. And why I care.

From Keith Haynes, Walking on Sunshine – Swansea City 2010/11 (2012) pp. 12-13

The battle for top spot of an eighteen year olds Premier League of interests was pretty intense in December 81. Music (well, more precisely a sad obsession with The Clash) took pole position, closely followed by girls, beer and The Swans. School work was used to fighting its annual relegation battle.

The offer of a cheap weekend in Paris with my first serious girlfriend had taken me away from the Leeds season opener and the unbelievable Latchford hat trick had haunted me ever since. What kind of Swans fan was I really?

To add insult to injury, the only chance of having any cash in my pocket came as a Saturday boy in British Home Stores. Brilliant to have 15 pound a week to buy vinyl - crap to miss quite so many home games.

Still I was in the right place when Chelsea rampaged through the town. I took my role on the cheese counter so seriously that I was nearly decapitated by a large Gouda hurled by a Blues supporter. Should have known that discerning West Londoners preferred softer cheeses.

So midweek games were the chance to catch up. Having endured 10 prior years of torrid afternoons versus Hartlepool (though the 8-0 game was good!) Rotherham (God, remember the 4-4 draw?) and a particularly bad cup game vs Bognor Regis (more rioting Chelsea fans for some reason) I felt the club owed me some quality .

I grew up with Herbie Williams, Dai Gwyther and Jeff Thomas skying a penalty over the West Stand. Watching Ante, Charlo and the James brothers made The Vetch feel like a different planet.

My first ever game at the Vetch was 27 December 1971 vs Villa, bizarrely in Division 3. I remembered scary Brummies, dressed in hats and boots from A Clockwork Orange, and we lost.

So to 15 December 1981. Swansea 2 - Villa 1. To be watching the Swans ten years on play the defending Champions off the park. To watch us go top of Division One and know that we were allowed to yawn every time Bluebirds mentioned 1927 (again). To know we would stay up in the top flight even with Dai Davies between the sticks. Well, it was magic.

The Swans stayed in my top three from then to now. That day I heard that I had won a University place. The next day I was nearly expelled for the worst hangover in school history.

But that was all ahead. That night we sang we were by FAR the greatest team ...and for the first time ever we were right.

Ed Sims

By car, train and plane

I've gone mainly with the away travel club and with friends, but I've also travelled by car, train and plane.

Arwyn N. Woolcock (57), Swans100 survey

From an early hour to-day thousands of people queued outside Swansea High-street Station waiting to be marshalled into six special trains which British Railways put on for the big match between Swansea Town and Cardiff City at Ninian Park this afternoon,

Most of them wore white rosettes, many carried giant wooden rattles and one or two had portable radios slung from their shoulders.

South Wales Evening Post, 27 August 1949

A description of Swans fans in London for the FA Cup semi-final against Bolton Wanderers. The Swans were playing in blue that day. 2,300 went to support the Swans, including 710 from the Cardiff district.

The battle cry of every Welshman in London to-day was 'Play up the Swans.' Early this morning, the first excursion train rolled into Paddington. A number of railway officials, who have experience of Celtic enthusiasm, gathered to witness the human avalanche. Almost simultaneously, about 100 railway compartment doors opened, and in a moment the station was in the hands of the Welsh. Then the huge mass moved into the adjoining streets.

'WHO ARE THE SWANS?' Residents who had been awakened by the excitement looked out of their windows to enquire the cause of the early morning invasion.

'Who are the Swans?' enquired an old lady. A young man wearing an Ystalyfera muffler answered 'Wales!' The old lady banged the window down, and muttered something, but nobody cared what it was. Practically every excursionist wore a blue and white rosette, much to the chagrin of the enterprising hawkers, who had raided Covent Garden for a supply of leeks. Whether Paddington liked this happy boisterousness or not, it did not matter, as the crowd moved towards the West End, singing Welsh tunes with great gusto. The restaurants that were open made a roaring trade.

FROM ALL PARTS The excursionists seemed to have come from all parts of South Wales, a large contingent travelling from Pembroke. They were all in London to cheer and inspire the Swans on to victory. It was a stirring scene to see this large, cheerful-crowd bubbling over with enthusiasm. Inter-club rivalry was forgotten, and a former Llanelly Rugby forward was proudly displaying a saucepan covered with blue and white ribbons. The Vetch Field fraternity smilingly acknowledged the sweet compliment.

BOLTON'S HUNDREDS A few hundred Bolton supporters arrived in London last night and attempted to paint the West End red but they will be looking blue today.

It was a coincidence that the Swans' colours were similar to those of the boat race enthusiasts, and there were many knowing and sympathetic glances between the two sections. The Varsity drawl blended with the musical accent of the Welsh. They had one thing at least in common and that was the colours they sported.

THE SECOND ARMY The second army of supporters arrived shortly before eleven, and Paddington was filled once more with the native tongue ofWales. To the dismay of hawkers, who had increased numerically, all the new arrivals were wearing blue rosettes, daffodils or leeks. An ardent supporter carried a replica of the Cup, with a photograph of Fowler in front.

'IT'S WELSH, BILL' Close behind him was a batch of musical enthusiasts who were singing that well-known Swans' tune, 'Fow, Fow, Fowler'. A couple of Londoners listen intently, but the words were too much for them, and one remarked to the other, 'It's Welsh they are singing, Bill.'

A feature of the excursionists was the large number of ladies, and they certainly were not afraid to show their favours. Three of them wore blue hats and when a precious youth commented, "They have to see the Boat Race," the women of Wales promptly reminded him that they were members of the proletariat.

South Wales Daily News, 27 March 1926

I had a mate who was a real keen Swans fan and in the sixties he and I would sometimes hitch to away games. I thought this was really cool as it was a cheap way of travelling. One trip though we had a lift with a lorry driver who kept nodding off to sleep as he was driving! It frightened the life out of me so I always travelled to away games by public transport after that.

Rob Samuel (63), Swans100 survey

On the outward journey [to Manchester] there were five idiots who were caught throwing light bulbs out of the train, and two clowns who pulled the emergency communication cord and caused the train to stop for quarter of an hour at Llansamlet. ... We have been praised up to the hilt for our good crowd behaviour at away games and I am sure we are not going to let a few ignorant louts tarnish our reputation.

Match programme, Swans v Birmingham City, 28 November 1981

Explaining to your boss that your pet dog has just died and the funeral is on Tuesday is one way of getting off work at lunch time, but instead I go for the boring 'I think I've got the flu coming on, so I'd better go on home now' routine. A quick change out of shirt and tie and into the Swans away top, before sloping out the back door of the office to catch the last freedom moped out of nowhere, well the TITS mini-bus at least.

Love, Peace and Swansea City, 5 (March/April 1993)

What day is it? Saturday. What time is it? Five thirty a.m. Where am I going? High Street in a taxi. And then? City of Hull. Is it cold? You're bloody right it's cold! Am I mad? Probably.

It's the last game of the season, it's away, and that can mean only one thing: transit van city!! Six hours sitting in a corrugated steel floor resulting in rear-end so numb that a prod with a bayonet would be a mere pin-prick. But wait, this little baby's got seats! (cue everyone rushes over to van to marvel at the seats, "cooorrr look at them!"). It's not going to be so bad at all. After we'd all been certified insane for being up at this unearthly hour by a passer-by, we climbed aboard the two mini-buses and departed just after six.

Jackmail, 21 (1994)

Went to see Portsmouth in the cup down there. Couldn't get a ticket with the away fans so went corporate. We were in the home end – about 100 Swans fans I would say – but when we scored went up and all hell broke loose. Then we got escorted to the away end – Great Game – we won. Most important part was that it was my grandson's first ever football match. After the game, the Portsmouth catering manager asked if the children would want to meet the players as an apology from the club. So James's first game and he gets to meet all the players and had photos with Leon, Scotland, Nathan, Big Ash. I told him not to expect this every week. What a lucky first game. He has come ever since!

Paul Jones (52), Swans100 survey

It's Saturday 2nd Jan and while the vast majority of the 3,600 Jacks are travelling up to the big smoke by coach, a couple of us decide that the train and tube is the best option, best for sinking a few beers early and getting to the game on time anyway.

Jackanory, 11 (February/March 1999)

Routine: Travel up early on day of game. Check in to a Travelodge or Premier Inn. Lunch and a few beers. Games and a good few beers and a curry after. Long drive home Sunday!

Simon Short (47), Swans 100 Survey

Although my husband always followed the Swans he also followed Llanelli rugby. The chaos of club rugby fixtures gives us more time to follow Swans. Also now use away trips to visit parts of the country we wouldn't normally.

Anon (48), Swans100 survey

My first away game

My first away game was as a child in 1925. My first in awareness was in 1940 with a workmate when we travelled to Ashton Gate to see the Swans against Bristol City in a wartime league match. My memory is just one of bleakness and austerity.

John Conibear (89), Swans 100 survey

Just after the war. Couldn't afford it much then. First saw them up at Eastville, about 1,000 went up. I went by coach, the Queen's instigated that trip, Old Newcrews. Players drank there too. Paul and Burns were regulars.

Love, Peace and Swansea City, 5 (March/April 1993)

1949 against Bristol Rovers. We were both fighting for promotion to the Second Division. It ended 1-1. The train wasn't leaving Bristol until gone 10.00 so my friend and I went to see Ted Ray as Buttons in Cinderella. On the way home, youngsters who drunk too much caused mayhem on the train. Had to stop so many times, it was gone 4.00 am when we arrived home.

Eileen Morgan (77), Swans100 Survey

Ninian Park, 24 August 1951. Seemed to be a huge stadium compared to the Vetch, with plenty of seating. The result 0-0 and it was the first of many visits to Ninian Park. I am yet to go to the new stadium. I went by train with my girlfriend – we got married soon after and she (Hazel) still attends matches with me.

Tommy Vaughan (80), Swans100 survey

Not sure of the year but it was against Bristol Rovers at Eastville. An Easter game, it ended 4-4. About 1,500 went up. I usually went to Cardiff and you could mix then. In 1957 Cardiff came down from the 1st, Swans took up 9,000, we drew 0-0.

Love, Peace and Swansea City, 5 (March/April 1993)

We beat Liverpool. Great day and we sang "we beat them yeah yeah".

Anon (63), Swans100 survey

I went to Peterborough in 1965 with my Father, his Friend / Son. Had to travel on Friday night and stop off for an overnight stay in hotel. At the game a Swans supporter ran on to the pitch before kick off and places cut out cardboard Swan on the centre spot! Over 30,000 in the

ground and we drew 0-0. We lost the replay 2-0.

Anon (58), Swans100 survey

I think my first away game was at Crewe Alexandra in 1971/2, although I may well have gone to Ninian Park prior to that. I was threatened with a 'Karate chop' by an octogenarian in the stand who took exception to my obvious glee at the Swans going 2 nil up. He had to be restrained by his son (who was probably sixty) and a steward.

Paul Williams (57), Swans100 survey

One of my first away games was Liverpool FA Cup 1971. We were in the paddock at Anfield singing "Toshack is a fairy". He Scored. Liverpool crowd sang "our Fairies are magic".

Clive Mitchell (58), Swans100 survey

Cardiff, Welsh Cup 1974. Was blown away by ALL the Swans fans young and old just chanting SWANSEA SWANSEA over and over again as the team played well against 2nd division Cardiff. Not many at the game but we were loud & proud. Went with a friend.

Jack Flack (52), Swans100 survey

Away at Torquay United 1976. We won 2-0. We were a small crowd huddled together desperately whilst a torrent of stones landed on us, hurled by enraged Torquay fans. We were like the 300 Spartans at the Battle of Thermopylae but with flares, tank tops and no shields.

Phil Roberts (50), Swans100 survey

Watford 1978. Being scared! Buying a programme and trying not to speak too much, even though I was in the Swans end - the illogicality of fear! I went with three mates on the Supporters Bus and didn't get home till 2am. Good stuff for a 15 year old! I think Ross Jenkins scored in a 2-1 loss. I haven't got the programme anymore.

Keith Roberts (48), Swans100 survey

Against Lincoln City in 1979. Took a long time to go to away games - away trips in 70s seemed very linked to trouble at games and don't enjoy long coach trips. Drove over from Mansfield where we were staying with mother-in-law and sat in the stand behind the goal. We lost to a relegation threatened side; in a rare tactical blunder Tosh

My first away game

played himself and Waddle up front despite the howling gales blowing from the East coast. All our crosses got blown off course! The ground itself was small and basic - even more so than the Vetch. We could see the travelling Swans contingent surrounded by police at the top of the open side terrace - no away ends then.

Peter Dawson (55), Swans100 survey

Plymouth Argyle in 1979. Travelled with a mate from school and his Dad on the train and watched from the stand rather than the away end. A really exciting adventure. [Afterwards, I went to] Most away games with mates, always on supporter buses. Considering the crowd violence back then it surprises me that I was allowed to go.

Simon Short (47), Swans 100 Survey

Sheffield Wednesday 1979. 0-0 draw, 2 buses of Swans fans, on my own, my bus window hit by a glass when passing a pub, walking for what seemed like a mile from bus to ground with a policeman on horseback leading all the home fans to see where we were.

Simon Stranaghan (48), Swans100 survey

Bristol Rovers 1979. It was freezing and the Rovers fans threw frozen pies at us! Went by Double decker bus! The old service type one with bench seats and the platform at the back to jump on/off. Took forever to get to Bristol.

Huw Mellor (46), Swans100 survey

The first away game I attended was at Preston North End when Swansea won 3-1 and secured promotion to the first division. I just remember the emotion of winning and getting to the first division. The only other away game I attended was against Liverpool at Anfield during their first season in the first division. So many Swansea fans turned up that they closed the gates leaving many hundreds maybe

thousands outside the ground. There were police horses who were pushing the crowd away from the entrances. I ended up going to sit on the bus and listen to the game on the radio.

Paul Davies (50), Swans100 survey

Mid 1980s. It was at Cardiff on the open away terrace and wondering why fans had umbrellas when there was no chance of rain. We soon realised when we had to shelter from the coins and stones being thrown over when we were kept in after the match.

Paul Ashley-Jones (45), Swans100 survey

1999. Travelling up to York on the supporters' bus for 6hrs. Standing in an open terrace behind the goals, we lost 1-0 and it rained all game. It wasn't the best of starts.

Geraint Davies (28), Swans100 survey

Portsmouth 2009. Caught a train to the match with a few friends. We were forced to go into the ground 2 hours before kick off. The atmosphere from the away section was electric

William Price (19), Swans100 survey

Swans fans at Brentford

Away day memories

In October 1978 myself and my wife returned to Gatwick after spending our honeymoon in Corfu. We returned, coincidentally, on the night that the Swans were away to QPR in the League Cup. What an incredible quirk of fate. So, I persuaded Sue that we may as well nip across London to watch the game. No hardship really.

Anyway, this was my first visit to Loftus Road and I didn't know the stadium layout. We were walking past a line of shops with the ground behind when a bloke out of a group that were walking towards us deliberately bumped me in the shoulder as we were walking past. I ignored him and carried on walking. After a couple of hundred yards it became obvious that we'd gone the wrong way so we turned around and walked back. And who should be walking towards us but the same group of lads.

So I walked up to the same bloke who had bumped me and said 'excuse me mate, can you tell me where the away supporters go'. He went a funny colour and spluttered something like 'shit, you're a Swans supporter. I'm sorry I bumped you pal (splutter, splutter), I'm from Morriston myself'. He then showed us how to get in the away end.

It really tickled me that, with all the problems surrounding football at the time the only person who tried to cause any trouble, that I saw, was another Swansea lad and none of the thousands of home supporters who were milling around.

Perhaps the bloke I've described will read this and remember the event. Not exactly seismic in the overall scheme of things but it's still something that I remember when I go back through my Swans supporting days.

By the way, the Swans lost 2-1 and Robbie James hit the bar with one of his thunderbolts.

John Young

I went on a supporters coach to Anfield in 1964. We stopped at a lay-by /cafe on the way there. One of the party wrote on the dust on the back of the coach; roses are red, violets are blue, Liverpool 1, Swansea 2. This remained on the back of our coach all the way into Liverpool. Of course it turned out to be a very prophetic rhyme.

Mike Davies (67), Swans100 survey

A particular memory again revolves around the 1964 FA cup game at Liverpool. My father drove us up to Liverpool and the car broke down near Llandovery. He hired a replacement car to get us there and on the way back fell asleep momentarily at the wheel. We crashed through a hedge in the countryside ending up in a field and as it was so dark couldn't see a way out so he exited the same way as we had gone in. Through the hole in the hedge. Alive to tell the tale and ready for the semi final at Villa Park which we lost to Preston.

Anon (60), Swans100 survey

Travelling to Plymouth and coming back on train without buffet car sharing a compartment with a family who proceeded to eat their way back while myself and friend ostentatiously shared a packet of polo mints.

Rob Lewis (56), Swans 100 survey

Being locked out of Anfield in 81/82 after Shankly had died; then being given a stand season voucher by an old lady (because I was on my own and she'd got nervous of the queues I think) and watching the game from the Kemlyn Road Stand with the Liverpool fans! The surge down the Kop after Dai Davies decked Terry McDermott for grabbing the ball out of his hands was spectacular. An amazing 2-2 draw (though I missed the first goal) and a surreal experience. Our bus got lost on the way to the ground as well.

Peter Dawson (55), Swans100 survey

Getting locked out of Anfield in '81. Over 6,000 travelling Jacks locked out. My Dad and I did manage to get on the Kop for a while but it was horrible. We left at half time.

Rob Jenkins (46), Swans100 survey

Going on one of Ugo's midnight starts to Hartlepool in the middle of winter, probably around 1987. The coldest place I had ever experienced! We arrived at something like 6.30am. The only place we could find open when we got there was a snooker hall so we spent most of the day there trying to warm up.

Adrian Byrne (45), Swans100 survey

At Birmingham City, the vast majority of Jacks were more interested in shouting 'Dougie, Dougie, Dougie, Out, Out, Out' than watching a game had travelled many a mile to see.

Voice of the Vetch fanzine, issue 2, 1990

I witnessed Swansea's record defeat at the hands of Monaco in 1991 – 8-0, oh why do we do it? The game for us was inconsequential, as we did the conga behind the goal in Monaco of all places! This had to be the biggest party atmosphere ever seen at an away end at a European game. The French TV director kept panning to the mad Jacks behind the goal as the party went on and the hapless Mark Kendall let in goal after goal.

Howard Richmond, in Keith Haynes & Phil Sumbler (eds)
Vetch Field Voices (2000), 67

Frank Lampard jnr playing for the Swans and coming over at the end of the match to shake hands with us. There were only 53 away fans there.

Alison Shingler (31), Swans100 survey

Peterborough Away 2000. Pre match, most Swansea fans got (without realising) enticed into a local bar gay. Watching the older fans faces' was priceless. We had come off the back of I think a record 7 clean sheets only to find ourselves 2 - 0 at half time. The Swans were attacking our goal second half and scored 3 of the luckiest goals you will ever see to win 3-2. I think the winner went in off Cusack's backside!

Tom Lloyd (30), Swans100 survey

Beating Orient away in our desperate season - Cutler performing miracles and Tatey having a blinder and thinking to myself as I left the Swans fans who were going home 'I THINK WE'RE GOING TO BE ALLRIGHT'.

Keith Roberts (48), Swans100 survey

My aim is every away game but I usually end up missing 3-6 every season (mainly on Tuesdays).

Becca Williams (19), Swans100 survey

The green, green grass of home: eighty years at the Vetch

Whenever I hear Tom Jones sing 'The green, green grass of home' I think of the Vetch Field. This is very odd considering that when I first heard the song, I had already been going to the Vetch for over forty years.

First of all, I went in my father's arms and sat on his lap in the Centre Stand. My first visit would have been in 1925 and I actually went to my first away game in August 1925 – at Fulham. My parents were visiting the great Wembley Exhibition, but they could not miss what was the Swans' first away game in the Second Division.

We stayed in the Centre Stand for a few years until the 'Eighth wonder of the world' was completed in 1927-8. I mean, of course, the Double-Decker, later known as the 'West Stand'. It really was a sensation, a cantilever stand with an apron big enough to give protection to about two-thirds of the terrace accommodation below. The great experience was the wonderful outlook as, unlike all other stands, there were no pillars to obstruct the view.

It was not long before the family season tickets were transferred from the Centre Stand to the Double Decker. It was also about that time that I was getting old enough to know what was actually going on on the field and to adopt my own heroes from the men in white. The West Stand was 'home' until 1931 and I remember one of the last games I saw from that viewpoint was against Everton. I am proud to say that I actually saw the great Dixie Dean that day. There were also two ex-Swans in that Everton side who trounced the Swans by five goals to two.

From then on, I cut away from my family and began my journey around the Vetch. It was all new experience for me to be allowed to go off on my own. I sampled the terrace 'under the double-decker', the Bank in all its facets, the Town End (the East Bank) and even the Enclosure.

Once inside the ground, the 'field' customer had no restriction – he could find his way to any standing viewpoint. He could pass from the Bank to either end and vice versa. In fact, it was popular for fans to gather behind the goal the Swans were attacking in the first half and go to the other end in the interval.

Railway sleeper terracing was provided at the Town End and access was from Glamorgan Street. At the top of this terrace was only a light wire fence between the ground and the back gardens of the houses. Several of these houses, with home-made structures, were able to gain excellent views of matches and it was rumoured that some were charging for accommodation. Eventually the building of the East Stand put and end to what might have been a thriving cottage industry.

Before a game, the crowd gathered steadily for an hour or so; at the end they all left together. At Swansea, it seemed that the entire crowd made a bee-line for Oxford Street, and on match days it was common for the crowd to surge line abreast across that thoroughfare up to the market and beyond. There is one other feature of the after-the-match dispersal that ought to be mentioned. The front of the Bank above its railway sleepers was bad, but you should have seen it at the back. Whereas people going in would approach the Bank from the ends and climb to a convenient spot, in the rush to get away at the final whistle most climbed to the top and scrambled down, black ash and all. It was bad enough on a dry day, but when it rained there was a terrible mess. On really bad days rivers poured down the Bank and the ash was liquefied.

Along the front of the Bank and the Town End there was an iron railing fence about three feet high. There was no vandalism or serious bad behaviour but on days of big crowds this fence was under some strain. There were a few occasions when crowd pressure caused sections to collapse and I remember the odd time seeing people being passed over the heads of the crowd to waiting St John's ambulance men. On such occasion youngsters were allowed to sit inside the fence.

Crowd behaviour was usually very good. There would be the occasional gentleman who had had too much to drink. The inebriated were treated with indifference by the crowd unless they became offensive in language or demeanour. Then they were put in their place – no violence, just a few appropriate words. Bad language was not tolerated, and anyone using foul or abusive terms was immediately shouted down by those around them.

John Conibear (written in 2005)

Supporters of the Swansea Town football team in 1928 against Cardiff City in the final of the Welsh Cup at Ninian Park, Cardiff.
Back row: Arthur Lewis, Joseph Wilcox, Sam Parkin, Front row: George Taylor, Sydney Lewis, William Joseph and Stanley Goodwin.

Swans Memories

Vale Park 1969, the all white of Port Vale versus the all red of Swansea City. It was quite an eventful 0-0 draw, The Swans hit the post and the left back was Vic Gomersall. It won't be remembered in the history of either club, but in my own football history, it was the day when it all started, when an English lad from Shropshire began a 40-plus years' allegiance with one club. As a 7 year old I used to have a club a week, Wolves, West Brom , Man Utd. I did support Man City for a number of months, but something clicked at Vale Park that November afternoon, maybe it was family influence, my Dad being from Swansea, a supporter since the 1930s, and my brother, older than me, having supported The Swans already.

From then on it was highs and lows. I was at Spotland in the mid-70s when The Swans finished in the bottom four of the league for the first time, it was the era of massive flared jeans and long hair, and some tough looking Swans fans advising the the opposing fans what they were going to do with their effing heads! Jeff Thomas was the stand out player of those dark times. He seemed to do everything including serving in the Swans Club Shop. Another abiding memory of the early 70s was sitting in the double decker, Swans coming out in a pure all white strip with the big black swan on the left chest. There seemed to be a set move each game. If the Swans kicked off the ball would end up with Carl Slee who would thump it left footed into the North Bank.

Another great memory was the Swans playing Rhyl in the FA Cup. There were the Millington brothers in goal, Tony for the Swans, Granville for Rhyl. The Swans were cruising in the game, two or three up , Tony had little to do, and fans in the enclosure were chucking him sweets. He was picking up one of these sweets in the back of the net when Rhyl had a rare attack, and he only realised this when the ball went flying past him in the top left hand corner.

Things got better for The Swans in the late 70s when I avidly followed them from Shropshire. The season before the arrival of Toshack I compiled a scrapbook of cuttings sent to me by my Auntie who lives in Dunvant , from the South Wales Evening Post. That was the season when Harry Griffiths really started to turn The Swans fortunes around. It was also the start of replica kits and I was keen to get the all white with black trim Bukta kit that the Swans wore. This wasn't so easy to get in Shropshire. However my local sports shop, Bristow Sports, came up trumps and ordered me one in September. I was happily wearing it by Christmas.

The great ascent started from there. There were some great games including The Swans' 8-0 defeat of Hartlepool with George Smith, an ex-Swans, going berserk at his Pools team mates. I had my first pint ever in the Vivian Arms, Sketty the night The Swans went up to the second division having beaten Chesterfield. There was the strange game against Middlesbrough in the FA Cup when The Swans dominated but lost 4-1 at home.

But in 1981 the promised land was reached. It also coincided with my first year at Polytechnic in Sheffield. As a small boy and beyond I had suffered from constant pee taking from glory hunting Leeds fans about my supporting lowly Swansea. Therefore when the Swans beat Leeds 5-1 in the opening game of 1981-82 season I thought I was going to die on the way home to Shropshire from Swansea, so excited I was at the prospect of seeing all the Leeds fans I knew. The following week we went to West Brom and in the car we followed the Swans coach along the Birmingham Road, Robbie James was seating in the back seat of the coach. I was thrilled when he responded to my thumbs up. A few months later I was going over the snake pass from Sheffield to Stoke to meet up with my parents to see the Swans. I was with some other lads from Sheffield Poly, excited by the prospect of seeing The Swans go top of the league for the first time ever. That excitement disappeared under a cloud of smoke when the big end went under the 1970 Allegro we were travelling in. The game against Southampton near the end of the season was a top of the table classic, when Ante Rajkovic totally outclassed Kevin Keegan, and at the same time gave Nigel Stevenson some technique training on how to pass the ball back.

After that high, the great descent! Some bad times, including seeing the Swans arrive at Walsall in a fleet of cars, and the game against Leyton Wingate when only the main stand was opened, as we thought that was the last we'd see of The Swans as they faced liquidation. My Dad, who retired around this time, had as a present, a framed list of autographs of The Swans, at the top of the sheet was ' Swansea City Football Club (In liquidation)'. The one bright note from the Leyton Wingate game was the appearance of a 16 year old, Andy Melville!

However, we survived and trips to Swansea, and away games in the West Midlands and beyond thankfully continued. A couple of trips to Twerton Park Bath, really hit home the saying 'the otherside of the tracks'. You'd walk through palatial Bath, go under a rail bridge and you'd be in pre-fab land as you approached sub-Southern League standard Twerton Park. Bristol Rovers would play their usual aerial bombardment game which would phase The Swans, along with the surroundings.

Another trip to West Brom in the early 90s will always remain with me. The Swans 2-0 down with much of the second half played brought on Steve Thornber, and miraculously The Swans turned it around to win 3-2. However what sticks in the mind was the substitution of Alan Davies, innocuous at the time, but who the following week took his own life.

A first trip to Wembley for the Freight Rover Final v Huddersfield was particularly emotional especially when the Swans emerged from the famous Wembley tunnel

A mini-revival took place under Frankie Burrows, a great manager, after initially being very sceptical due to his Cardiff roots and perceived liking for the long ball game. Nothing could have been further from the truth. The Swans played some great stuff, with players like Des Little and Jimmy Gilligan being outstanding. That team's fortunes culminated in another encounter with West Brom in the play-off semi final when The Swans outplayed West Brom at The Vetch, going into the second leg 2-0 up with minutes to go, when Andy Mcfarlane kneed the ball into his own net. The Swans played well in the second leg, and when Micky Mellon was sent off for West Brom, The Swans looked like they would get back into the tie, only for Colin West to be sent off minutes after coming on.

Fast forward a number of years, and a significant shift for me moving to Edinburgh. Local trips for me were now to Hartlepool, Darlington and Carlisle. My enthusiasm for the Swans north of border attracted a few friends and colleagues to take the trip down south with me by train and car. The 'Jacks in Fife' as the group were christened, enjoyed some memorable days away. Bottles of beer were often a feature and at one game at Darlington we left a number of bottles behind a gatepost for the duration of the game thinking we would not be allowed into the George Reynolds Arena with them. After the game we were pleasantly surprised they were still there and enjoyed them on the trip back north. Trips to Hartlepool were usually accompanied by getting soaked before and after the game. Of course, in more recent years the trips have been to more illustrious venues like Preston North End and Newcastle. With Newcastle it was a great experience as long as you weren't that bothered at seeing

individual players. In the game in the championship a few years back, apart from seating in front of some penguins, we were also informed after the game that the Newcastle goalkeeper had been replaced at half time, all we could see from the orbit of the away end was some dot in an orange shirt.

Two occasions in the last 10 years illustrate the incredible lows and highs of supporting The Swans. For many years I went to Sheffield with my girlfriend to see the final of the World Snooker Championships. In May 2003 this coincided with The Swans 'league survival game' with Hull City. My brother and Dad were at the game. All I could do was sit in a wicker basket chair in the guest house in Sheffield listening to reports on the radio, looking at Grandstand and getting texts from my brother. My brother's texts were a few seconds ahead of the BBC, therefore a few peeps on my phone was then accompanied by a score flash on the TV , or a radio up date from The Vetch. Such was the turn of fortunes in the game. By the end of it I realised I'd unravelled one of the arms of the chair.

Then in May 2011, the trip to Wembley for the play-off final was I feel the pinnacle of a Swans occasion. The singing of The Swansea City song was highly emotional. I could hardly sing it. It reminded me of following the Swans all those years, seeing that song performed live before a Cardiff game in the 70s, it put it all into context. The game itself was just incredible and a carbon copy of the game 8 years before. This time though I wasn't in a wicker chair but in the stadium celebrating for over an hour after the game. That game and occasion can only realistically be bettered if The Swans won the FA Cup, and who knows such has been the topsy turvy way of life supporting Swans that could happen in the future!

John Richards

The Swans supporters sing

Apart from the natural advantage of playing on one's own ground, if you have never seen a crowd of Welsh enthusiasts you will not be able to realise the electricity they can put in the air. You will see it on a minor scale this afternoon, but multiply that three times and you will have a rough idea of the whole-hearted enthusiasm which the Swansea supporters can put on show at their own ground.

Arsenal v Swansea Town, match programme, 28 January 1950.

At the moment many supporters are not only staying away from matches themselves because of the obscene language, but if they do attend they do not bring their wives or girl friends.

Match progamme, Swans v Northampton Town 3 December 1977

The Chelsea F.C. Chronicle, 25 August 25 1928

> ## OUR VISITORS:
> ## Swansea Town.
>
> The Swans are noble birds, as any student of ornithology will tell you. They have tough bills, as long as those of a seaside landlady, and the strength of their " wings " is such that they have frequently been known to break a home team's record. They did that to Chelsea three seasons ago. Swans are popularly supposed to sing only when about to die, but the Swans' supporters sing, and very tunefully, when the stately bird is very much alive. Daffodils are not in season just now, but leeks are coming on strong, and these, coupled with the sweetly plaintive songs of leek-wearing supporters of the gallant Welshmen, are calculated to draw tears from the eyes of the sturdiest Sassenach.

They deserve even greater support than we've been giving them. At least one of the chants from the boys at the back of the North Bank "Swansea City are Magic" comes to us all as we watch Curtis and Co. bamboozling the opposition. Why not conjure up some magic of your own, lads and bring your absent friends into the "Magic Circle" at the Vetch. I am sure that once they have been they will be regulars.

Swansea City v Rochdale match programme, 10 September 1977

One point has been brought up to us at our Committee meetings. It is that many supporters feel very strongly about the use of obscene language during the chanting by certain members of the younger set. Please lads, chant as much as you like and as loud as you like,

but please consider that our support is gained from many members of the opposite sex; wives, sweethearts and even mothers, not counting the older citizens. Please lads, moderate your language and make the Vetch a pleasure to come to.

Supporters' Club notes in Match Programme, v Rotherham United, 12 September 1978

As we approach this season, let us remember the vital positive role we in the crowd have to play to support the side with good old-fashioned Swansea hwyl.

David Farmer in match programme Swans v Lincoln City, 22 August 1978

So as a new season arrives it will undoubtedly bring with it a new spate of terrace anthems. The North Bank faithful will again sway to the monotonous 'Ole, Ole' song which proved to be a hit with all 92 league clubs last term. It was less complex than others, very easy to remember – 'Ole, Ole, Ole, Ole, Swansea, Swansea'. We had a brief encounter with the 'celery' song which drifted from the terraces of Stamford Bridge across to us, this wasn't a favourite at the Vetch however. Unlike the 'horse' song which most eardrums welcomed, it went 'To my horse, to my horse, singing goodbye to my horse'.

Jackmail, 3 August 1988

Whatever happened to the North Bank racket? These days, the boys on the bank generate very little noise – can this be the reason behind our mysterious home form. We used to out-sing all before us, but no one makes the effort any more. Come on North Bank. Sing For the City!!

Jackmail, 14 (December 1990)

There is less atmosphere on the North Bank this season than on the Moon. So far this season Wrexham, Merthyr, Exeter and even Barnet have made more vocal noise than the North Bank. The place is like a graveyard. Seeing that most of the boys are banned or in jail; thousands prefer shopping on a Saturday; kids have to pay a fortune to enter, there is a lack of nucleus from which an atmosphere can be generated. Added to that, the lack of flags, loo rolls, confetti and horns (ok, there was at the Barnet game), mean the Vetch is becoming quiet, drab and boring, just like Ninian between 1988 and 1991.

Letter to The Jack, 6 (April 1994)

PRESS AND PUBLIC RELATIONS

with CHRIS SMART

By now you will, no doubt, all have heard the new Swansea City song, written and recorded by 26 year old Llanelli man, Roger Evans. This brilliant young singer could unquestionably go places and his hitherto mundane life as a computer operator could well be dramatically transformed, almost overnight, as I am sure it will be after this record gets the success I know it deserves. Both sides of this release are attractive to music lovers and already the response for the record in the club shop has been quite tremendous. I would reiterate my appeal of last week to sports fans to buy the record just as soon as possible. The producer of the record, Mervyn Reed from Swansea, has put in some tremendous work to get this off the ground, so for the sake of everyone, please support this project, not just because we want support, but do sincerely believe that this record is worth buying and treasuring.

Swans v Plymouth match programme, 31 March 1979

The Singers, they were great, shouting out support and some of the funniest chants I'd ever hear. I wanted to become a North Bank singer.

Lee Davies (38), Swans100 archive

In later years, the North Bank, which held over 5,000 of the ground's 12,000 capacity, was the focus of the most noise. In terms of what songs are sung, the North Bank could be loosely divided into three sections:

Subject of songs/chants on the North Bank

East end	Middle section	West end
	Pro-Swansea	Pro-Swansea
Pro-Swansea	anti-English (occasional)	anti-English
	anti-Cardiff (occasional)	anti-Cardiff

Of course, these sections were not neatly defined and blurred into one another, particularly at the better-attended matches where space was limited. Nonetheless, any regular of the North Bank (or indeed anywhere within the Vetch) would have recognised these divisions and consciously chosen where they stood on the terrace in accordance with how comfortable they felt with the songs and chants that would surround them. The west end of the North Bank was significant in that it was the part of the ground nearest the away stand and thus the best location to taunt visiting fans.

From Martin Johnes
'We Hate England! We Hate England? National Identity and Anti-Englishness in Welsh Soccer Fan Culture',
Cycnos, 25 (2008), 143-157

We are attempting to stamp out any form of racist chants including those used by English fans visiting the Vetch when references to a sexual act with a sheep is highlighted.

Letter from Mike Lewis (Swansea City General Manager) to
Heather Moyes, 27 September 1999

The Swans supporters sing

Why do some people want to turn football into a game watched by corporate freeloaders, where the only noise you hear is a polite round of applause whenever a goal is scored - no matter who scored it. I've been to premiership grounds and there is a total lack of atmosphere as true supporters are priced out of the game. I much prefer grounds with an atmosphere. Quite frankly I enjoy chanting derogatory comments about Cardiff, I feel I have the right to question the decisions made by officials and yes, give abuse to players. If I think calling Damon Searle a scummer helps my team win then I'll do so. If anything else it is a great stress reliever.

www.scfc.co.uk guestbook, 21 September 1999

I know these chants are supposed to be aimed at the opposing fans but what exactly do the people who take part in these think that the English players who make up the majority of OUR team think? How does it make them feel? They are not deaf and insensitive. Why should they stay with the club and have to listen to that sort of abuse week in week out? Would you want to play in front of fans who are just as offensive to you and your country as they are to players in the opposition team? They don't suddenly become Welsh when they sign for Swansea City and they don't leave their own pride at the Severn Bridge toll booths.

www.scfc.co.uk guestbook, 3 February 2000

Anti-English chants are perfectly valid in my book. Most of them are quite amusing and they get banter going between the supporters which is good. Where we have to be very careful is in saying 'just keep up the noise – doesn't matter what you chant etc' That's a dangerous green light to the large number of racists and the easily-led that Swansea have as regular supporters. Technically I guess, some of the anti-English stuff could be regarded as racist, but I don't really think so. However, ANYBODY chanting racist filth from a Swansea City standpoint deserves everything they get (which unfortunately these days means virtually nothing and probably a pat on the back from their colleagues) and must not (even inadvertently) be excused.

www.scfc.co.uk guestbook, 9 February 2000

My Swans

For an auspicious start, I was born in C*rdiff. By sheer luck, my father was a Swans fan. Like most reading these stories their Swansea City supporting lives will have begun with their father taking them by the hand one day and saying: 'Son, do you fancy watching the Swans today?'

I'm no exception, and my father, a fan since he was a lad, took me at the age of seven to the Vetch Field to watch Burnley in the old Division Two – League One in new money – on a cold, wet, eery 5th of February 1993 night.

It was a joy on three fronts – I was going to see my first live, real football match. It was a night on which I was allowed to stay up extra late! It was a Friday night 'under the lights'.

I only came to fully appreciate how special Swans games are 'under the lights' in the years following, but I was absolutely hooked. I still remember the scoreline – a 1-1 draw – but I have sadly forgotten who scored for the Swans. And this was the beginning of what has become a most enthralling and engaging passion which shows no sign of ever abating.

The more I think back the more I wonder how I ever got hooked as I had Manchester United this and Liverpool that shoved in my face by the cooler kids at primary and then secondary schools. Easily would be the word to describe how I could have been swayed by peer pressure.

But I take incredible pride now from the fact that I stuck with the club I love and that has given and taken away from me in equal, unforgettable measure. It also makes me smile no end to speak to some of those lads who in school laughed at me supporting the Swans 'coz they're rubbish', but who now have seen the light and claim to have supported the Swans for years! I know that I saw the light on that dark night in February 1993 with my father, and feel a sense of belonging to a club I know thousands of fellow Jacks also do every Saturday.

A highlight for me was my first season ticket. It was a Christmas present one year for the forthcoming season, and I was thrilled to be able to go every other Saturday and midweek to the Vetch Field in the old East Stand upper and take my seat for every home game!

The high of Wembley in 1994 made me realise the jubilation one can feel when their club achieves the unthinkable. Relegation from Division Two to the basement Division Three in 1996 couldn't deter me from wanting to go to see my team, and that no matter what,

rightly or wrongly I was in now. No going back!

What followed relegation, after the blip that was Kevin Cullis – historically the worst manager ever to have been given the job at any club, was something of a glimpse of later success with Jan Molby coming in and steering us back to Wembley in 1997 against Northampton Town. I cringe now thinking of the referee allowing John Frain to re-take his infamous last-gasp free-kick, a kick I felt in the gentleman's vegetables then and still do today. It was to be the first time in my memory that I have cried at a Swans match, but not the last.

The Swans made it 'big' again in 1999, drawing with West Ham United in the FA Cup for a replay at the Vetch. I was absolutely gutted to miss the away trip to Upton Park on such a memorable night as it turned out, but the family queued in shifts all night and into the next day for the tickets to watch what became the stuff of legend in the clubs illustrious and continued history – THAT win over Frank Lampard, Joe Cole et al thanks to a wonder strike (or what is still to me a wonder strike) courtesy of Martin 'Psycho' Thomas. The atmosphere at that game still gives me goose bumps so many years later.

We would see our first league title in years just a year or so later when John Hollins produced the most effective but boring team I'd seen in some time to win the old Division Three title at Rotherham United. The happy memories of that day and season were only checked by the tragic loss of fellow Swans fan Terry Coles. Despite not knowing him or anyone he knew most probably, I felt sad for him and his family for he was a fellow Jack.

Fans of that era will remember all too well the disastrous times under one Tony Petty, and long may his like stay away from our fine club. What happened under his 'tenure' should not have to be experienced by any football fan in the world. It was almost as if I was faced with losing a member of the family knowing at the time that each game could be our last as a club, culminating in THAT game against Hull City to stay up from the grasps of Conference football.

I have only ever truly dreaded going to the Swans once in my life. That Saturday in May 2003 was that one time. I did not even want to face the inevitability of getting out of bed for fear of triggering off a series of events which would see us eventually relegated out of the Football League for the first time in our history. Some may see this as irrational, and I can agree wholeheartedly with that!! But I cannot truly explain in words, as the above rambling will testify, how much this club means to me and how much I love every match I go to and celebrate every goal like it's the winning goal at the Champions League final.

The joy I get from a Swans win puts a smile on my face for days, to which my wife-to-be will wholeheartedly agree. But that win over Hull City in May 2003 is only one of two times I have cried celebrating a Swans win. The second, also in May, followed only 8 years later in my third Wembley trip in the famous white replica shirt.

I have left just the one home game early after a gut full of losing at home to Bury 3-1 – but each of which has a special place in my heart because it was an opportunity to see the team I have loved since that first game in 1993.

I have taken my place on the North Bank, in the Centre Stand, and up in the East Stand to watch the Swans and seen some great players – Stuart Roberts, Jason Smith, Matthew Bound, Lee Trundle, Martin Thomas, James Thomas from the Vetch Field era; stood in all four stands and watched the great likes of Nathan Dyer, Scott Sinclair, Freddie Bodde, Joe Allen, Jason Scotland, Angel Rangel and Ashley Williams in the latest Liberty Stadium era.

The last year or so following the Swans has been something of a 'pinch me' series of events firstly getting to the Championship – somewhere we had been widely tipped never to reach – and then unbelievably into the dizzy heights of the Premier League and to the top half of the table. I still remain resigned to waking up one day to the end of one incredible dream!

It has been something of a reality-checking exercise as a testimony to our amazing success that in recent games I've felt almost disappointed to lose against Manchester United and Everton at home, and not take all three points against Liverpool at Anfield. I almost blame myself for doing so and hark back to those lonely days watching us lose 4-1 at home against Kidderminster Harriers. But it has solidified even more (as if it needed doing in the first place) that this is my team for life as I'll still be there come hell or high water watching my team.

I hope that should I have children, I can take them to the Liberty Stadium to their first Swans game, and kick off the emotions in them that I first had in 1993 and will experience for the rest of my days. And that they support the Swans towards their bicentenary and write of their passion as I have tried to do above.

I have a lot to thank my father for, and something I thanked him for on his death bed following our second title in my lifetime in 2008. He would so dearly have loved to see us in the Premier League.

I smile fondly now at the Friday night in 1993. I suppose it was the fact that it was a game of football, but also the opportunity to do something with my father - just me and him, and later with him and my younger brother. It was "boys time" for which I am so grateful.

I mentioned above that my favourite Christmas present was a Swans season ticket, but the greatest ever gift I've received to date? My first ever Swans match ticket...

Jon Osterland

It's nostalgia time again folks! Dig out your Fila top, zip up your Lois cords, spin some Wham! on your turntable and allow us to take you on a gentle spin back in time to April 1984. Pull up a chair and share a fond memory from a mis-spent youth. RGW tightens his trim-trab and begins —

The promotion bubble had just burst and Swansea City were in the grip of the halcyon-days hangover. The team contained a few weary stars from the said period and was still, at least on paper, a strong one. However with the advent of papier-mache pitches not yet upon us and the Swans performing on grass week-in week-out, Les Chappell's braves managed to put together an impressive tally of defeats/debacles. The support, despite the results, was still holding up admirably, and the future was not as bleak as it was... if you know what I mean! Saturday for the hordes who travelled over from Neath was still most-definitely "Swans-Day", the Neath Station platform packed with eager youths all boasting the latest labels to parade around the North Bank (and impress the girls it has to be said). I bump into some of my old fellow travellers from time to time, the ones who still live locally that is. It's a sad tale of mortgages and children, unexplainable apathy and even in some cases defection to the oval-ball! That said, it only takes a few jars with the "old heads" and the memories come flooding back. The special trains to Plymouth (remember that one?), Deepdale (oh happy day), the pubescent memories of Sham 69, all-dayers on the bevvy for a tenner, Dai Davies shoving a left-hook on Terry McDermott at Anfield. A sentimental winding journey taking in the Falklands spirit, and the Angel in Neath before re-furbishment. All this winds inevitably towards the 21st of April 1984, Easter eggs, a Dean Saunders double-strike and scenes in the city that made last season's cup clash look like the teddy-bears' picnic.

On the morning of the big game I recall going to town at about 10.30 to have a cooked breakfast before making the train, always make sure you have something substantial before you go drinking as my grandfather used to say. The visiting Cardiff 'specials' weren't due to hit Swansea until 1, so catching the 12.10 seemed a safe bet. "A few of the boys have already gone down," grinned the ticket-puncher at Neath, a man renowned for the Bluebird badge permanently pinned to his lapel, along with his bizarre sexual preferences. "Oh aye, how many then?" I enquired, striving to maintain an air of blind indifference. "A good thousand or so" came

the smarmy git's reply, "a few got off in Neath to go Jack-hunting, but don't worry they've gone now." "F*** off you lying twat" I retorted with all the contempt a fifteen year old can muster, and breezed past onto the platform. For anyone familiar with Neath station you will know that in order to reach the West-bound platform you have to cross the tracks via the covered footbridge. We mounted the steps in high spirits and rounded the corner where we were quite disconcerted to discover that a Cardiff element had indeed been in Neath earlier, for sprayed along the walls in blue paint was the legend 'CARDIFF SOUL CREW'. The first thing that struck me was what a ridiculous statement to make; quite obviously they wanted the world to know that they were a battle-hardened army of thugs, instead by choosing the name 'soul crew' they succeeded in conjuring up an image of a motley band of medallion-wearing Luther Vandross impersonators!

Anyway, off the train ten minutes later in Swansea and nothing untoward was evident, just the usual Saturday shoppers, along with the customary gaggle of teenagers trying to pluck up the courage to go into Dai & Pie's tattoo parlour. We made our way down High Street window-shopping, leering at anything in a skirt, and putting on that much-practiced teenage "I'm hard as f***" strut that always appears at big games and Neath's September fair. We passed the Army recruiting office after the obligatory glance into the window and daring one another to sign up. We rounded the corner of David Evans when my world suddenly fell crashing around my ears, for there stretched out in the park were literally thousands of 'visiting' fans. I know there is a natural Welsh tendency to exaggerate when one looks back on fond memories of a long-lost youth, but there were thousands of 'em! Mostly decked out in Lyle & Scott or Pringle sweaters with the then mandatory Nike Wimbledon trainers. My first thought was to run, but on finding my feet rooted to the spot I decided to pretend to window shop in Aquascutum. Two minutes passed and to my disappointment nobody took a blind bit of notice of me. Here was I thinking I looked the archetypal football casual, but they didn't bat a sodding eye-lid. I walked up and down a bit in the hope of getting hit - nothing hard but something to leave a little bruise to show the boys I'd been rowing with Cardiff. But to no avail, they just weren't interested in making me their first scalp, so off I tramped feeling a failure down toward the Quadrant.

...And there it was! My first sightings of the phenomena they call

football hooliganism. Hundreds running back and forth, bricks, bottles flying, police dogs barking, yobbos chanting, brawling, it was all there. I gleefully allowed myself to be swept along by the crowds down toward the Grand Theatre, out into the Quadrant bus park, along to Mumbles Road, back again up Dillwyn Street to the Queens, then back along William Street to the Mumbles Road. Being fifteen and living in some sort of dreamworld I was in my element. All the stick I took in school, the shite I had to take off my parents, all the hate I had built up for months was let out in one glorious explosion, like an old locomotive letting off steam.

When we finally got into the North Bank, there was a mass of bobbing heads, rushing up to the fences chanting, spitting, threatening, it was electric. Despite the tight policing about fifty Cardiff 'fans' had managed to get into the far right end of the Bank. Naturally all hell broke loose, people punching left and right, bodies crashing down on to the concrete steps, an unhealthy squash up against the cold mesh fence, which was on its last legs as were the barriers of the West Bank. I was punched in the eye by a bloke who, on spotting my Swansea lapel badge promptly apologised before diving back into the fray. Surely South Wales' Chief Super was now rueing the day he said "Swansea - Cardiff? Saturday? Why not!". The last time these two met there were similar scenes, with a jumped-up Eric Bristow playing Bullseye from the North Bank and carrying out acapuncture on a nearby copper. Lessons had not been learnt. Oh, and whilst all this was going on there was the small matter of a relegation dog-fight, unfolding on the field. We found ourselves two down in less than half an hour, not that a sizeable chunk of the crowd were really that interested. The situation was so dire that Wyndham Evans took the law into his own screw-on studs and threw himself into a crazy 50/50 ball which left him being carried off. Furthermore Pascoe, then a slightly-built youth with a crap haircut was taking a leaf out of the nutters' on the terraces book and giving Karl Elsey a good feed. There was still sporadic madness on the terraces. "Drink is the root cause of all these troubles" said Cardiff Managing Director Ron Jones, who then went on to explain how the hooligans must have drunk lots of Coca-Cola at an early age which had unbalanced their psyche.

Back on-field it was all-square, courtesy of Saunders and Walsh, two Swans who later went on to play, albeit briefly, for our now crumbling opponents. Colin Pascoe, on the contrary a pure Jack with

no blemishes on his career was weaving some trickery on the right flank, dancing a gay jig past the bungling Bennett and sweeping the ball across to the aforementioned Saunders who, despite being sandwiched between two blue shirts, slid the ball beyond the reach of Dibble to clinch it with just five minutes left. A gaggle of two-fingered gestures are offered from an otherwise stock still West Bank, the North however resembled a mass of jellies on springs on a bouncy castle. Yes, take that.

Some three hours later I was back in the Angel in Neath, drowning my jubilation, the proud owner of my longed-for bruise. Telling anybody who was prepared to listen how I had done it single-handedly fighting off twenty of 'em! After stop-tap I made my way home, drunk, sore but happy, only to find that one of my father's friends had been at the match and told him what I had been up to.

The end-result - a matching pair of black eyes and no pocket money for a whole month; but what the hell, it's not every Saturday you get the chance to make terrace folk-lore!

Rhys Williams
From Jackmail, 21 (September 1992)

A 'part of youth culture': hooliganism

There was a lot of trouble in the 80s and 90s. Not proud but it was part of youth culture at that time throughout the country at football.

Mark Griffiths (41), Swans100 survey

Lively scenes were witnessed at Stebonheath Park, Llanelly, on Tuesday evening at the close of the West Wales Senior Cup final between Llanelly and Swansea Town. Immediately the final whistle sounded hundreds of spectators from the cheap side ran on to the playing pitch, shouting epithets at the referee who eventually had to leave the ground under the cover of darkness disguised in the uniform of a police officer. Considerable excitement prevailed during the match, which was won by Swansea by a goal after extra time had been played. The crowd, which numbered about 4,000, had repeatedly demonstrated their disapproval of the rulings of the referee, and scarcely had the play finished when a big portion of the crowd clambered over the railings and ran across the pitch in the direction of the grandstand. With trouble brewing a number of police officers, some of whom were in plain clothes, assembled near the entrance to the dressing rooms.

Mr. Simpson [the referee] was hustled as he walked off the field, and had only just disappeared into the official quarters when the main portion of the excited crowd reached the entrance. For a long time they set up a menacing attitude, while there were a few bouts of fisticuffs between supporters of the respective teams and the police had to interfere.

All attempts to disperse the crowd were unsuccessful until police reinforcements, which had been telephoned for, arrived on the scene, but it took nearly half an hour to clear the ground. In the meantime the referee remained in the dressing room, while attempts were made by the crowd to force the side doors near the main gate, and these had to be protected by balks of timber.

South Wales Daily Post, 2 May 1923

In 1935 at a game against Bolton Wanderers a young man threw a large stone (described by some as half-a-brick) at the referee who was struck on the knee. The offender was apprehended with the full assistance of the crowd and later charged and convicted.

John Conibear (89), Swans 100 survey

What a great pity that the first game of the season was spoiled by the disgusting behaviour of a lunatic fringe of so called 'supporters'. These hooligans are not supporters of Swansea City A.F.C. They do not come to watch the game but to incite others to cause trouble and inconvenience for the genuine supporter. We have a rule in our Constitution that any member of the Supporters' Club behaving in such a manner as to bring the name of the Supporters' Club or the Swansea City A.F.C. into disrepute will cease to be a member. This rule will be strictly enforced against any offender as we all wish to disassociate ourselves from such behaviour.

We have never before seen anything quite like the scenes last Saturday and to highlight the normal behaviour of the Swansea City supporter we have to quote the fact that during the whole of last season, the Supporters travelling to all away games on the official and unofficial transport behaved in exemplary fashion and were a credit to themselves and to the people in charge of them. Acclaim and praise as to their conduct at the games themselves have also been received from the Club Officials of the teams played.

Many wives and young daughters and sons are members of the Supporters' Club. Are we to allow these hooligans to spoil their entertainment and even prevent them from coming to our Matches through fear of assault and injury?

**Supporters Club News in match programme
v Doncaster Rovers, 23 August 1977**

During the 1977/8 season there was quite a bit of trouble on the North Bank. For some reason the police used to have a heavy presence amongst the home supporters and occasionally trouble flared. On one occasion I remember being dragged out of the crowd by an officer from the SPG and escorted to safety – the officer was my next door neighbour.

Phil Roberts (50), Swans100 survey

Skin heads were the fashion when I started going to the Vetch. In my second game a kid next to me got punched several times because he would not give this skin head his scarf!

Mike Mee-Bishop (54), Swans100 archive

It was quite frequent around late 70s/early 80s though I was usually good at keeping away from it. Remember the Cardiff games and the visits of Chelsea in the Second Division as being a bit scary; had to duck a brick once coming out of the North Bank after an 80s derby. Nearly got caught in a surprising punch up on the North Bank at a game v Middlesbrough just before relegation fron Div 1. At the Liberty have occasionally seen visiting fans run at Stewards in the NE corner, but apart from Cardiff mostly pretty peaceful. I don't look for trouble.

Peter Dawson (55), Swans100 survey

I was taken as a small boy by my father to watch a game. I can remember standing on old railway sleepers to watch the match. That memory is quite vague, but the first game I can remember properly was against Workington and there was a sparse crowd and I think the Swans lost. But also I enjoyed joining in the singing and larking about on the North Bank with boys of my own age (I was 15 or 16). I made quite a few new friends that day.

As a boy (not now) sometimes we might have a wander about after the match to look for away supporters. We usually ended up getting chased by the police, it was always a great laugh. A few of us sneaked under the double decker by pretending to be away supporters (Bradford) and after mixing in with their boys started a big scrap. We were all thrown out by the police but were hailed as heroes by our contemporaries on the North Bank.

I think my first away trip was to Newport County in the Welsh Cup. We went up by train and were all searched and shepherded to Somerton Park. We all "stormed" the turnstiles and got in without paying and then chased their lads off their own "end". We all treated Newport County with great contempt and thought of them as some sort of in-bred country cousins to be despised. The Swans hammered Newport and it summed it all up for us they were real low-lifes who deserved it (we thought). I now wish that Newport were back in the English league system fighting for the Welsh cause in that competition.

I think as I have matured I am able to see the bigger picture for instance how teams like manure are strangling the smaller clubs like the Swans. I tend to watch the game more now and not the opposing supporters. Also I am more knowledgeable about the football itself and enjoy the game more. It's not so visceral as it was when I was a kid.

Peter Murphy, written in 1999. Swans100 archive

Spent one evening before a Cardiff game in Swansea Workingmen's Club playing snooker. About 20 Cardiff Fans came in and proceeded to steal the balls to throw at the North Bank. That was about 1978/79.

Clive Mitchell (58), Swans100 survey

Back in the 70's/80's virtually every game was a matter of taking your life in your hands and running the gauntlet, literally at most away grounds.

Huw Mellor (46), Swans100 survey

Saw lots of trouble. The only time I really got into a problem was at West Ham circa1980 when we went into the ground through an away turnstile. However inside the ground there was no segregation. The match was sponsored by some new fangled lager and sold at half price! During the match we got attacked. The few police on the terrace were not particularly interested. When I remonstrated with one his reply was 'if you're not hard enough you shouldn't come to West Ham!'

Nigel Jarman (59), Swans100 survey

Liverpool away '82, Northampton away '87, Reading away '93 and Cardiff away '93. Hate violence. End of. Most frightening was actually

Jackmail 1989

SWANSEA CITY AFC LIMITED
OPEN LETTER TO ALL SPECTATORS

At the same time as the Club has been enjoying recent success on the field, a number of incidents have unfortunately occurred, which have brought the good name of the Club into disrepute. In particular:

● Obscene chanting and racial abuse have been used
● Spectators have invaded the field of play
● Objects have been thrown at officials and players

While accepting that the vast majority of our fans behave properly and reasonably the Directors of the Club are concerned about the increase in bad behaviour.

I am therefore writing to you to re-state our policy on these matters.

Spectators conduct in the ground is governed by the Football League Ground Regulations. Copies of these regulations are prominently displayed around the ground, an extract of which is copied on the back of this letter.

ANY PERSON ATTENDING A CLUB MATCH WHO IS FOUND GUILTY OF THE ABOVE OFFENCES WILL BE EJECTED FROM THE GROUND. IN ADDITION, THEY WILL BE BANNED FROM THE GROUND FOR LIFE, AND IF DEEMED NECESSARY, THE CLUB AND/OR POLICE WILL PROCEED WITH A FORMAL PROSECUTION.

I would ask for your support in helping us to eradicate this unacceptable behaviour.

DO NOT ALLOW THE FEW TO SPOIL MATCHES FOR THE TRUE SUPPORTERS.

Steve Hamer   *13 February 1999*
Chairman

---

when the Leeds supporters ran riot in the market, overturning the stalls and terrifying everyone.

Eileen Morgan (77), Swans100 Survey

Firstly, let's start by saying that a fair percentage of our following that day [against Leyton Orient] were not regular Swansea fans. As is the case with every first away game, people who wouldn't normally attend travel just for a day-out, a 'few' beers and, unfortunately, a punch-up. ... To be fair to the Swansea fans on the terrace they were well-behaved and the usual fine amabassadors of the club. Okay, so it's been said that they 'ripped' the gate off the away terrace exit. This is untrue. The fact is, if the police insist on keeping fans inside a ground fifteen minutes after the end they can expect a bit of pushing and shoving - any damage to the gates was caused by restless fans crushing against it. Nine were involved in the aggro that went on outside.

The usual hooligan element was swelled by the appearance of the 'casual' once-a-season thugs and they must have numbered two hundred plus. They left the grandstand early intent on causing trouble and attempted to steam into the Orient bank – failing to do this thanks to a heavy police guard they then ran around throwing missiles at all and sundry. However, as we made for our car we observed a lone Swansea fan getting struck over the head repeatedly by a policeman's truncheon. Takes two to tango?

It took a good twenty minutes for the thugs to be shuffled away from the ground to Leyton tube station. It has to be said that on that day Swansea 'fans' did cause trouble - we can only be thankful that the thugs only turn out in these numbers once or twice a season.

Jack Mail, 14 (December 1990)

You can't just let visiting supporters be set on week after week. If these activities continue at the Vetch then Swansea won't be a place supporters will wish to visit. And the good, friendly atmosphere that honest Swansea Jacks have created over the years will be shattered.

Jackmail, 14 (December 1990)

It wasn't a pretty sight, says an exiled Jack, but considered he'd only just escaped a knifing, the football fan should consider himself quite lucky. He sat there, still in shock, trying to piece together within his battered skull, the events that had nearly led to a night in casualty,

---

the least violent of the four - Northampton away on St.Valentine's Day 1987. Colin Pascoe's header meant we were the only team to do the double over them that season. Their fans weren't too happy and tried to storm our buses. The drivers locked the doors but kept the engines and ventilation systems running, meaning our bus was being filled with the carbon monoxide from the bus right in front of ours, with everyone beginning to cough and splutter. Terrifying at the time!

Robert Dixon Miles (42), Swans100 survey

We were in the First Division. I was on my way home from the game

'....... left the ground, police escort vanished after about five minutes, turned up a dark street, only four of us now, where's the station, suddenly there they were, loads, out of breath, we didn't want any hassle, someone thumped me from behind, tried to stay on my feet, useless, hit the floor, boots came in, someone yelled 'get the blades out', staggered up, got up, got away, somehow. Left the other three behind, hope they're OK...'. Sadly, this extract isn't an extract from 'Steaming In' or 'Bloody Casuals' or any of the other confessions-of-a-soccer-hooligan books currently on sale. No, this is 1993, this is Swansea.

Love, Peace and Swansea City, 5 (March/April, 1993)

Hooliganism is the problem of society and government, not football. Football is only a devise used by trouble makers. Take away the football and another outlet would be found.

The Jack, issue 6 (April 1994)

Cardiff in the 90s, in the FA cup, was probably the worse. I can remember taking the bus from Pontardawe and when arriving in the Quadrant you could feel the tension in the air. It was electric. The North Bank was a huge mass of sound and movement. I ended the game nowhere near where I started watching. Afterwards, the Kingsway was like a scene from Beirut or something. Even so, my abiding memory is Jimmy Gilligan picking up the ball one side of the stanchion, moving out of my sight and unleashing a stunning shot to score the winner. Pandemonium.

Richard Davies (40), Swans100 survey

The police consistently over reacted to football fans at that time but I once witnessed the most ridiculous ground banning I have ever seen before or since, it was at Bristol City and we had gone into the ground early so it was pretty empty. In the away end (as you do) two fans behind were ejected for "you are looking over there all the time" presumably towards the Bristol fans. They had done nothing nor uttered a word but out they went.

Paul Williams (57), Swans100 survey

Brentford away. 2000ish. A drunk Swans fan kept climbing on the advertising and the police kept telling him to get down. In the end they lost patience and grabbed his arms to lift him out. Cue chaos.

Fans around him grabbed his legs and tried to pull him back. There was a surge from behind me as people rushed to help. I was swept off my feet and pushed forwards. The police had their batons out and were hitting those holding on to the fan. I was getting pushed closer and closer to the police hitting out. I thought **** and elbowed my way out of trouble.

Anon, Swans 100 survey

A golf ball landing on the side of the pitch when we played Cardiff at my first home game. Fans ripping out advertisement boards and chucking missiles at the linesman when he awarded Carlisle United a penalty against us in 2003. Swansea & Luton fans scrapping on the pitch in 2002 following Luton's promotion at The Vetch, and Swansea and Bristol fans charging at each other separated by a large line of police officers outside The Vetch after Trundle's last minute penalty winner in 2004.

Jack Carter (19), Swans100 survey

A jumper and other memories

I like the Liberty Stadium. The perfect example of a modern, multi use 21st Century Stadium, it's always a real pleasure to go there. But the Vetch? Well that was different. I absolutely loved the Vetch. For so long it was the very centre of my life and was the most important place that I would visit. I've never been into religion, but the Vetch became my cathedral, my own particular place of worship. My first service was 1973, with my mam, where the Swans beat Lincoln City. I was eight years old. A love affair began. There are two things I remember as clear as a bell about that day; my new scarf, bought by my mother that very morning from the market – red and white. Lincoln City wore red and white... the scarf never saw the light of day again. The second thing was the tunnel. We sat right next to it and I was able to stand in my seat, peer down it and could hear all its sounds – the doors slamming, the studs on the concrete, the shouting, the laughing and, best of all, the swearing. From that moment I knew that I wanted to live in that world, the world that took place inside that dark, narrow tunnel. There was only one way to achieve that dream, I had to become a footballer.

It's a whole other story as to why my dreams of representing my beloved Swans were so cruelly stolen from me, denying me the opportunity of experiencing that unimaginable thrill of running down that tunnel, emerging into the sunlight and hearing the fans chanting my name. Suffice to say, the real reason those dreams remained unfulfilled, was because I was crap.

Still, if football wasn't going to deliver my dream of experiencing that dark and secretive world of the dressing room area of the Vetch, I knew a man who could. Or more accurately, my grandfather did. Harry Griffiths. Now as all of you know, Harry was a living legend whose life, tragically, was cut short at the dreadfully young age of just 47. It broke my heart. My grandfather, Fred Ridge, treated Harry like another son. Fred was the secretary of the Heathcliffe Club at Heathfield in Mount Pleasant, which was a regular watering hole of Harry's. I've lost count of the number of times that I'd be kicking a ball against the wall of the club, when Harry – always beaming through the features of his weather beaten face – would walk over with my grandfather, shouting "give us a kick then you clogger" and for five minutes I'd become the footballer I always dreamed of becoming. Harry would tell me stories of his playing days, of his great friend John Charles and tantalise me by saying "work on that left foot son, and then you might make it.....great players use both

feet." I absolutely adored him.

One day outside the club, he came over and introduced me to a tall bloke he had with him. "Dave, come and meet our goalkeeper – his name is Jimmy." I shyly said hello as this man shook my hand and picked up my football and squeezed it between his massive hands, as goalkeepers tend to do. At the time I had no idea what a significant part this man would play in the future of the Swans. He was only on a three month loan at the time from Manchester United and would return to them, before arriving back at the Vetch over ten years later, via Arsenal and Aston Villa. You may remember him – he remains the finest goalkeeper I have ever seen in Swans colours – his surname was Rimmer. So as my new mate got me to kick some shots at him on the road at Heathfield – not many joy-riders to worry about in Swansea in the early 70s – Harry asked me the question that was to make my life up to that point. 'Is your mam taking you to the game on Saturday son?'

"Yes" was my instant reply.

"Good. Well I've got a nice surprise for you. After the game, tell her to bring you to the tunnel entrance and I'll bring you in so that you can meet Jimmy again and all the lads. Would you like that?"

Would I like that? Had Harry lost his mind? "Would I like that?!" My god, I would have given anything to visit the holy of holies – the dressing room.

Harry burst out laughing at my response – or rather – total lack of one. I hadn't made a sound in reply, just stood there open mouthed and just about managed to nod in agreement.

"Good, see you Saturday then son," he ruffled my hair, off he went and Jimmy turned and lobbed me the ball with a beaming smile. I dropped it.

Well I was only eight and a half.

I have no memory whatsoever of who the Swans played that Saturday. I just remember spending almost the entire match watching Harry in the dugout, desperately hoping he'd look over at me, give me a smile and the thumbs up that he hadn't forgotten his promise. But nothing, absolutely nothing. When he walked back in at half time, he must have passed within five yards of me and my mam, scuttling past in his tracksuit and sweatshirt, carrying his little black Bukta physio's bag, but again, no glance our way, no smile. Nothing.

This was the pattern when he came out for the second half and at the end of the game. I just wanted to shout his name out as he walked down the tunnel at the end, but the manners I'd been given by my mam and dad ensured that my trap remained – if not shut – silent. As all the players left the field and the fans drifted off – there were probably less than 3,000 in those days – I looked at my mam with tears in my eyes.

"He's forgotten hasn't he?" I asked, rapidly approaching blubbing point.

"He's a busy man love – especially today, but he told your grandfather last night that he was taking you in, so let's go and stand by the tunnel and see what happens."

I felt a little better hearing that, it was one thing making a promise to a little kid, but telling my grandfather – a hard, honest man – well that was sealing the deal in concrete as far as I was concerned.

So we stood there, waiting, and I snuck my first steps onto the hallowed turf. I made sure none of the groundsmen were looking because I knew it was probably wrong, but it drew me toward it like a magnet. I sneakily placed one foot onto the edge of the pitch, with the other firmly on the red gravel that ran all around the outside, then, checking nobody was looking, raised my other foot and stood fully on the edge of the pitch. I looked down and the first thing that amazed me was firstly how dry and dusty the edge of the pitch was, and secondly how many circular stud marks were left deep into the turf and dried mud that I was staring at – there were hundreds and hundreds of them. I took another step and moved over the touchline and stood on the field of play proper. I looked up and saw a now empty North Bank way ahead of me over the far side of the pitch, and to my right I looked at the tiny East Bank with its scruffy railway sleepers as steps that were hidden slightly by the nets of the goals. Everything looked so much bigger now as I looked round the ground.

"Oi, get off the pitch!"

I froze. I turned around slowly and there was Harry, beaming as usual.

"Work on that left foot son and you'll be there one day. Now, are you coming in here with me or are you gonna stand there daydreaming all day?"

I smiled and ran straight to him. I know it might be hard for non-sports people or non-Swans fans to understand, but I simply cannot describe the joy I felt as Harry grasped my hand and led me up that tunnel, and into the sacred and secret area of the dressing rooms. I

was so happy I thought I would burst.

"Got your autograph book Dave?"

I pulled it straight out of my anorak pocket and showed him proudly.

"And a pen?"

My face hit my boots. Harry burst out laughing... "Come on then, lets find you one in my office."

Harry's office wasn't what I might have thought an office would be like. It was the boot room, and remains the best office I have ever visited in my life. There was loose mud all over the floor – full of holes made that afternoon by the studs of the boots from which the mud had fallen. Across one wall was a swathe of football boots and trainers, all hanging from six inch wooden pegs. The boots were all shapes and sizes – all black, no electric blues or lime greens on show – and the only brands I remember were Adidas and Puma. I was totally star struck with this raw football environment. There was also a small treatment bench, a little desk and some shelves with all sorts of bottles and bandages laid out on them. There was also a half empty (or full!) bottle of whisky next to a bottle of liniment. I was in a daze of complete wonderment.

Then, Harry turned with a bic pen in his grasp, beckoned me with his hand, and said "right, want to meet the players then son? Follow me."

He walked across the bootroom, opened a door, turned left and called me in. I froze to the spot. All I wanted to do was go in and see these heroes of mine, but was just hit by a tidal wave of shyness. Harry, recognising that this may be a moment just a little too intimidating for one so young, held out his hand, pulled me gently towards him then whistled loudly.

All the players looked round, and Harry announced to them all, "Right lads, I want you all to meet a good friend of mine. His name's David Brayley and he might well play here one day, so be nice to him and sign his autograph book. Oh, and mind your language too or I'll give you a bollocking."

I shyly looked up and saw my first smiling face – Jimmy Rimmer. "Hiya son, still playing are you?"

"Yes" I stammered and blushed in reply.

"Let me sign that for you then."

I was off and running.

But there was one quite surreal post script to the story. As I was

A jumper and other memories

passed by Jimmy around the dressing room from player to player, they all had one thing in common....they were all completely bollock naked. Aged eight and a half, I'd never shared a dressing room with anyone up to that point in my life. I hadn't yet played team sport nor experienced the unique atmosphere of a sporting dressing room. I'd never seen another man naked – not even my dad! Yet here I was, walking amongst this dressing room of strangers, in a blue anorak, black and white bobble hat, hand outstretched offering a bic pen and autograph book, and them putting down a towel to expose themselves fully to this young boy, wandering around their sweaty dressing room like a startled rabbit. It was bizarre to the extreme. I'd

have to stand there, wait while somebody like Pat Lally or Dave Bruton noticed me or finished drying themselves, then they'd drop their towel, take my autograph book off me, rest it on their leg and I'd watch them write their name, as I'd desperately try to avoid looking at their cock, which hung there just a few inches from the cover of my autograph book. What amazed my eight year old mind the most was how brazen they all were, strutting around without a care in the world, as naked a jaybirds, just laughing, joking – and swearing – as I just stood there trying to look anywhere apart from the area of their cock and balls. Trouble was, I was only about four foot tall at the time, so pretty much everything was on eye level. Still, I was a lad on

a mission and I was determined to get everyone's autograph – naked or not. And I'm pleased to announce that I did, and have happily remained largely unscarred by the experience!

I had to wait another seven years for my next experience of the tunnel and dressing room area of the Vetch, and whilst, thankfully, there was not a Swansea City penis in sight, all did not go to plan.

It was December 1980 and I'd managed to win a competition in the short lived Swansea published sports newspaper, the Sports Gazette to win a Swansea City official club jumper. I'd received a letter saying that along with the two previous weeks winners, the three of us were getting presented with our jumpers, the following Tuesday evening at 6.45pm. It was a fantastic thrill to be told that I'd won – but when I read where the presentation was to take place, I nearly passed out.

The Vetch.

That eventful Tuesday evening, John Toshack's Swans were playing their fiercest rivals, who would almost match Swansea City's unprecedented march up the divisions between 1977 and 1981 – Watford – owned by Elton John and managed by Graham Taylor.

I couldn't believe my luck. Since my first visit to watch the Swans in that Lincoln City match in 1973, I'd only missed a handful of home games, and now I was in possession of a letter instructing me to be at the Players' Entrance at 6.45 where I would be met by a Club Official and taken inside the ground, down the players tunnel and out onto the pitch where I would be presented with my jumper. By John Toshack, who, in common with all Swans fans of that era, I absolutely idolised. Still do in fact. I wasted no time in telling my mates – lifelong Swans fan Rob Dawtrey amongst them – and telling them that I wouldn't be able to join them all on the North Bank as usual that night, as I'd be on the pitch getting presented with my jumper by Tosh, and would then, I assumed, be taken to a VIP seat in the centre stand to watch the rest of the game. I was chuffed – the boys were green with envy.

And so came the night. Mam dropped me outside the Vetch, I got out, and walked toward the Players' Entrance, stopped, and waited outside. This was going to be my moment – the closest I'd ever get to being a Swans player, a walk down the players entrance on a match day. I was excited beyond belief. Within a couple of minutes out came the club official, collected me and the other two people to be presented with our jumpers, and walked us into the ground. I was in

a daze. Here I was, just 15 years old and walking in the footsteps of giants. I'd recently read "The Swansea City Story" by Brinley E Matthews, and the names I'd committed to memory like Billy Hole, Ivor Jones, Reg Weston, Jack Fowler, Ivor Allchurch, Joe Sykes to name just six, had walked the path I was now making, several thousand times between them. The official swept us in, past the Secretary's office, the Boardroom and the Referees room, then best of all, past the home dressing room, whose door was slightly ajar. As we went past the room I slowed down slightly to hopefully spy and see or hear something fascinating that I could tell the lads in school the next day. Just as I slowed down and peered through the crack in the door, I heard a loud scream of "you f***ing wanker" coming loudly back at me. To paraphrase the clever words of Oscar Wilde, I absolutely shit myself. I scurried off after the others, not knowing to this very day whether someone was abusing me or whether it was a regular pre match war chant. I like to think it was the latter. Obviously.

Anyway, out we went onto the pitch. Heaven. I walked out of the tunnel – a strange experience – it was lit bright by fluorescent lights at the top, then went quite dark halfway down, before the floodlights outside kicked in as you emerged out across the ash pitch surround, and up onto the turf. We were led by the official, about twenty yards out, just to the edge of the penalty area. I gazed around hoping to see a friend or two in the stands, but the sea of faces betrayed no familiar ones. Then we had a typical Swansea welcome which started quite quietly over at the corner of the North Bank and radiated along it in no time. I was thrilled. Until I made out what they were singing. "Get those wankers off our pitch, get thooose wa-ankers off our pitch" followed by howls of laughter. Great. Then the next bit of bad news. The official announced that Tosh was busy, and wouldn't be making the presentation, but Graham Taylor would. Graham Taylor? I was going to get slaughtered by the boys – I'd told them Tosh was doing it and I was going to get autographs the lot, but now it was the manager of our biggest rivals, Graham bloody Taylor. Then, following quickly, was the next cock up.

Now I should point out here that for the bulk of my life I've had problems with my surname. It's become a bit of a standing joke with my friends. Personally, I can't see it. If you've managed to stick with this story so far, then I'm assuming you can read. My surname is Brayley. It's not that hard. Bray-ley. Ea-sy. But in my time, I've been

A jumper and other memories

called Bradley, Brimley, Bramley, Bentley, Bratley and Bailey amongst many, many others, it never ceases to amaze me. I could understand it if my surname was Hadziabdic or Rajkovic – easy names to get wrong I'd have thought. But Brayley? Well it's not too challenging surely?

Well it was for the f***ing stadium announcer.

The finest public moment of my short life, taking place in front of my peers, friends and relations was announced as follows:

"Ladies and Gentlemen, out on the pitch tonight, receiving their Swansea City jumpers, courtesy of winning the weekly competition in the Sports Gazette are, Ceri Evans of Upper Killay, Peter Stephens of Manselton and David Barley of Three Crosses."

David Barley. David f***ing Barley. I didn't live it down in school for weeks. In the last fifteen minutes, on the greatest day of my life I'd been called a f***ing wanker by one of my heroes, I been called a wanker by about four and a half thousand fans, and now a retard with a microphone couldn't read the word Brayley. Champion.

Anyway, as I stood feeling more and more bewildered by each passing moment, out came Graham Taylor – carrying our jumpers – to a rapturous Swansea reception...... "Are you shagging Elton John....arrrrrre you sha-ha-ging Elton John."

Got to give it to Graham though, he was not fazed in the slightest. He was a truly lovely guy. He presented us with the jumpers, had a quick chat with each of us and had photos taken individually – nothing was too much trouble. I've had a soft spot for him ever since, even at the height of his turnip phase. At least he was bothered to come out and give us the jumpers – unlike my hero Tosh. Not that I'm bitter.....it was 30 years ago, I'm over it now.....

Anyway, Graham bade us his farewells, smiling as ever, very firm handshake and he cuffed me around the back of the head which was nice – I think – and off he disappeared down the tunnel to the sounds of a Swansea take on Elton John's classic "Saturday night's all right for fighting" reworked as "Saturday night's all right for shagging Elton" – nothing if not original.

So that was that. I breathed in the atmosphere of my last few seconds on the pitch as the photographer took our names for the paper – "no, no, it's B-r- ayley, not B-ailey" I corrected as he was writing it down incorrectly - "all right son, keep your hair on", he stroppily replied. Still, I wasn't bothered anymore, and made a slow 360 to take in the full panorama of my personal field of dreams. As I

just completed my leisurely pirouette, taking in the full glory of the way the Centre Stand made its way up to the Double Decker and across to the vast North Bank, the official approached me – "Ready then son?"

"Yes fine" I replied.

"Where are you watching the game from?" he asked.

A little disappointed that I wasn't being whisked off to the Boardroom or the VIP lounge, I really wanted to cheekily say "the Centre stand please" but being a well brought up polite lad, I just told him where I always watched the game – "North Bank sir."

"Ok, follow me" he said.

So I did. Instead of walking across the rest of the pitch in front of the goal to the corner of the North Bank, where there was a small gate in the fencing that allowed you into the Bank which was quite full now as there was only about 15 minutes until kick off, he turned, and walked back the way we came, across the brightly lit pitch, across the small ash surround, back up the dark players tunnel, into the falsely lit corridors, past the home dressing room – now firmly closed thankfully – out past the Board room, Chairman's office and Secretary's office, outside, back through the players entrance and out onto the road.

"All the best son."

And off he went.

I was in shock. I was left standing, once again open mouthed, out on the road beneath the dark high walls of the prison, right in the middle of the swirling crowds.

Holding a jumper.

Two minutes before I'd been within ten yards of the penalty spot of the pitch – the very heart of this sporting venue, now, with only about 15 minutes to kick off, I was outside – alone – realising that there was no free seat for me tonight. I had to rush around to the North bank – and pay to get back in! The final indignity.

Bloody nice jumper though. Embroidered badge and 100% polyester. Nice. I wore it to school every day for about two years.

It picked up more static than a lighting rod.

Dave Brayley

Spectators will always get something extra: Cardiff City

In the sporting rivalry between Swansea Town and ourselves spectators always get something extra which adds to the interest of a game when the sides meet and this afternoon's match should be of vintage.

Cardiff City v Swansea Town, match programme, 2 April 1949

The recent successes of Swansea Town have added interest to this afternoon's visit of the 'Swans,' when we renew friendly rivalry with the West Wales club, and supporters of both teams will enter into with zest the traditional partisan flavour which is the spice and life of football gatherings whenever representative teams of Swansea and Cardiff pit their skills against each other.

Cardiff City v Swansea Town, match programme, 24 March 1951

We have received several enquiries as to whether some effort will be made to prevent a clashing of fixtures as far as Swansea Town and Cardiff City are concerned.

Asked for his views on the matter, Swansea Town manager Billy McCandless told the 'Evening Post' that he had been in touch with the Football League on this very issue and has asked whether, as far as possible, the home fixtures of the two clubs could be arranged on alternative Saturdays.

He was fairly confident that the request would get a favourable consideration – a statement that will be received with pleasure by followers of the game in this area, many of whom are already contemplating seeing some of the City's most attractive home fixtures.

South Wales Evening Post, 6 May 1952

I have nothing against Cardiff – I wish them well. But there are a lot who hate them - pity!

Tommy Vaughan (80), Swans100 survey

I always remember my first game against Cardiff City ... they beat us 1-0, the goal that was scored was by the first black player that I ever saw after the war. His name was Tommy Best. He scored the goal that beat us 1-0. The return game, at the Vetch, was round about Christmas time, but I didn't have a ticket for the game – it was all ticket then, down there, the first time we played Cardiff. I was

outside the Vetch Field, looking there, feasting on the atmosphere, and just before the kick-off, a police sergeant come out, he had about 8 or 10 tickets in his hand, and he said "Anybody want a ticket?". And I was one of the first. I had a ticket, and I got in there, it was only about 10 minutes to kick-off and the ground was absolutely full. In them days, it wasn't like it is today, there was a terrace, a rough bank as I was saying earlier, and you could go up the bank and it was just like a wall of people there. A couple of the men looked at me, and said "you're not going to see much by here son", they said, and they shouted out and all of a sudden the big bank opened up like the Red Sea like in the Bible, and the next thing I was on the front, right on the front of the game. And the Swans beat Cardiff 5-1.

Roy Griffiths (73), Swans100 archive

Due to the poor transport communications between the Rhondda and Swansea then, my early seasons (the late 1940s and early 1950s) of watching league football took me to Cardiff City which was more easily accessible. When transport facilities improved in the late 1950s then I soon directed my attention and support to Swansea where my loyalties have remained ever since.

Brian John (73), Swans100 survey

I have nothing against the team, it's the supporters I don't think much of.

Eileen Morgan (77), Swans100 Survey

We would mix with the Cardiff fans, have a load of banter, with a sweeps being organised to see who scored the first goal.

Peter Miles (76), Swans100 survey

Having experienced wonderful Derby matches in the Fifties, the present rivalry has nothing to recommend it. The booing of Ramsey, Captain of Wales, at the Arsenal match, for example, was appalling. Aspects of the rivalry among a small section of fans can only be described as psychotic.

David Lewis (67), Swans100 survey

Have probably hardened my views about Cardiff since the Swans have become more successful in recent years. In the past was not

overly concerned about Cardiff but now keen to see the Swans having the upper hand.

Anon (62), Swans100 survey

Whilst the games between us usually have an extra edge, I feel Cardiff are just one of the 'other' 91 teams in the league. They are not deserving of any special status.

Andy Reilly (58), Swans100 survey

I do not consider myself quite as extreme as some of our fans but I am not keen on them. However the local derbies were great and winning was even better. I am one of the people who would like to see Cardiff in the Premier league with us.

Paul Williams (57), Swans100 survey

I always want them to lose but feel a bit guilty about it! On match days I am totally absorbed by the rivalry but as a non-violent person

that stays on the pitch. The history of trouble is upsetting but as a committed supporter it's hard to distance yourself. I like Cardiff as a place but I think that the sense that Cardiff has been favoured by greater prosperity and investment over the last 20 years has added to the bitterness – it's not just about football.

Peter Dawson (55), Swans100 survey

Have no interest in Cardiff, feel they get too much tv and radio coverage in Wales compared with us, at least that was the case until we got to the premier league.

Anon (58), Swans100 survey

They hate us and we hate them.

Anon (58), Swans100 survey

I used to watch Cardiff City when the Swans were away 1969 to 1972. My mother would only let me travel as far as Cardiff. I think the rivalry that has developed since late 1970's is OTT. 'Tis only a game.

Clive Mitchell (58), Swans100 survey

My heart says they're an important club to beat, whereas my head says they're just another small team in a lower division ;-)

Tim Douglas (54), Swans100 survey

I think the friendly rivalry is good but not the so-called hatred between supporters. We are the only two Welsh teams in the Football League so should enjoy each other's successes.

Alan Hughes (56), Swans100 survey

Following a number of unsavoury incidents with followers of Cardiff City, I have little respect for them and their club.

Gary Fisher (49), Swans100 survey

I think that good healthy rivalry and healthy banter is wonderful. It makes for an interesting workplace. It's when the children of all ages hijack the great history of rivalry and turn it into something poisonous that I find truly depressing. To the idiots I would just like to remind them that most of our heroes have played for Cardiff City.

Keith Roberts (48), Swans100 survey

I wish I could be magnanimous towards Cardiff. As a proud Welshman, I feel some pride in Cardiff as a place, but I find I cannot enjoy it when they have any success as a team. The same goes for the Blues rugby team. That said, I despise the hatred that some people feel towards the other team, and can see no reason to feel so strongly about it. It's not as if the players have much connection with the places any more. I was once a juror on cases of football violence involving a Swansea v Cardiff match (which I had also been to see, and witnessed people being chased down the street by other fans) and found it all so senseless.

Anon (44), Swans100 survey

Not being Welsh I don't have the hatred towards the fans but I hate the arrogance of the club, how they spend beyond their means and how the media always focus on them and not the Swans.

Jeremy Lunn (43), Swans100 survey

I work with Cardiff City supporters and they will (sometimes) admit that they are envious about the way our club is run. The Supporters Trust ownership bit in particular. They hated the bad headlines when Ridsdale was Chairman and us getting to the Premiership was the final straw. I'm sure they think that's only a matter of time before our positions are reversed. It's not helped by the Welsh media who favour them all the time. But its important for Welsh football that we have at least 2 clubs playing at Premiership/higher Championship level. As long as we are on top of course!

Julie Hopkins (43), Swans100 survey

Carnage, fighting outside the Canton Stand on our way in, Swans fans on the Bob Bank, Cardiff fans setting off CS gas or a smoke bomb. Police allowing dogs off the lead in our end. Joe Allon headbutting Terry Boyle. Singing on our way out and the boiling hot weather. We were caught in a picture in the Evening Post on the Monday on the Grange Town End looking mad.

David Richards (42), Swans100 survey

Ying yang, Black/white, Christ/Antichrist, Matter/Antimatter I hate them with a passion but realise that to truly love something you must realise the horror of their opposite.

Steve Close (47), Swans100 survey

In the Falklands, Cardiff City and Swansea City fans fought and died together. In normal life we live and work together. Why should this change going to a football match, especially a Wales match.

Letter to Love, Peace and Swansea City, 5 (March/April 1993)

For you to say that Cardiff City fans are jealous of Swansea City is really sad, but then that's your mentality for you. Really speaking the only emotion Cardiff fans have for Swansea City FC is hatred not jealousy. In the same context as I hate Margaret Thatcher and Gyles Brandreth, I dislike them but there is no way I am jealous of them.

Al, Cardiff. Letter to Jackmail fanzine, 16 June 1991

I hate them, been brought up to! Since I've been old enough to have a mind of my own they've not done much to convince me they're capable of earning any respect from me! Terrible fans, biased media.

Can't stand them!

Clare Ridley (37), Swans100 survey

Honestly, it's of little interest to me and never has been. They are just another team who happen to be located nearby. Hate doesn't come into it. The hatred part - where it exists - reflects more on that group of fans than the clubs themselves. Are they even true football fans? I don't know.

Jamie Borley (34), Swans100 survey

I always hope they'll do worse than us. The clubs will always be connected due to the proximity and understanding we have of each other as supporters whether either of us like it or not. I was surprised how glad I was when they lost the play off final against Blackpool.

Anon (33), Swans100 survey

I love the atmosphere and build up to a derby game and the atmosphere at the game is always phenomenal! You can feel the rivalry in the crowd and it is this that makes them so enjoyable. I have no bitterness towards Cardiff as a club but I always want the Swans to have the upper hand on them, I'd love to see a Welsh derby in the Premier League but I would not want to see Cardiff in the Premier League unless we remain there also, which we will! So proud that we were the first Welsh club to make it!

Carl Smith (30), Swans100 survey

I love the rivalry between the two clubs. After the Swans result, Cardiff is the second result I always look for.

Geraint Davies (28), Swans100 survey

I have been brought up to love Swansea, hate Cardiff, so that is my view on them. I would love them to get to the premiership with us though so we could beat them on a world stage in the biggest league in the world in the biggest derby in the world.

Daniel Williams (22), Swans100 survey

My Cardiff Hell

Being a Swansea supporter and studying in Cardiff for three years was never going to be easy to begin with; especially when you're one of those types who shoots his mouth off about the Swans every five minutes. The first indication I had of how tough things were going to be happened when a guy from Chepstow ridiculed me for pinning up a Welsh flag daubed with SCFC in my room. Ill feeling grew as I found out he was a closet bluebird, this mounted every time the guy celebrated when the Swans lost, we exchanged blows more than once. Still we had to get on, we shared the same house!

November '88 and the first Swans v Cardiff encounter since I'd been living in the capital arrived. I set off with a mate for Ninian, I soon learnt it wasn't that wise a thing, to stand out in a bright red coat amongst the 300 Jacks on the Grangetown end. Mercifully a police escort up through Canton to Riverside and then the city centre prevented any injuries to the two of us.

A less than friendly encounter with locals took place on an away trip to Merthyr. On boarding a sprinter at Cardiff Central, my mate and I gingerly avoided the bluebird supporters who were also going up. Yet as we sat down we were joined by an obscene local, and judging by his appearance he was definitely under the influence.

He asked if we were going to the match, we told him yes. He then asked where we were going in the ground, we told him we didn't know. He said if we showed him our ticket he'd tell us which part. I handed the ticket over, a bad move. As the guy compared his ticket with mine, it dawned upon him that they were different colours, which meant only one thing. Shit, I thought.

'You're effing Jacks!,' he replied, 'I hate Swansea, my brother still harps on about his jail sentence after the ruck in 1987'. Oh hell, oh bugger. The conversation continued along the same lines all the way to Merthyr, with a few threats here and there. On arrival at journey's end I sprung out of my seat like Bob Beamon and mingled as best as I could. My mate and I shot through Merthyr bloody quickly. You're just not safe anywhere these days.

It was a visit to the Arms Park to see Wales play West Germany that I next encountered a tight situation with apes from Cardiff. Not content with sitting next to my mate who was decked out in a Swans t-shirt, I spotted one of the editors of this fanzine and greeted him by yelling, 'Yes, the Jacks are here'!.

That wasn't too clever, because I then got tapped on the shoulder, I turned round to see two or three hundred Cardiff knuckleheads behind me. Quick talking managed to delay a bashing. They threatened to get me after the game and told my mate to take his Swans t-shirt off or he'll set fire to it! The speed by which we left our seats and the ground at the end of the match has gone down in the annuals of history and is even recognised by Norris McWhirter in 1989 Guinness Book.

For a while things quietened down, Swansea weren't playing too well, and Cardiff were crap. My Swansea RFC shirt got me a few glares in the city centre, and provided I didn't wear my footie top outside Roath I had nothing to be wary of.

The game at Ninian Park in 1990 however was slightly more unnerving. I stayed in a mate's house in Cyncoed and walked to the game. A corner shop provided the ale, so I ambled down decked out in a mid 80's Fila top with an SCFC tour of Europe t-shirt underneath. Passing the Ninian Park pub and the Bob bank my hatred of the scum grew, as did the tension I was feeling. Bracing myself for trouble I turned the corner and walked passed the not so grandstand. On making it onto the terracing I met up with a few of the lads and succumbed to the atmosphere.

From the moment Hughes scored, till Wadey struck the second I was caught up entirely in the game, only pausing to remove my sweater, (show my colours like) at half-time. It was after I and 2,500 others had informed the bluebirds they were going down, I noticed my Fila top had been nabbed. A little aggrieved but not too concerned over losing the out of fashion item, I waited to filter out.

It was only then I realised my predicament, I was to meet Stuart (my mate) outside the 42nd Street pub, attired in an SCFC Euro t-shirt. My salvation came in the shape of a Llanelli rugby shirt lent by an understanding 30 year old after I explained my sorry situation. I left with the tail enders (not normally wise) and was probably only saved a beating by two reasons. 1) The time we were kept in the ground at the end and 2) Most of the Scum were already on their way to Barry Island!

So I managed to make my way slowly and surely through Cardiff via Canton .... no problem .... to the Crest Hotel .... fine .... Cathays .... great .... Death Junction (City Road/Albany Road) .... shit!! Three locals wearing outdated and dodgy CCFC tops were loitering on Albany Road. They yelled out 'Rugby twat', and looking at my newly acquired Llanelli top, assumed that I wasn't from Cardiff.

They continued to hurl abuse then came the proposition, 'Oi twat, do you like football'. I carried on walking up the road, ignoring them. Another shouted 'Have you been to the match ?'. I knew they wouldn't let this lie, and despite looking ahead I sensed they were crossing the road. However a car pulled up before they caught up with me. It was Stuart in his Nissan, he'd just been down Miss Millie's in City Road. He opened the door. 'Hang on a sec', I said, 'but get ready to shift fast'. I then turned to the three Cardiff lads who were now only 30 or so yards away, took off the rugby top and bellowed 'Surrr-wanzee', and dived into Stu's car. It was lucky we didn't hit any lights as the car was chased all of 200 yards to the corner of Albany Road and Penylan Road.

I behaved after that, in fact I never chanced it again. I was even a bit fearful of meeting the 3 bluebirds in Roath at some future moment. I never wore Swans clothing again. Not even for the Welsh Cup Final versus Wrexham at the Arms Park. But even here danger loomed, for in buying tickets for the game off the Welsh F.A. we were situated on the Wrexham side of the ground (we had Robins one side of us and about 100 Cardiff boys the other). Yet the only threat came from our fellow Jacks, as we left the ground walking towards the mass ranks of Swansea boys. It was only thanks to Rik and Paul recognising us that we weren't put in an uncompromising situation.

My last dicey moment came before the Wales v Brazil game at Cardiff. As I walked into the Bluebell on High Street with Nick and Paul (two rugby lads from Neath and Barry respectively) I was greeted by, 'You Jack bastard' from Elliot, a moronic Leeds fan I knew, and Spencer an acquaintance from Gwent. Elliot meant it in jest, Spencer I'm not to sure about as he's a committed bluebird.

As everyone in the pub turned round, colour left my face. 'Oh bugger', I thought! Suddenly Spencer's glare changed. 'Fancy a pint you div ?', he shouted intentionally. Nick yelled 'Wales, Wales' and Paul took off his jacket to show his Cardiff RFC shirt. Thankfully the hard, scowling faces turned away and a few joined in with Nick shouting 'Wales' at the tops of their voices.

One guy (who I later learnt was from Porthcawl and was covered in CCFC tattoos) mouthed off at me about the episode on Swansea beach. 'Hundreds of them, only ten of us' he said but I wasn't going to be drawn. Cardiff is not an easy place to be a Jack. I've since returned home, life is so much easier these days.

Jackmail, 4 (January/February 1993)

I'll have a pint of Dark

I remember the early starts for games at Doncaster and Barnsley. Usually one coachload with maybe another dozen or so by car. Always stopping off for a few pints on the way home at Derby or Birmingham. XXXX would sing in pubs before games to get people to buy him pints. The away fans were so few that we would often be handed tickets by the players outside the ground. We rarely paid. One Easter we left Swansea at midnight, drove to London to watch the morning kickoff on Good Friday at Brentford, then to watch Chelsea play Luton in the afternoon where my mate went to sleep on the Shed. A night out in the West End, then off to Watford for the game on Saturday afternoon. I think we lost both games and I had my scarf pinched by a Swans fan outside Vicarage Road. Hey ho. It seems extraordinary that we would travel the length of the country to watch division one games and just paid on the turnstiles. We never bought tickets. I remember the minutes silence at Anfield for Bill Shankly and how the Liverpool fans were outraged the Swansea support (10,000?) hadn't respected it. What most people don't know is that one nutter in the Swans support shouted out 'Burn the Bastard" half way through and the sound the Liverpool fans had heard were the swans supporters rounding on the individual concerned. Unfortunate. I remember the disbelief at Toshack's appointment. I remember the first time I saw Jeremy Charles play. How good was he? I remember being introduced to Mel Nurse in the entrance lobby at the Vetch minutes after he had signed from Swindon in 1969. It was very easy to be in contact with the players in those days. I even watched the reserves away once – at Reading. We won 6-2. One of my early heroes was Geoff Thomas. I met him at Mumbles Cricket Cub a few years ago. What a thrill. Although I never made it, whenever the Swans were playing near Leeds, the small band of away support would always make an effort to stop off at John Charles' pub where he insisted on playing his own records (made when he was in Italy) which he had on the juke box. I'm told they were terrible. I remember the minute silence for Roy Evans and Brian Purcell at a game against Doncaster. There were 5 or 6 Doncaster fans on the North Bank who began to sing God Save the Queen during the silence. They didn't get past the first few bars. Another world. I saw Kenny Morgans play in a Boxing Day friendly on Ashleigh Road about 10 years ago. I believe therefore I may be one of the last people to have watched a Busby Babe play a game. Kenny of course played for the Swans after Munich. There was a power cut in the supporters club at Somerton Park one year. All conversation stopped. For a moment the place went absolutely quiet in the pitch black and then a Swansea voice piped up at the back somewhere…. "I'll have a pint of Dark". You couldn't make it up. I must write it all down sometime.

Anonymous (55), Swans100 survey

Clouds of darkness, clouds of despair

I am sure that I am not alone in taking a view of the Swans which charts the club's fortunes over the last thirty years or so within terms of reference marked out by weather patterns and atmospheric conditions in South West Wales, the rain capital of Britain. Others of course have sought their explanations and patterns elsewhere. I remember one fanzine article which argued with great conviction that the team's league position always bore an exact correlation to the meat content of the pasties on sale at the Vetch (bring back the bakers Davies of Mumbles, all is forgiven); and there are those who suggest that the lamentable performance of successive generations of PA announcers lies at the very heart of all the club's problems over the years. But I have long taken the view that any follower of Swansea Town or City is quite capable, like me, of having water on the brain. This is because our snapshot images and memories of the Vetch Field are more often than not shaped by recollections of long-forgotten games played out against a background provided by damp, dismal, windswept days and nights. Drizzle drifts past floodlight pylons across a quagmire pitch and into the faces of the poor deluded fools who sit in the East stand in the mistaken belief that they are somehow going to find shelter from the elements. Water cascades down the dolls' house roof of the Centre Stand, falling past broken guttering and eventually forming glistening pools on the red shale running track. On the pitch, white shirts turn brown, and would-be tacklers slither from the turf and into advertising hoardings. The Vetch, living up to its name, slowly becomes a muddy, churned-up vegetable patch. And all the time, silently and out of sight, the puddle that always forms between the gateposts at the exit from the North Bank grows into an enormous lake which lies ready to claim hundreds more shuffling, grumbling victims who have not yet mastered the art of the thirty-foot leap from a standing start.

Huw Bowen
**From Keith Haynes (ed.), Come on Cymru 2000!: New Football
Writing from Wales (2000)**

It's not often one is lucky enough to choose a football team to support. In the UK one is born into a club and you live and die by that club. I was fortunate enough to have grown up in Cape Town where if you change the team you support no one will mind, too much.

Having been lucky enough or dumb enough to have lived in many cities around the world, Swansea has certainly become my favourite. I recall watching the Swans v QPR in November 2001 and experiencing and feeling the passion of the fans. That's when I realised that we had something special.

Fast forward ten years and Swansea is in the Premier League. Who would have thought that all those years ago? Not many. We always had the belief and the desire to become a Premier League club, and in life if one desires something enough it normally comes true. If one puts the required amount of energy and effort towards it, something can happen.

The away board rooms have been interesting to say the least, my typical dress code is jeans and a t-shirt and if I really want to dress up then a sports jacket comes along with my sunglasses. Now you can imagine that doesn't really go down well in most board rooms.

It certainly used to work when we were in the lower leagues. I arrived at the Southend match thinking I was Jonny cool in my standard gear only to be told by a brawny bouncer that I would need to sit with the home fans, well I tried to explore other options and eventually got led away to a special room where I had the option of leaving or putting on a pair of black tight trousers that looked like they were last worn at a funeral. The next week Chelsea played at Southend in the FA cup and to my horror I saw on the TV my Russian colleagues in the board room smiling wearing blue jeans!

Our first away game in the Championship was an exciting affair, the butterflies were flitting around and everyone was nervous. I was excited to be at the game, especially since it was in London and almost a home game for me, but due to various personal reasons that I won't describe here as no one would believe me, I arrived 5 minutes before the end of the match with Messi's beautiful cousin!

Onto the Premier League and at the first away game v Manchester City I had brought along bankers from New York to attend. Being that we only get a limited number of seats to the board room we opted to go in the guest lounge. When we walked in there I was greeted by King Kenny.

My first reaction was no photos please BK, but I know I have a lot of mates who are staunch Liverpool fans, so I said Kenny, look I don't mean to be a groupie but can I have a picture for my mates. To which he replied, sure sonny where are you from, I can barely understand you!! Touche Kenny, all the best! Then went into the board room to say hello to my fellow directors and the Manchester City CEO at the time came over to say hello to me and says please come join us with your guests (We had spent some time at the world cup together in South Africa), the next week he was a goner! Such is life, we can never take things for granted and certainly in modern football there are not many that remain in the same position for all that long.

The season wore on and each away game brought with it another flight, another train or taxi to get somewhere, but I wanted to be a part of it in a special way and to really experience what we had spent ten years building towards.

I remember Norwich away, purely for the reason when Norwich were at the Liberty the steak we gave their celebrity chef would have bounced off the floor if dropped. Our Chairman graciously went across to say hi and said could he swop the steak for some fish please, It's very good! To which a smile the length of the Gower was transmitted back.

The away match at Norwich was payback and the pie we received waiting outside the make shift board room made the steak look edible. Entertaining to say the least, the hospitality however was very pleasant otherwise.

Along we moved to Liverpool away and the excitement kept growing. I brought along a lifelong friend who was a staunch Liverpool fan, I opted to train it up instead of driving with him and after being at the station in London an hour after the departure time and we hadn't moved yet I realized there might be a small problem. The hundreds of Liverpool (and Swansea) fans were not happy, my options of getting to the game were running out and as time marched on even driving there wouldn't have gotten me there in time. When my mate suggested a helicopter and an 8,000 pound one way ticket to arrive at half time I knew it was time to watch the live streaming. Which I did and ended up jumping on one of Richard's (Branson) planes back to Cape Town that evening.

At Manchester United, I arrived late as usual, and thought I was in our home board room. Their CEO and ten of us at the table, and Sir Bobby on the next table with his family. The CEO (who was my

neighbour in London) greeted me with a handshake, saying the usual Brian! A great atmosphere and an incredible experience and then they took a picture with us with last year's Premier League title. Sad to say it never returned.

When I looked at the table and saw our names typed up on place cards alongside the Manchester United Logo I realized how far we had come in a relatively short period of time so to speak and I also realised that we never want to lose the position we have of being in the Premier League and will do all we can to retain this status! The one thing I did put in my pocket though, was John the Dutchman's

place card! I have never seen a Dutchman get so worried in so short a space of time. I think he either had it sold on E Bay or tagged for his Swans museum!

Let it be told I did return it due to some severe pressure from Sir Bobby, as the Dutchman wouldn't leave him alone and he had to sign 300 pictures of himself! Sir Bobby that is!

All we can hope for is that next season's away end will be just as adventurous and colourful as last season's was!

Brian Katzen

Swansea After I Die

A Jack knocked on the pearly gates,

His face was lined and old,

He stood before the man of fate,

For entry to the fold.

"What have you done?" St Peter asked

"To gain admission here"

"I've been a Swans supporter, Sir,

For many a long year"

The pearly gates swung open wide,

St Peter rang the bell,

"Come in my son, and choose your harp,

You've had your share of hell!"

E Chapron

Supporting the "Swans" for nigh on 50 years has brought so many conflicting emotions I do not believe there is another club anywhere in football that has experienced the highs and lows, and ups and downs, that we have, what a rollercoaster ride it has been, and probably will continue to be.

Paul Williams (57), Swans100 survey

Is there anything better than to see those white shirts take to the pitch?

Anon, Swans100 survey

What would we be without Swansea City Football Club?

Simon Stranaghan (48), Swans100 survey